A LIFE BY
MISADVENTURE

COLIN M. BARRON

authorHOUSE®

AuthorHouse™ UK
1663 Liberty Drive
Bloomington, IN 47403 USA
www.authorhouse.co.uk
Phone: 0800.197.4150

Published by AuthorHouse 10/16/2017

ISBN: 978-1-5462-8259-4 (sc)
ISBN: 978-1-5462-8260-0 (hc)
ISBN: 978-1-5462-8258-7 (e)

Cover Photo by: Charalambos Iacovou
www.fotokinisi.com

Print information available on the last page.

CONTENTS

FOREWORD

I first met Colin Barron in 2008 when he delivered a weekend training session in Thought Field Therapy (TFT) to health care personnel, which was organised by my wife, Phyll. Since then I have met him at a number of TFT trainings and conferences and was delighted when he asked me to write the foreword to *A Life by Misadventure.*

Colin was born and educated in Greenock, Scotland, and qualified in medicine at Glasgow University in 1979. Whilst at medical school, he developed his journalistic talents as a student magazine editor, publishing many and varied articles, and was also well known as a cartoonist. After spending more than five years as a hospital doctor in Glasgow, he left the NHS to set up and run a private nursing home with his first wife, Alison. He developed an interest in hypnotherapy and subsequently TFT, selling the nursing home in 1999 to become a hypnotherapist and TFT practitioner. He was the first British practitioner to qualify in Voice Technology TFT and was a popular TFT trainer. His teachings were formal but, like his writing, were spiced with a clever and irreverent sense of humour.

He has wide interests that include reading, walking, cycling, films, military history, and aviation. Apart from some 150 articles appearing in student, medical, and other publications, his first book was Running Your Own Private Residential and Nursing Home (1990). Other more recent publications are The Craft of Public Speaking and Planes on Film (both released in 2016) and Dying Harder: Action Films of the Eighties (2017).

A Life by Misadventure is typical of his writings, providing intimate details of people and situations, like any good story, but amidst the grief and sadness there is also the humour that can make a difficult situation tolerable.

The story is about two people who met in midlife and became soulmates. However, their life together was changed forever after a devastating illness struck one of them. The tragedy was worsened by the knowledge that this could have been prevented by timely intervention for a rare but curable condition. Such a predicament can create negative, unhelpful emotions of blame and anger – or at least a desire for recompense. As the story progresses, and as the situation shows signs of stabilising, new tragedies occur. Despite everything, the couple survive and adjust to their new circumstances with the crucial support of family members and friends. The carer in the story demonstrates the benefits of maintaining good physical health, despite his own major setbacks, and allows time to care for himself.

The narrative is told in great detail, exploring the strengths and weaknesses of the characters and taking the reader on a journey over many years. The remarkable thing, though, is that this story is true.

The book is an easy and gripping read, told with great detail (which informs us about the character of the writer) and interspersed with humour. The book demonstrates how the writer coped with adversity and shows that, with commitment and a change in lifestyle, anything is possible. This should encourage people facing similar troubles or caring for others, who need to recognize the perspectives and values of those they look after. For the general reader, it illustrates that we have an inner strength that can be drawn upon to survive difficult situations if we share love and respect.

A Life by Misadventure is therefore a story of two people's struggle against impossible odds and how their great love for each other endured despite the terrible tragedies that affected them. I hope you find it as compelling a read as I did.

Dr Howard Robson MA, MB, FRCP, TFT Adv.

Retired Consultant Cardiologist and Physician

August 2016

INTRODUCTION

In 2010 I was the happiest man on this planet. I had a beautiful, intelligent, articulate wife. We had been together for eleven years and married for eight of them. We enjoyed many things together – cycling, walking, eating out, the cinema, and foreign holidays. We lived in a roomy modern house. I drove a Jaguar while Vivien had a Nissan Micra. I had a dream job as a self-employed hypnotherapist. I couldn't believe how lucky I was.

Then on 20 May 2011 Vivien collapsed unconscious in her bath. She was rushed to hospital where a massive stroke was diagnosed. Later, after carrying out an echocardiogram (ultrasound scan of her heart), doctors discovered that the cause of her stroke was a rare heart tumour. Later still it was found that she was also blind in her left eye. The cause of the blindness was a central retinal artery occlusion, also caused by her heart tumour. Vivien had life-saving cardiac surgery to remove her heart tumour, but she was left with severe brain damage and partial blindness.

It has always been my view that this tragic sequence of events could have been avoided if Vivien had been investigated more thoroughly by the Rheumatology Department at the Scottish General Hospital, and I have laid out my case in the chapters that follow. Vivien's stroke was preceded by twenty-one months of strange symptoms and signs (largely attributed to vasculitis) which should have rung alarm bells but didn't.

The fact that the Rheumatology Department at the Scottish General Hospital now carries out an echocardiogram in every case of vasculitis (or suspected vasculitis) as a direct result of Vivien's stroke is – as far as I am concerned – proof that a terrible mistake was made. To this date the NHS have never admitted that they did anything wrong. Nor have they (or the consultant concerned) ever issued what I would consider to be a proper apology for their error.

By July 2015 I had completed a book, Vivien's Story, which detailed how we met, our happy life together, the series of clinical errors which led to

Vivien's stroke, her incomplete recovery, and our fight to get financial compensation.

I was all set to take this to a publisher when I was struck down by a near-fatal heart attack, as a result of which I spent four months in hospital and had two cardiac operations. Happily I survived due to the skill of the medical and nursing staff at the Scottish General and Scottish Heart Hospitals. On 30 November 2015 I got home to start the long, slow process of recovering from a severe heart attack and cardiac surgery.

But what was I to do about Vivien's Story? Initially I thought of scrapping the whole project, but then I came up with an alternative plan: I would write a second, shorter book, Colin's Story (about my own experiences of heart disease and being treated in the NHS), and then publish both books in one single volume titled A Life by Misadventure.

I would like to make one thing clear. I am not anti-NHS, anti-doctor or anti-nurse. I once worked as a junior hospital doctor, eventually becoming a Registrar in Ophthalmology, and have always been a great supporter of the NHS. I also come from a medical family. Both my parents were doctors, as were my sister, brother-in-law, and uncle. My brother's first wife is still a practising doctor, and I have many friends who are members of the medical profession.

Nor am I a fan of the 'compensation culture' in which people receive vast payouts for trivial injuries. Nonetheless, I believe the present system of compensation for the victims of medical accidents is unfair. The requirement that claimants prove negligence according to the Hunter v Hanley test (in Scotland) or the similar Bolam test (in England and Wales) means that many compensation cases fail even though on a common-sense basis they seem to have merit.

Right from their first day of training, doctors are taught not to criticise other members of the medical profession. Rather like the Freemasons, doctors do tend to stick up for other doctors even when they don't know them. As one litigation solicitor put it to me very succinctly: 'The medical profession tends to close ranks when faced with a complaint.'

This can cause problems in medical litigation cases, as some supposedly 'independent' medical reports are clearly biased in favour of the NHS and designed to exonerate the doctor who is the subject of the case from all blame. Indeed, it is possible for a personal friend of the doctor who is the subject of a medical negligence claim to do such a report, providing they declare that they know that person.

I think the solution is for the Government to introduce a no-fault compensation scheme similar to that which operates in Scandinavian countries, which would avoid the need to prove negligence in court.

I also think that Health Authorities and NHS Trusts need to review their protocols for the investigation of vasculitis, and I have made some recommendations in one of the appendices at the end of this book. It is my hope therefore that many positive things will result from the publication of this book and that, as a result, what happened to Vivien will never happen to anyone else.

I believe that this book is very balanced in its approach. *Vivien's Story* contains some criticisms of her investigation and treatment, but *Colin's Story* is overwhelmingly positive in describing my own experiences of NHS care, without which I would not be alive today.

Colin M. Barron

September 2017

Note – some names of individuals and hospitals have been changed for legal reasons

PART 1

VIVIEN'S STORY

What will survive of us is love.

—Philip Larkin

PROLOGUE

4 August 2015, 4.30 p.m.

I was dying. Oxygen mask clamped firmly to my face, I lay on my back in the ambulance as it sped through the rush hour traffic on the M9.

Just fifteen minutes earlier I had been told that my 'indigestion' – which had been troubling me for four days – was actually a massive heart attack. How was this possible? I had never smoked a cigarette in my life. Didn't drink much. Ate a heathy diet. Exercised almost every day. I particularly enjoyed cycling. I didn't have high blood pressure or diabetes. No one on either side of my family had ever suffered a heart attack. The only risk factors I could think of were that I was a bit overweight and under stress through caring for my disabled wife.

I knew that I had suffered a heart attack – or to give its correct medical name, a myocardial infarction. An infarction is the medical term to describe the death of an area of tissue due to a cutting off of the blood supply. What nobody knew then was that the infarct had caused the ventricular septum – the muscular wall between the two main pumping chambers of the heart – to rot away. Even a hole the size of a match-head can be fatal. I had one the size of a 10p piece. Unbeknown to me (or anyone else), blood that was supposed to be circulating round my body was now pouring into my lungs, flooding them and making me breathless.

I had only hours left to live. If I could make it to the Scottish Heart Hospital and be put on some kind of life support machine, I might survive. If not, I would die.

As I hovered between life and death, I reflected that what was happening to me was merely the latest chapter in an extraordinary personal journey that had started almost seventeen years before.

CHAPTER 1

A NEW BEGINNING

Wednesday, 17 December 1998

It was 7 p.m. when the phone rang at my home in Doune. Even before I picked up the handset, I recognized the number on the caller display. My girlfriend, Fiona, was calling. We had had an argument earlier that day, so I answered with a feeling of trepidation.

'How are you?' I said meekly, anticipating the inevitable furious response.

'What do you think? I'm livid. What goes on between me and Sam has got nothing to do with you. You and I are finished, Colin. It's over.'

Fiona was referring to an incident earlier that day when her ex-boyfriend Sam had arrived unexpectedly at her shop just before me. Even though some months earlier she had told him she never wanted to see him again, he had a habit of turning up every few months in an attempt to worm his way back into her affections. On this occasion, he had spent the whole afternoon with her, despite my protests. Fiona undoubtedly found this quite flattering, though I regarded Sam as one of those jobbies you couldn't flush away. Like these unpleasant faecal floaters, he kept coming back again and again.

Over the next twenty minutes, I did my best to placate Fiona and calm her down but to no avail. She ended our telephone conversation by making it clear that our relationship was finished, that she didn't want to see me again, and that our plans for Christmas together were over.

I put down the handset, stunned. We had broken up once before in the previous year, but it really was over this time, and I knew we would never get back together again. I felt upset and angry that yet again she had put her ex-boyfriend's feelings before mine. Yet in my heart of hearts, I knew that we were not really meant for each other. We were totally different in temperament and in interests and had nothing in common, so perhaps what had happened was for the best. I even wondered if this upsetting incident might lead to better things for me. As Napoleon Hill said, 'Every situation of adversity contains the seed of a greater benefit.'

As I would shortly discover, that is exactly what happened.

I didn't sleep that night, tossing and turning. Just like the old song goes, breaking up is hard to do. And you always feel worse when you are the one who's been dumped rather than the person who has initiated the split. Yet by the next day, I felt better, and after speaking to my best friend, Michelle, I decided that I would go to the Inter-Varsity Club Christmas dinner dance the following evening.

I didn't know it at the time, but a new and most wonderful chapter in my life was about to begin.

The IVC had branches all over Scotland, and I had been a member of the Glasgow club for some months. It was a social club aimed at people who had been to university, and I had enjoyed many of its varied events.

The outside temperature gauge on my car dashboard was showing seven degrees Celsius as I parked my dark-blue Citroën Xantia V6 outside Esquire House in Anniesland, Glasgow, where the IVC dinner dance was being held on Friday, 19 December. There were only six days left till Christmas, yet it was quite mild for the time of year.

I was still feeling a bit down that evening but tried to put a brave face on things. A few of my friends were there, including Michelle and David Carlile, who'd been at university with me. I had met David in September 1977 when he was just starting first-year medicine and I was about to begin my fourth year of the same course. I had recently been appointed editor of Surgo, the Glasgow University medical journal, and David was interested in joining the team. We worked together on Surgo over the next two years and remained firm friends ever since, as we shared a lot of common interests, including James Bond, Monty Python, Doctor Who, and eating a lot.

The first half of the evening was a traditional three-course Christmas dinner followed by coffee and mints, and then we all had to leave the hall for twenty minutes while staff moved the tables to allow the dancing to start. As I was standing outside the hall with my friends, I happened to notice an attractive woman with shoulder-length reddish-blond hair and long legs, which she showed off in a short, black minidress. She looked about thirty-eight. Some months later, Vivien told me that people said she looked a bit like Helen Mirren, though I thought she more closely resembled Diane Keaton in Annie Hall. It was the first time I ever saw Vivien, the woman who was to transform my life.

After this brief interlude, we all went back into the main hall for the second half of the evening. I danced with a few of my female friends and then returned to my seat to sip my drink. By then, it was getting quite late. As the end of the evening was approaching, I noticed that the attractive woman with the long legs had sat down at my table. She looked over at me and smiled. I smiled back and continued sipping my drink.

'Do you work with David?'

I looked up. These were the first words that Vivien ever spoke to me.

'No, I don't. I run a private nursing home.'

We started talking, and then after a couple of minutes, I got up from my seat and sat beside her so that I could hear her better over the loud music. I was flattered that she wanted to talk to me. Was I really a babe magnet? At the age of forty-two and getting a bit thick around my middle, I thought I was more of a fridge magnet! Some months later, Vivien revealed that she only started chatting to me as a way of escaping the unwelcome attentions of a man who was trying to get off with her.

We talked for fifteen minutes, and during this brief conversation, I learned a lot about Vivien and discovered we had a great deal in common. We were both forty-two, though she looked a few years younger. We had both been to Glasgow University. Like me, she enjoyed cycling and had been married before. She lived in Bearsden and worked as a learning support teacher in Coatbridge. I realised that something was happening and that I should ask her out. Unfortunately, other people arrived at the table, and our conversation was interrupted. Not long after that, she had to return home. I kicked myself for not getting her phone number, but I was sure I would meet her again.

I had not made any arrangements for Christmas 1998, because it was originally planned that I would go over to Fiona's family in Glasgow. However, as that was now off, my ex-wife, Alison, and her partner, Robert, very kindly invited me to spend Christmas Day with them and their children at their house in Galashiels.

I now found that I was not thinking about Fiona. My thoughts were all about Vivien, who I believed represented my future. Over the next three weeks, I attended a number of IVC events in the hope that I would meet her again. I didn't have to wait long, because on Tuesday, 12 January, at 8 p.m., I walked into the Mitchell bar in Glasgow's Charing Cross and nearly collided with her. Her face lit up when she saw me, and it was obvious that she remembered me. Much later, she told me that she had also been thinking about me a lot and was hoping that we would meet again.

This time, I was much better prepared than I was at the Christmas night out, as I had brought a notebook and pen with me. After chatting for a couple of hours, during which we totally ignored everyone else in the room, I got her phone number.

The following night, I rang Vivien at her home in Bearsden. Her eleven-year-old daughter, Gillian, answered and then passed the phone to her mother. I asked Vivien if she would like to meet me for a drink on Friday night, and we agreed to meet in the Glasgow Marriott Hotel.

I turned up for our date a few minutes early, and Vivien arrived on the dot at 8 p.m. The evening went like a dream, and it was clear we had a tremendous rapport with each other. At 10 p.m., I walked her to her car, and as I went to kiss her on the cheek, she kissed me passionately on the lips. I knew there and then that she was the one for me and that this was the beginning of a wonderful romance.

The following Sunday, 17 January, Vivien came over to my house in Doune, and we drove to Gleneagles Hotel in Auchterarder for afternoon tea.

Our next date was on Tuesday, 19 January, at the Ashoka Indian restaurant in Bearsden. Vivien asked me to meet her there rather than have me pick her up at her house, as she was afraid one of her children would make a 'crass remark' like 'Are you my mum's new boyfriend?'

The following weekend, I had to travel to Birmingham, as I was doing a course in hypnotherapy with the British Society of Clinical and Medical Ericksonian Hypnosis, which consisted of twelve weekends' teaching, one per month for a year. I found I was missing Vivien terribly and was really glad to see her again the following Tuesday, 26 January, when we had dinner in the Tickled Trout in Milngavie.

By February, I was spending every weekend with Vivien and her two children at her house in Bearsden. Situated in Montrose Drive with beautiful views of the Campsies, the property was a 1970s split-level house with two bedrooms, a bathroom, and a lounge upstairs and two further bedrooms, a TV room, a bathroom and a kitchen–dining room downstairs. The only snag was that the house was directly below the flight path of planes taking off and landing at Glasgow Airport.

'You get used to the noise,' said Vivien as a Boeing 757 screamed overhead, rattling the windows.

I did a lot of DIY jobs for Vivien around her house. One of the first was fitting a bolt to her bedroom door so we couldn't be interrupted by her children during our moments of passion. 'No more coitus interruptus,' I quipped as I tightened the last screw.

One night as we lay in bed together, Vivien opened her heart to me. 'You've made me ... very happy,' she said. 'Now I have a future.'

Our relationship continued to grow stronger. In March I passed my hypnosis exams with flying colours, and I set up my own hypnotherapy business. In July we went on holiday together for a week to the Hotel Montechoro in Albufeire in the Algarve. As Vivien's children – David, 13, and Gillian, 11 – were too young to be left on their own, they stayed with their father in Eastbourne.

We always got on wonderfully well, but I soon discovered that Vivien did have one fault: she had a terrible temper. The first time I ever witnessed it was in the spring of 1999 when she was suffering from a sore back. One Sunday morning Vivien put some eggs into a pan of boiling water for our breakfast and then sat down to eat her muesli, obviously in some pain. A few moments later she asked Gillian to take the eggs out of the pan and put them in egg cups. When Gillian seemed to struggle with this high-tech task, Vivien screamed at me to get off my backside and sort out the problem, her face contorted with rage.

Half an hour later, as she was soaking in her bath and feeling a bit more relaxed, she called me into the bathroom and for the first time (at least in my presence) uttered what was to become her catchphrase: 'I am sorry I was such a cow!'

Yes, Vivien could lose her temper, and when she did, her whole facial appearance changed. As her facial muscles tensed up, lumps appeared in her forehead, making her look a bit like the Klingon Lieutenant Worf in Star Trek: The Next Generation.

Probably her worst temper tantrum occurred in August 1999 when we went cycling around Arran. I had originally intended that we cycle north from the ferry port at Brodick, go through Lochranza and then cut back to Brodick across the centre of the island using the so-called String Road. It was a hard run with a lot of hills that would normally have taken me four hours.

It was a beautiful hot, sunny day as we cycled anticlockwise around the north half of the island with the sea to our right and, after having a bar lunch at the Lochranza Hotel, we set off on the second part of our journey.

Not long after starting on the String Road, Vivien threw her bicycle down onto the tarmac and started screaming at me.

'I can't cycle any more. This is all your fault! It was your idea!'

Trying to stay calm, I did my best to placate Vivien. One solution I offered was for us to cycle to the nearest phone box (we didn't have mobiles back then), chain our bikes to a railing, and call a taxi to take us back to Brodick. Then I could come back the next day with the car to recover the bikes. Yet Vivien refused to consider this option. Instead, we had to walk the full length of the String Road – seven miles, uphill all the way – in the hot sunshine with me pushing both bikes, one on either side.

If you have ever watched the scene in the war film Ice Cold in Alex where John Mills, Sylvia Syms, Harry Andrews, and Anthony Quayle hand-crank and push an Austin K2 ambulance backwards up a steep hill in the Libyan desert in the summer heat, then you can imagine what it felt like.

Vivien was furious that day, but at least she calmed down and apologized eventually, but from that moment on, I used to refer to her anger episodes as 'Arran moments', and some years later I had a T-shirt made up for her with the words 'I Am Sorry I Was Such a Cow' printed on it and suggested she wear it when she wanted to make up after an argument.

For some unknown reason all the great loves of my life have been fiery women, prone to bouts of anger. Why this should be I do not know. It is not that I am attracted to such women; it is more that this kind of person seems to be drawn to me!

By this time I had agreed to sell the Ashlea Nursing Home, which I ran with my business partner and ex-wife Alison, and on 1 September 1999, the deal was done. The following month I went on holiday again to Ibiza with Vivien, and this time David and Gillian came with us. A few weeks later a new century dawned, and as I gazed out of the window at the hundreds of fireworks exploding on the Glasgow skyline just after midnight on 1 January 2000, I realized it wasn't just the start of a new millennium but the beginning of a new and very happy era in my life.

CHAPTER 2

WEDDING IN THE SUN

If 1999 had been a good year for me, then 2000 was even better. Early in the New Year I learned a remarkable technique called Thought Field Therapy (TFT) – invented by American psychologist Dr Roger Callahan – which involved-finger tapping on the body's energy meridian points. Originally developed as a phobia cure, it was also a very effective treatment for many other psychological problems such as anxiety, depression, traumas, and stress. At the time I studied it, I was still one of a very small number of British therapists who used the technique. The very first TFT practitioner in Britain was Ian Graham, who started using the method in 1996. A few years later TFT was to become very well known when top TV hypnotist Paul McKenna discovered it and incorporated it in his books, articles and TV shows such as Sky TV's *I Can Change Your Life*.

In the autumn of 1999 I had used some of my share of the proceeds from the sale of Ashlea Nursing Home to become a bondholder with the Holiday Property Bond organization (HPB). This involved the purchase of a bond for £8,000, which entitled us to take holidays at a number of HPB apartment complexes and villas around the world. It was a bit like a timeshare except that you were not restricted to one particular property.

In April 2000 the two of us went on holiday to HPB's facility at Biniorella, near Camp De Mar in Majorca, and the following August we had another HPB holiday with Vivien's children on the island of Gozo, off the coast of Malta.

By this time we had become engaged and we agreed that we would get married in the summer of 2002. Neither of us wanted a big family wedding, so we decided we would get married abroad, during a summer holiday, with David and Gillian as the only guests.

We also had some discussion about where we were going to live together. By now I had a thriving hypnotherapy practice in the Stirling area and also saw some patients at the Glasgow Nuffield Hospital. I didn't really fancy living in Bearsden because of the constant aircraft noise, so we agreed that we would look for a house in the Stirling or Dunblane area. Eventually Vivien discovered that some large houses were being constructed in Dunblane by Bryant Homes, so we put down a deposit on a property which was to be ready by the end of 2001.

In preparation for this move, Vivien got a new job as a learning support teacher at Central High School starting in March 2001, and Gillian became a pupil at Dunblane High School, while David was at a boarding school in England.

In November 2001 I travelled to California to train in Voice Technology TFT with the creator of TFT, Dr Roger Callahan. Voice Technology TFT (VT) was the ultimate form of the therapy, as it involved an objective diagnostic method which enabled people to be treated over the telephone anywhere in the world. The fee for this one-on-one training over the course of a week was $100,000, making it probably the most expensive therapy training in the world at the time.

Vivien and her two children moved into our new house in Dunblane on 30 November 2001, and I followed two weeks later, once I had sold my bungalow in Doune.

We got married in Cyprus on 30 July 2002 in the charming little village of Pegia a few miles from Coral Beach Resort, near Paphos. The only guests were the holiday firm representative, David, and Gillian, with the latter doubling up as Vivien's bridesmaid. We'd gone for an all-in-one holiday package which involved flights, hire of a small villa and a rental car, and all the necessary wedding paraphernalia such as photos, video, cake, champagne, and flowers. Vivien wore a traditional white wedding dress, while I donned a dark blue M&S cotton summer suit, light blue silk shirt without a tie, and brown slip-on suede shoes.

The wedding was held in the open air in a beautiful garden close to Pegia's town hall with the local marriage officer, Demetris Kappetzis, conducting the ceremony. Cyprus is very hot and humid in the summer, and this day was no exception as the temperature topped 43°C. A look at the wedding photos shows that we looked like a couple of red lobsters, our skin shiny with sweat. After the ceremony was over, we drank some champagne and posed for photographs and then headed off to Coral Bay for our wedding breakfast. Our budget didn't extend to a proper wedding limousine, so we had to make do with our rental car, a white Renault Megane Mark 1 with a 1.4 litre petrol engine (which happens to be Alan Partridge's least favourite car).

It was rather cramped for a wedding car, but at least it had air conditioning. We had our wedding breakfast in the Coral King, a large restaurant in the centre of Coral Bay.

A few days later we flew back to the UK as man and wife and settled down to married life in our beautiful new house. There was only one other thing we felt we needed to make our domestic life complete, and that was a couple of pets. For some time I'd been keen to get two kittens, and one type of cat particularly fascinated me, an American breed called the Maine Coon. These cats could grow to be extremely large (twenty pounds for females and thirty pounds for males were quite typical), and the largest domestic cat in the world (at the time of writing) is a red Maine Coon called Leo.

In August 2002 we visited a couple of cat breeders and eventually chose two male Maine Coon kittens which we named Oscar and Jasper. In late October we collected them from the breeder in Dundee, and they became much-loved members of our family.

Jasper was the more affectionate of the two and became very fond of me. He particularly loved to keep me company when I was in the bath; he would sit on the edge and flick water at me with his paw or else lick my scalp as I reclined in the water. Sadly, Jasper did not live long because in March 2004 he developed a rare and serious illness called Key-Gaskell syndrome, and as a result he had to be put down. It was one of the greatest traumas of my life, and I cried for days after he died.

Several weeks later we purchased another Maine Coon kitten called Kiki. Although she had the same dark grey and black colouring as Jasper, she had a totally different personality, as she hated being stroked and cuddled, and she never purred. She also had a tendency to throw up occasionally, which the vets thought was due to a food intolerance.

At that time my hypnotherapy, TFT, and training business was doing very well, so in September 2003 I traded in my Citroen Xantia for a nearly new Jaguar X-Type. We also enjoyed many more relaxing foreign holidays. In July 2003 we had a two-week break in La Gomera in the Canary Islands. David didn't accompany us on this occasion, and it was also to be the last time Gillian would come on holiday with us.

Over the next few years we visited the Algarve, Southern Spain, Gibraltar, Morocco, Lanzarote, Crete, Madeira, Egypt, Cyprus, and Majorca. Life was good for both of us, and at times I couldn't believe how fortunate I was. I was married to a beautiful woman, had two lovely stepchildren and a couple of adorable cats, lived in a large modern house, drove a luxury car, and made a good living doing something I enjoyed.

However, there was a dark cloud on the horizon. Vivien had a few health problems, and in the summer of 2009 she developed the first symptoms of an ailment that – although originally thought to be minor – ended up nearly killing her and brought an end to the perfect life we had enjoyed.

CHAPTER 3

IN SICKNESS AND IN HEALTH

Vivien had suffered from minor health problems since her mid-thirties, particularly allergies. Some years before I first met her, she had developed oedema (swelling) around her eyes, which appeared to have been an allergy triggered by the accidental contamination of her local water supply by diesel oil. She had been taking the antihistamine drug Zyrtec for a few years to counter this but, despite this medication, had occasional flare-ups of the condition.

She was also prone to allergic skin rashes almost anywhere on her body and had to use hypoallergenic products and special bedding. In the spring of 1999 she developed a sore back and saw an orthopaedic surgeon at a private hospital. He concluded that she had degenerative disease of her lumbar spine, for which no treatment was possible, so that August I took her down to Swindon for three days to receive hands-on healing from one of my friends, Geoff Brooks. This proved highly effective, and her back remained pain-free for years afterwards.

However, in 2009 Vivien developed the first symptoms of a condition that nearly killed her. On 24 July she was working in the garden on a beautiful day when her left hand became red and itchy. She asked me to look at it, and I said I thought it was probably an allergic reaction to a plant that she had touched, which I believed was a reasonable diagnosis, bearing in mind her medical history.

On 27 July she saw her GP, who agreed she had some kind of acute allergic reaction. He prescribed the antihistamine drug Piriton and asked her to come back if there were any further problems.

Despite the Piriton, Vivien's condition worsened, and she developed redness of the fourth and fifth fingertips of her left hand along with swelling and tenderness. On 4 August she was seen by another GP, who made a diagnosis of vasculitis (inflammation of the blood vessels) and started her on a course of oral prednisolone at a dosage of 60 mg a day for five days. This treatment appeared to be effective, and within a few days the swelling and redness diminished.

On 28 August Vivien developed severe pain in her right thigh. I took her to the Accident and Emergency department, where they diagnosed bursitis of the right hip joint. Vivien was advised to take anti-inflammatory medication and discharged home. Again, this treatment appeared to be effective, and within a week or two her symptoms subsided.

On 1 September Vivien's left big toe became swollen, red, and painful. Three days later she was seen by a GP registrar who diagnosed gout and suggested she take ibuprofen for a few days.

Vivien had no further health problems over the next few months, but then on 8 March 2010 she attended the Health Centre once more after developing a rash on her left hand. She saw her GP, who described the rash in the case notes as a 'purple blanching rash on the ulnar [inner] aspect of the fifth finger of her left-hand'. The GP prescribed betamethasone cream, which Vivien used for a few days.

Within a few weeks the rash had flared up again and on 26 April 2010 Vivien was reviewed by another of the GPs. He prescribed oral prednisolone at a dose of 60 mg a day for five days and also ordered a number of blood tests. Once again the 'vasculitis' settled down in a week or two. In view of the recurrence of her 'vasculitis', Vivien was referred to a Consultant Dermatologist for further investigation.

Around this time there was another stress in our lives. My –eighty-nine-year-old mother, Nancy, had been living on her own in her house in Greenock for many years without any kind of support. However, in the past couple of years I had wondered if she had started to develop dementia. Her behaviour had become very odd, and she seemed to have great difficulty remembering things.

My concerns were shared by my brother Alastair and sister Sally (who at that time was a practising GP in the New Forest area of England), so in January 2010 we had my mother assessed by her GP, who agreed that she had developed dementia. By March we had made arrangements for her to receive support at home from the community care services.

Unfortunately, her condition deteriorated rapidly and by the middle of April it was clear that she could not stay in her own home much longer, as she was at risk of injuring herself. On a number of occasions, she had turned on the gas hob without igniting it, forcing us to have her gas appliances disconnected. She was also unable to drive her car or go shopping, so in mid-April her social worker advised me that I should seek a place for her in a nursing home as soon as possible.

As it happened, there was a private nursing home called Altnacraig just 150 yards from my mother's house. The owner was a lady called Sheena Todd, whom I had known for over twenty years. I phoned Sheena and asked if it would be possible for my mother to be admitted to Altnacraig as soon as possible. Sheena visited my mother at home and carried out an assessment. She agreed that my mother needed nursing home care, and we decided that the admission date would be 28 April 2010, as I needed a little time to make all the necessary arrangements.

Vivien requested a day's compassionate leave to help me move my mother into Altnacraig. It proved to be a stressful and tearful occasion for both of us. My mother was so confused that she quite happily accepted her transfer to Altnacraig without protest and settled in quickly, telling everyone that she was living in a 'hotel for old people'. My brother Alastair, who worked as a civil engineer in Dumfries, also took a day off work to help us.

Unfortunately, Vivien was acutely distressed at the thought of her mother-in-law being taken into care, even though this was absolutely necessary. Her emotional state was no doubt exacerbated by the high-dose corticosteroids she was taking. Corticosteroid drugs have many side effects, including euphoria and even mania, and I noticed that when Vivien was taking these drugs, she became even more emotional than usual. 'I don't want to ever go into a nursing home,' she said to me that evening. 'I don't want to end up like one of these people in the nursing home, disabled and unable to do much for myself. If I ever end up like that, I want you to give me a little blue pill!' She wasn't talking about Viagra; she was suggesting I commit euthanasia on her if she ever ended up like my mother. It was an uncannily prescient comment in view of what happened to her just over a year later.

A few days later, on 2 May, Vivien had another flare-up of her vasculitis, this time affecting her left lower leg. She was seen by an out of hours doctor who noted a patch of mottled red skin on her left lower leg. Prednisolone treatment was restarted, this time at a dose of 30 mg per day. Vivien's altered emotional state returned as a result of the steroids, and she announced that her emotional reaction to my mother's nursing home admission had been her 'epiphany'. She started wearing a crucifix (even though she had never been a Catholic) and said she was thinking of going to church every Sunday. She also announced that she wanted to book a function suite in a hotel in Glasgow so that we could renew our wedding vows in July 2012, exactly ten years after our marriage.

Two days later Vivien was reviewed by a GP. She reported that she felt very unwell while taking steroids, and the GP agreed that these could be gradually reduced in dosage and then stopped.

The following day the GP emailed Dr Brown, consultant dermatologist at Central General Hospital, to ask if Vivien could receive an earlier appointment in view of the many recent episodes of vasculitis. The following day Vivien was seen by Dr Brown at the hospital's dermatology outpatient clinic. In his letter to the GP practice following this consultation, Dr Brown noted that she had had a recent flare-up of the vasculitis and suggested a gradual reduction in her corticosteroid dose. He also noted that blood tests had shown an elevated neutrophil (white cell) count and a raised erythrocyte (red cell) sedimentation rate (ESR). Dr Brown also said he was unsure about what type of vasculitis she might have. No follow-up appointment was arranged at that point.

On 24 May Vivien was reviewed by her GP who noted that the vasculitis was now settling down and agreed that the prednisolone dosage could be gradually reduced.

Six days later, on the afternoon of Sunday, 30 May, Vivien was tidying her bedroom when she suddenly became unwell. 'Colin, I'm dying. I'm dying,' she screamed. Immediately I ran into her bedroom to find out what was wrong. Vivien told me that she felt dizzy, and the whole room seemed to be spinning round and round. She also felt nauseated and was sick a couple of times.

I wondered if she might be suffering from labyrinthitis, an acute viral infection of the inner ear, and phoned NHS 24. A little while later an out of hours GP called round, examined Vivien, and came to the same conclusion. The GP gave Vivien an injection of Stemetil (a drug which counters nausea) and prescribed a course of Stemetil tablets, to be used for a few days.

Two days later Vivien was reviewed by her GP, who noticed that her symptoms had now disappeared. In fact her dizziness had settled within a few hours, and she had returned to work as normal the next day.

On 3 August Vivien had another flare-up of her vasculitis in her left hand and was seen by her GP again. At that point she was not keen on a further course of corticosteroids owing to the unpleasant side effects. On 26 August she had yet another episode of vasculitis, this time affecting her right hand. This time she was seen by a different GP, who described the rash in her notes as 'purpuric' (a purpuric rash is one which results from bleeding into the skin from small capillaries). The GP discussed Vivien's case with a senior partner, and prednisolone was restarted at a dose of 60 mg per day. Four days later Vivien developed swelling in the left side of her face which was thought to be a side effect of her steroid medication.

On 9 September 2010 Vivien was seen again by Consultant Dermatologist Dr Peter Brown. He suggested reducing the steroid dose and – in view of the unusual presentation – decided to refer her to Consultant Rheumatologist Dr Norman Green for further investigation. He also noted that it would have been helpful to carry out a skin biopsy of these rashes to determine if they really were vasculitic, but since the lesions had faded prior to his consultation, he felt the opportunity to do a biopsy had now passed.

On 17 September Vivien was seen again by her GP with yet another recurrence of vasculitis. This time he decided to increase the dose of prednisolone to 30 mg a day.

By this time Vivien was on long-term sick leave. She had gone back to work as a teacher at Central High School in late August, but within a matter of days she had gone off sick again. In reality it was the symptoms of the high-dose corticosteroid treatment, rather than the vasculitis, which were making her feel so unwell, as she suffered a number of horrible side effects from her steroid treatment. As well as the aforementioned mental agitation, which at times was almost like a mania, she developed severe insomnia. This was so bad that her GP eventually prescribed the sleeping tablet Temazepam, to be taken as required. The Temazepam gave her only four hours of sleep a night, and she was left feeling very groggy during the day.

On 24 September she was reviewed again at the Health Centre by one of her GPs, who increased her prednisolone dose to 60 mg a day. The GP also contacted Dr James Smith, one of the two consultant rheumatologists at Scottish General Hospital, and started Vivien on alendronic acid, calcium carbonate, and omeprazole in an effort to reduce some of the side effects of her steroid medication.

On 6 October Vivien had her first outpatient consultation at the Scottish General Hospital with Consultant Rheumatologist Dr Norman Green. He noted that she had suffered many side effects from high-dose corticosteroid therapy, so he decided to change her medication to azathioprine 50 mg per day, in addition to the corticosteroids which were to be gradually reduced in dosage and then stopped. Azathioprine is a so-called immunosuppressive drug, which reduces the activity of the body's immune system and thus is helpful in some cases of vasculitis, which is an autoimmune condition. Unfortunately, it is a highly toxic drug, similar to chemotherapy agents, with many serious side effects, including liver and bone marrow damage and an increased chance of patients developing certain types of cancer.

Six days later Vivien had another recurrence of her vasculitis and was seen by a GP registrar, who noted that she had a rash on her left palm.

On 13 October Dr Green contacted Dr Brown by fax. He speculated that the cause of Vivien's vasculitis might never be found and also suggested that her raised white cell count might be due to the corticosteroid therapy.

On 26 October Dr Green wrote to Vivien's GP. He mentioned that cervical ribs, which were more prominent on the right side, had been found on Vivien's chest X-ray and said he would get an opinion from a vascular surgeon. He also said that 'neither Dr Brown nor I have actually seen the lesions, and we cannot be sure they are vasculitic'.

Cervical ribs are a common abnormality in which people have an extra pair of ribs originating from the cervical (rather than thoracic) vertebrae. Although they often don't cause any problems, they can sometimes press on blood vessels and nerves, causing symptoms in the hands. They might have explained rashes in Vivien's hands but not in her feet. Nor could they account for any of her other strange symptoms.

On 8 December 2010 Dr Green saw Vivien at the rheumatology outpatient clinic for the last time. He said he now believed the cervical ribs were probably unrelated to her symptoms as Vivien had also had rashes in her feet. However, he said he still wanted Vivien to see a vascular surgeon for an opinion on them.

Dr Green then told Vivien that she couldn't have vasculitis, as there was no sign of inflammation in her blood tests. Vivien then asked him what was wrong with her, and he said, 'I don't know.' Despite his doubts about the diagnosis, she was advised to continue with 100 mg of azathioprine daily for another six months, with a review appointment arranged for June 2011.

On 20 December Vivien was reviewed once more by her GP. Her prednisolone had now been reduced to a dosage of 5 mg on alternate days. Although her rash had now settled, she reported pain in her thighs, calves, and feet for the previous five days. Her GP carried out a physical examination and noted no abnormalities. In the notes he suggested that the cause might be viral myalgia (painful inflamed muscles caused by viral infection). On 5 January 2011 Vivien was seen again by her GP. At this point her vasculitis had settled, and she had stopped taking corticosteroids though she continued on azathioprine. Her GP noted that she had had a hot, red swelling on the medial (inner) aspect of her right foot the previous week.

Vivien started a daily diary in 2011, although she only kept it up till mid-January. On Thursday, 6 January, she wrote, 'feeling better … and intend to spend more time with people in 2011 esp Mum & Gillian.' Four days later she reported, 'Period came today. Quite heavy. Thank you, God.'

On 24 January Vivien had another review with her GP. He noted that she was suffering from anxiety, disturbed sleep, and vivid dreams and was having to go to the toilet frequently to urinate. She also reported some loss of hair. Her GP thought all these symptoms might be due to the side effects of azathioprine and decided to write to Dr Green to express his concerns.

On 25 January Dr Green wrote to Vivien's GP and suggested that – in view of the side effects – Vivien should reduce her azathioprine to 50 mg a day for one to two months and then stop.

Eight days earlier Vivien had been seen by a vascular surgeon at Central General Hospital. After examining Vivien and taking her blood pressure in both arms, she wrote to Dr Green and the GP practice to say that she felt that Vivien's cervical ribs were unrelated to her hand symptoms.

On 21 February Vivien was reviewed by her GP. By this time the azathioprine dose had been reduced to 50 mg a day, and Vivien was feeling better. Her vasculitis had settled down, and he also noted that she had reported pain in her left knee, the cause of which was unknown.

On 14 March Vivien developed an uncomfortable facial rash and was seen by one of the GPs, who felt this was a possible allergic reaction to the azathioprine. Vivien was prescribed fexofenadine HCL and topical hydrocortisone 1 per cent cream. After the other GPs discussed her case, it was agreed that the azathioprine could now be stopped. On 17 March Vivien was reviewed by one of the GPs. He noticed that the facial rash had improved, though she had reported pain in her right shoulder.

On 8 April 2011 we went on holiday to the Lake District. We stayed three nights at the Ivy Lodge Hotel near Keswick, which was owned by the Holiday Property Bond organization. The weather was unusually hot and sunny for the time of year, and we had a lovely time visiting several tourist attractions in the area. On the Saturday we had a cruise on Lake Windermere and then went for a long walk followed by lunch in the garden of a local hotel. The next day we visited the James Bond Museum and the Movie Cars Museum in Keswick (a few months later I discovered that both of these museums closed down a couple of weeks after we visited). We also explored the Cumberland Pencil Museum and enjoyed walking about in the sunshine, eating ice cream cones, relaxing on the shingle beaches of Lake Windermere, and just enjoying each other's company. It was quite a long drive there and back, so we shared the driving chores. We didn't know it at the time, but it was to be our last normal holiday together.

In late April Vivien developed a 'funny feeling' in her right hand and complained of difficulty in doing handwriting. I gave her a quick neurological examination – in particular checking the power in both arms – and could find no abnormality. I then asked her to write 'the lazy brown fox jumped over the gate' on a bit of paper. Her writing looked normal. I didn't think it could be anything serious, but all the same I suggested that she see her GP. On 3 May Vivien did so. The GP took a brief history and carried out an examination but could find no abnormalities. He asked Vivien to return in a couple of weeks for a follow-up appointment.

On 18 May Vivien was reviewed by another GP. She had reported a slight improvement in her handwriting problem. He carried out a thorough examination, which included listening to her carotid arteries in the neck and her heart. He noted no abnormalities. He also suggested that her hand symptoms might be caused by her cervical ribs and said that he would refer her to a neurologist if there was no improvement in two weeks.

Fifty-one hours later, Vivien collapsed at home. Both of our lives were never to be the same again.

CHAPTER 4

THE DAY OUR LIVES CHANGED FOREVER

Almost everyone over fifty-five can recall what they were doing on 22 November 1963, the day President John F. Kennedy was assassinated. In more recent times, 11 September 2001 – the date of the World Trade Centre atrocity – is remembered for similar reasons.

Friday, 20 May 2011, is a date I will never forget. It was the day my wife nearly died – the day she lost the ability to speak. It was the day she had a massive stroke, the day our lives changed forever.

That Friday started just like any other workday. We rose about 7 a.m. and had breakfast together, and then at 8.20 a.m. Vivien set off for Central High School – where she worked as a learning support teacher – in her silver Nissan Micra. She finished work at 3.30 p.m. and then went shopping in Morrisons, stopped at the filling station, and arrived home at 5.10 p.m.

For dinner Vivien made grilled squid and steamed asparagus. Then, rather unusually, we washed this feast down with a bottle of champagne, aptly named House of Vivien, which her brother, Andrew had given her a couple of weeks earlier as a fifty-fifth birthday present. After dinner I did the dishes while Vivien made some phone calls, and then at 7.20 p.m. I was snuggled up to our Maine Coon cats Oscar and Kiki, looking forward to a couple of hours of television viewing, when Vivien popped her head through the doorway.

'I'm going to have a bath,' she said. It was the last thing she would say for several weeks, the final words she would ever speak in her normal voice.

At 8.25 p.m. I had a feeling of vague unease. Something was wrong. Vivien had gone for a bath an hour before, and yet there were no sounds of her moving about and closing doors and opening wardrobes and drawers, the sorts of noises she would normally make after bathing, so I decided to investigate. I looked in the bedroom; she wasn't there. Nor was she in the en suite bathroom so I went along the hall to the main family bathroom where she usually had her bath. I tapped on the door, asking if she was all right. There was no reply. Gingerly I opened the door – which fortunately had been left unlocked – and got the biggest shock of my life.

Vivien was slumped motionless in the bath, lying on her left side with her head just above the water. 'What's wrong, darling?' I asked. There was no reply. I asked her again. Vivien responded with a gurgling sound. She was trying to tell me something but couldn't manage it.

Deep inside her skull Vivien was screaming in terror, but the words wouldn't come out. Millions of brain cells that once formed her speech centre had died from lack of oxygen and were turning to water.

What the fuck is happening? I must be dying! Get an ambulance, you moron. For Christ's sake, do something – don't just stand there!

Vivien could think the words but could not speak, as the brain structures required to perform this task no longer existed. Suddenly the theme music from Holby City started blaring from the TV set next door, which told me it must be exactly 8.30 p.m.

For a moment I thought that Vivien was suffering from concussion after slipping in the bath and banging her head, but then I realized it must be something far worse. Quickly my doctor's training from the seventies took over, and I assessed Vivien in an objective, professional manner. I remembered the acronym ABC, which stands for airway, breathing, and circulation, the first things you check when assessing a casualty.

I discovered that Vivien was paralyzed down her right side. This finding – plus the fact she couldn't speak – told me that she must have suffered a stroke affecting the left hemisphere of her brain. Immediately I pulled out the bath plug, grabbed the nearest phone, and dialled 999.

'Which service do you require?'

'Ambulance,' I blurted out. 'I think my wife has had a stroke.' As quickly as I could, I gave the operator all the necessary details and then unlocked the front door and shut the cats in the utility room, as had been requested.

Three minutes later the First Response paramedics' Ford Fiesta van screeched to a halt outside our house. Immediately the two-man team raced upstairs to the bathroom and got to work, starting with the insertion of a cannula into Vivien's left arm. A few moments later the ambulance crew arrived and soon the ambulance crew, the paramedics, and Vivien and I were all crammed into the small bathroom. If it had not been such a desperate situation, it would have been comical, rather like that scene in the Marx Brothers movie A Night at the Opera when a huge number of people squeeze into a small ship's cabin.

The two teams dried Vivien's wet body with towels and got her into a special lifting harness to hoist her from the bath without injury and then carried her to the ambulance. As they left, they told me to follow them to the hospital as soon as possible and bring some clothes and toiletries with me.

Hurriedly I found a small overnight bag and packed it with a few essentials. In my panic I had great difficulty in determining the difference between Vivien's bras and her knickers. I couldn't find her toilet bag, so I emptied one of my own and shoved a few basic essentials into it.

Just a few minutes after the ambulance had left, I was on my way to the hospital. I chose to take Vivien's Micra, as I thought it would be less likely to be vandalized in the Central General Hospital car park than my own Jaguar X-Type.

It was a beautiful warm spring night as I belted down the M9 motorway at 70 miles an hour heading south, and Stirling Castle looked majestic in the golden light of the sunset. I was amazed that I was able to drive safely because hundreds of anxious thoughts were passing through my mind. How serious was the stroke? Would she ever walk again? Would she end up in a wheelchair? Would she ever drive a car once more or ride a bicycle? Would we ever go on holidays again? Would her speech return? Would we ever have sex again? Was she going to live or die? How were we going to survive financially? If she lost her job and I had to be her carer, how would we pay our bills? And what had caused her stroke? Did she have high blood pressure? Or was there some kind of vascular abnormality within her skull? It would be six days before anyone would know what had caused the stroke, and when the true answer was known, it was something that most people had never heard of.

CHAPTER 5

VIVIEN'S LIFE HANGS IN THE BALANCE

Accident and Emergency department, Central General Hospital
Friday, 20 May 2011, 9.40 p.m.

After parking the Micra, I raced through the power-operated doors of the Accident and Emergency department and went straight to the reception desk.

'My name is Dr Colin Barron,' I blurted to the receptionist. 'My wife, Vivien Barron, had a stroke, and she came here by ambulance. Can I see her?'

The receptionist looked at her computer screen for a moment before replying. 'Your wife hasn't arrived here yet. The ambulance is still on its way.'

'But that's impossible. I left the house about ten minutes after the ambulance departed; it must be here by now, surely!'

'The ambulance crew may have stopped on the way to pick up another patient.'

I couldn't believe I was hearing this. My wife had suffered a severe stroke, which could kill her, and I was being told that the ambulance had stopped on its way to pick up someone else. Surely every moment counted? The receptionist looked at the screen again.

'I'm terribly sorry. I made a mistake. Your wife is actually here. If you take a seat, the doctors will let you know when you can see her.'

I turned around from the reception desk and took stock of my surroundings. Although it was a Friday night, the waiting room in the Accident and

Emergency (A&E) Department was still fairly empty, with just three or four people milling about. I had worked as a casualty officer in an A&E department about thirty years before, so I knew that the place would start to get busy after 11 p.m., when the pubs emptied. After that time most people attending casualty departments were there because of the effects of alcohol.

Now that I'd got to the hospital, my next priority was to let Vivien's family know what had happened. A sign in the A&E Department warned people not to use their mobile phones in the waiting area. I didn't want to go outside the building, in case the doctors and nurses were looking for me, so I was forced to use the single payphone in the waiting room. Fortunately, I had a few coins in my trouser pocket. Trembling with anxiety, I put 50p into the slot of the payphone and dialled my mother-in-law, May Thompson, in Bearsden, Glasgow. The phone rang four times before she answered.

'It's Colin. Something terrible has happened to Vivien. She's had a stroke.'

'Oh, my God!'

Quickly I told May what had happened: how I had found Vivien semiconscious in the bath seventy minutes earlier and how she had been rushed to hospital. I then learned that Gillian – who was working in Greenock and staying with May – had still not returned home from work, so I told May not to phone her on her mobile because I didn't want her to get upset and have a car accident. Instead I suggested that she gave her the bad news when she got home.

I then sat down on the hard, uncomfortable chair in the waiting room and awaited developments. After a few moments one of the junior doctors opened the swing doors leading to the clinical area and asked me to come through to the room where Vivien was being treated. She looked in a bad way, as she was drifting in and out of consciousness, and there was a drip in her left arm.

I went up to her and clasped her right hand. 'Everything is going to be all right.'

Vivien did not respond. Her face was fixed and immobile, but I knew that deep inside she was terrified.

There was nothing I could do to help, so I just sat by her trolley holding her hand and praying that everything would indeed be all right. After a few moments the on-duty Accident and Emergency consultant, Dr Barrie, arrived and explained that Vivien would need a CT scan.

A few minutes later Vivien was wheeled into the scanning room. 'Right, lady, we're going to have a look at what's going on inside your head,' said Dr Barrie.

The scan only took a few minutes, and shortly afterwards Vivien was taken back to the treatment room. The staff explained that contact had already been made with the on-call stroke consultant in Edinburgh who would be speaking to me by video link. There was a large flat-screen television and video camera at one end of the treatment room, and after a few minutes, an image appeared on the screen of a middle-aged balding man with glasses. Quickly the consultant explained the situation.

'You're probably wondering what's happened to your wife. We know from the clinical picture, and from the CT scan, that she's had a severe stroke affecting the left hemisphere of her brain. Now I understand that you last saw her in good health about three hours ago, is that correct?'

'Yes,' I replied.

'In that case we believe it may be worth using a thrombolytic drug to dissolve any clot that may be causing the stroke. It has to be used within about four hours of the onset of the stroke, so there is still time for this treatment to be carried out. If this treatment is successful, then it could result in your wife being less dependent in the long term than would otherwise be the case. There is a risk attached to this procedure, as with some types of strokes it can cause bleeding inside the skull which would be immediately apparent from a sudden deterioration in your wife's condition. So I will have to have your consent to carry out this procedure.'

Even though I was no longer in clinical practice in the NHS, I was familiar with this procedure as I had read about it in newspaper articles. It was now common practice to offer thrombolytic treatment to people who had just had a stroke. In many cases it could result in strokes being 'reversed' within twenty-four hours. This did not mean that such people always made a total recovery from their stroke, but it could result in a much lower level of disability in the future than they might otherwise face. I was also aware of the risks of this procedure.

'I give my consent. I'm quite happy for my wife to receive this treatment.'

'Okay, that's fine,' said the consultant. 'I should mention that your wife does appear to have suffered a very severe stroke, as she has a dense hemiplegia.' This refers to paralysis of one side of the body.

Soon after this Vivien received a dose of the thrombolytic drug through her intravenous cannula. However, there was no change in her clinical condition, either improvement or deterioration. I was still waiting by her trolley when my mobile phone went off. I looked at the display; it was Gillian. She was very distraught – as any daughter would be – to hear of her mother's illness.

She told me that she was coming to the hospital with her grandmother plus Vivien's sister, Margaret and her friend and flatmate, Alice. They would also pick up Vivien's son, David, en route and expected to be there within an hour or two. I told her that I would let her know what ward Vivien was going to be transferred to as soon as I had details.

An hour later Vivien was moved upstairs to the medical intensive care unit. Soon after this Gillian arrived with the rest of the family. Everyone looked stressed and tearful. By now it was well after midnight, and I was starting to feel very tired, but my mind and body were so racked with tension, there was no way I was going to sleep that night.

We waited in the corridor for half an hour before we were shown into the ward. Vivien was only semiconscious but seemed to be aware of our presence. She was now attached to monitors which constantly checked her pulse, blood pressure, and heart rhythm. At 3 a.m. one of the nurses pointed out that there wasn't any point in us staying all night with her, so we all agreed that we would go home to our beds.

It was 3.30 a.m. when I got back to Dunblane. For some reason the streetlights in my road weren't working, and in my rush to leave the house a few hours before, I had forgotten to turn on the external house lights. I had to fumble with my keys to get the front door open in the darkness. Immediately I went upstairs to the bedroom and undressed, washed my face, cleaned my teeth, and got into my pyjamas.

Normally I would have put Oscar and Kiki to bed in the utility room, but on this occasion I decided I would quite like their company, as I knew I would not sleep that night. So I let them roam free in the hope that they would come up on the bed and cuddle me. Unfortunately, things didn't work out as planned. Instead, the two cats sat in the bedroom doorway staring at me. All I could see in the darkness were the four yellow dots of their retinas. When I got up and approached them, hoping to pick up one of them for a cuddle, they both ran away and scampered downstairs, expecting me to feed them.

As predicted, I didn't get any sleep that night, as my mind was racing, so I rose at 7 a.m., had my breakfast, shaved and showered, and then got down to work on my computer.

My first priority was to let all our friends and family know what happened, so I sent an email to all our friends, and my sister Sally and brother Alistair, to tell them what had happened. I also set up a 'Group' in my email address book entitled 'Vivien Stroke Recovery' so that I could easily send out regular updates on how Vivien was getting on.

An hour later the phone rang. It was my friend Michelle, who had just got the news. 'What's the latest news?'

'She's being transferred to the High Depend ....' I couldn't say the words and burst into tears.

'OK, take it easy.'

I quickly recovered my composure.

'She's being transferred to the High Dependency Unit. There's a chance she could die.'

From my medical training I knew that 30 per cent of stroke victims die within a month. Michelle calmed me down and told me to stay in touch if there were any further developments. In the next couple of hours there were further phone calls from my brother Alastair and my sister Sally and some of our friends. Everyone was deeply shocked by what had happened.

Later that morning Gillian arrived, and we agreed that she would stay with me for at least a couple of weeks. She had asked for compassionate leave, and her employers had been very understanding. Gillian even offered to help out with the laundry, ironing, and cooking.

A few years before, when she was still a teenager, we had had a rather tense relationship, but all past animosities were now forgotten as we were working as a team to support each other and Vivien. I don't know what I would have done without Gillian in those first two weeks after Vivien's stroke. Our whole world had turned upside down, and we faced a very uncertain future. At worst Vivien could die. Even the best possible scenario was that she would end up seriously disabled and require care for the rest of her life. In these two weeks Gillian was a rock that I could depend on.

Later that day we went to visit Vivien again at Central General Hospital. One problem was soon apparent: we couldn't all visit at the same time, as there simply wasn't enough room round the bed for Vivien to have six visitors at a time. So Gillian drew up a visiting rota, arranging that at least one person would always be with her during all the permitted visiting hours. I eventually visited Vivien every single day, bar one, between the day of her admission to hospital and her discharge home almost three months later.

On Monday, 23 May, Vivien was transferred to Ward 16 at Central General Hospital. This was good news because it meant she was now considered to be at little risk of dying from the acute effects of the stroke. Unfortunately, Ward 16 was an old-fashioned ward which was scheduled to close down in a few weeks, and she was in a large room with seven other people of both sexes. There was little ventilation in the room, and like most hospital wards, it was overheated. From time to time the nurses would pull the curtains round one of the beds to allow a patient to use a bedpan, and within a couple of minutes the room stank of faeces. In one corner of the ward was an old man who was clearly in a bad way, as he was making a terrible groaning noise. I wondered how on earth anyone could sleep with this commotion in the background. The staff were obviously doing their best to provide a good standard of care despite poor accommodation and were probably looking forward to the day when they could move to brand new facilities at the Scottish General Hospital.

The day after Vivien's transfer to Ward 16, she had her first session with her physiotherapist, Alison, who declared that she had suffered what was known as a total anterior circulation infarct (TACI), the most severe form of stroke. Alison explained that only 4 per cent of people with a TACI made a complete recovery. Obviously she would do everything she could to help Vivien get better, but nothing was guaranteed.

By the following day my anxiety had started to subside a little. It was clear that our lives would never be the same again, but at least Vivien had survived. But on Wednesday, 25 May, we received terrible news which made us realize that her life was once more in the balance.

CHAPTER 6

DEVASTATING NEWS

Vivien had suffered a very severe stroke but at least she had survived, and over the next few days, my life settled into a new routine. Gillian was now staying with me, so in the mornings we would attend to the housework, do the washing and ironing, and go food shopping. Afternoons and early evenings were taken up with visiting Vivien in hospital.

I still felt very stressed and upset and was having difficulty sleeping. So I rummaged in Vivien's bathroom cabinet to see if she had any sleeping tablets. She had been prescribed them the previous autumn when she was suffering from insomnia caused by high-dose oral corticosteroids. On a shelf I found five 20 mg Temazepam tablets in a partly used bubble pack which I took over the next few nights. Once they had been used up, I found I was able to sleep naturally again, although I was still having nightmares triggered by the current crisis.

By the middle of the following week I was starting to feel more relaxed, but then, on the afternoon of Wednesday, 25 May, we got some bad news. Following her stroke, Vivien had investigations to determine the cause. These included measures like blood tests, an electrocardiogram, a chest X-ray, and – most important – ultrasound scans of her carotid (neck) arteries and her heart.

That day, as we were visiting Vivien in Ward 16, one of the junior doctors approached us and told us that an abnormality had shown up on the echocardiogram (ultrasound heart scan). However, she refused to discuss details and said that the best person to talk to would be the stroke consultant, Dr Brian Sutton, who could speak to us the following afternoon.

My mind started racing. What could this abnormality be? Could it be a blood clot? I knew from my medical training that heart rhythm disturbances (such as atrial fibrillation) can sometimes cause a blood clot to form in the heart chambers, which can then break off and travel to the brain, causing a stroke. Another possibility could be some kind of disorder of the heart valves or a congenital heart malformation, such as a 'hole in the heart'.

That evening I phoned my sister, Sally – who at that time was still working as a GP in the New Forest – and explained what I had been told. Sally confirmed that a blood clot in the heart chambers was a possibility but then mentioned that the abnormality might be something called an atrial myxoma, a benign tumour of the heart muscle which, being friable, had a tendency to break up and discharge small pieces into the bloodstream (a phenomenon known as embolization).

Atrial myxoma. Could that be her problem? I remembered reading about this tumour when I was studying pathology at medical school, so I decided to find out more. I consulted my copy of Davidson's Principles and Practices of Medicine and read a few articles on the Internet and discovered that there were two kinds of atrial myxoma. There was a firm, smooth sort which often caused problems with heart function, so patients would often present with fatigue and breathlessness. More interestingly, the other type was described as gelatinous and friable – as Sally had described – and often released emboli into the bloodstream. This could result in the development of red fingertips and toes – often mistaken as signs of vasculitis (a condition known as pseudovasculitis) – and could even cause strokes!

The more I read, the more convinced I became that Vivien must have an atrial myxoma because she had many of the classic symptoms and signs of this condition. I was also surprised that none of the doctors who had treated her – including a consultant dermatologist and a consultant rheumatologist – had considered it in their differential diagnosis. Clearly a terrible mistake had been made. If only the doctors had thought about this possibility and carried out an echocardiogram some months before, then this whole tragedy could have been avoided as the myxoma could have been surgically excised before it could cause any problems.

The next day Gillian and I had a meeting with the stroke consultant, Dr Sutton, in a small room at the end of Ward 16. Dr Sutton was an extremely pleasant man with greying hair and spectacles who looked about forty-five. He started off by explaining that Vivien had suffered a very severe stroke, and the prognosis was not good. She was likely to suffer severe disabilities for the rest of her life.

He then explained that they had carried out an ultrasound scan of her heart and discovered that she had a benign tumour in the left atrium, known as an atrial myxoma, which had caused the stroke. In order to get an even better view of the lesion, they did a second scan, known as a transoesophageal echocardiogram, which required Vivien to be sedated in order that a sensor could be pushed down her oesophagus.

Dr Sutton explained that the atrial myxoma could be removed by open-heart surgery, but the problem was that Vivien had just had a stroke, which meant that it would be very dangerous to give her a general anaesthetic. He said that no anaesthetist would want to give her a general anaesthetic for at least two to three months. During this period she would be at high risk of having another stroke, as her myxoma could fire off another embolus at any time.

It was truly devastating news. Vivien had survived her stroke, but now we were being told that she was at high risk of having another one. There was also the possibility that further emboli could end up almost anywhere in her body, so she could end up losing a limb, going blind, or suffering further brain damage resulting in her becoming a 'vegetable'. If the next embolus was even bigger than the first one and blocked her aortic arch (a major artery emanating from her heart), she could even die!

Dr Sutton said that there was very little that could be done for her at this stage. He would put her on aspirin, which decreased platelet stickiness and just might reduce the risk of further emboli from clots forming on the surface of the myxoma. It would not affect the risk of emboli from bits of the tumour breaking off. He also said that if Vivien developed an embolus affecting one of her limbs, then it might be possible to carry out surgery to remove the embolus before the limb went gangrenous. But these were small comforts. As far as I was concerned, she was living on borrowed time, and I thought that it was virtually certain that she would have another embolus before the two-to-three-month period was up.

Gillian asked Dr Sutton what caused atrial myxomas, and he said that no-one knew. I was furious because as far I was concerned the NHS had made a terrible mistake in not diagnosing the myxoma despite nearly two years of symptoms. Vivien had seen about ten different doctors in the past twenty months, including a consultant dermatologist and a consultant rheumatologist. All the technical resources of Scottish General Hospital – the newest in Britain – were at their disposal, but they all failed to make the correct diagnosis. However, I knew there was no point in ranting at Dr Sutton because he was not to blame for anything that had happened in the past two years. He was only responsible for Vivien's care since her stroke.

We were stunned at the latest news and retired to the WRVS café at Central General Hospital to consider the implications. I bought two toasted cheese-and-ham sandwiches and a couple of soft drinks at the counter and sat down at a table in a corner of the café with Gillian. When I looked at her, she started to cry, and then, as if on cue, my tears started too. I wept like a small child. A dam of emotion had burst, and for fifteen minutes I bubbled like a baby, feeling as though I was going to drown in a sea of my own tears.

How could there possibly be a God? I thought. How could he let a thing like this happen! There were murderers and rapists and paedophiles in prison who lived to a ripe old age. Vivien had never done any harm to anyone, yet her life had now been destroyed, and she was at risk of dying. And there was nothing anyone could do about it. It was so unfair.

I decided there and then that there were going to be consequences for the NHS. Vivien had worked for most of her life and paid taxes, and yet the NHS had totally failed her in her time of need. From that moment I resolved to find out exactly how this dreadful mistake had happened and who had made the wrong decisions. And I was going to sue them and report them to the General Medical Council. Unfortunately, it was not something I could do right then; I would have to wait until I was ready.

As a therapist, I was aware of the need to forgive people who had done me wrong, but I wasn't in a forgiving mood. I certainly didn't feel like Mother Teresa of Calcutta; I felt more like Charles Bronson in Death Wish!

Eventually our tears stopped, and we managed to calm each other down. I had to remind myself of all the principles of positive thinking that I had learned in my training as a hypnotherapist. Things might be bad, but they were by no means hopeless. Although there was a high risk of Vivien having another embolus, there was always the possibility that this might not happen. She might survive the next few months without incident, have her operation, pull through this, and then make a good recovery.

I remembered what I had once read in a book on positive thinking. It said that if you are diagnosed with cancer and you are told that only 1 per cent survive this particular type of tumour, then you should always assume that you are going to be in that 1 per cent.

I also remembered some very sage advice that I had come across in Dale Carnegie's book How to Stop Worrying and Start Living back in the 1970s. One thing he had said was that if you thought of all the watertight compartments in a large ocean liner – which can be closed to prevent the ship from sinking when it is holed below the waterline – in a similar way you should live your life in 'day-tight compartments'. In other words, instead of worrying about what might happen in the future, you should simply concentrate on what you have to do that particular day and not think about anything else. Jesus said something similar in the Bible: 'Fear not the morrow because the morrow will take care of itself.' I found that thinking of these words gave me great comfort.

I had to take the view that, although horrible things might happen in the future, at least Vivien was alive and comfortable now, and we should rejoice in every day she remained in that state rather than worrying about what might happen tomorrow or next week or the following month.

This is a strategy that I have used successfully with many of my hypnotherapy patients. Many people live lives of misery, not because of what they are doing at that particular moment, but because they are either fretting about things that happened in the past or else worrying about what might possibly happen in the future. I have always believed one secret of mental calm is to focus solely on the present moment, but very few people do this. So people with the wrong mental strategies could be lying on a sunbed in Majorca with a glass of wine in their hand, about to have a lovely lunch, yet feel miserable because they are thinking about what they have to do back at work the following week. So I made a resolution that I would live my life in 'day-tight compartments' and focus on the present moment, as it was the only way that I could get through this current crisis. Furthermore, I felt that there were some things I could do to help Vivien, things that very few people would even be aware of.

CHAPTER 7

A LITTLE HELP FROM MY FRIENDS

In 2000 I learned an amazing therapy technique called Thought Field Therapy (TFT) – involving finger tapping on the body's energy meridian points – which was invented by American psychologist Dr Roger Callahan in 1980. Dr Callahan, who had been practising clinical psychology since 1950, had used various techniques to treat patients including cognitive behaviour therapy (CBT), which is still the main conventional psychotherapy used in the NHS. However, in the 1970s he became dissatisfied with the results of orthodox treatments and became interested in an alternative therapy called applied kinesiology (AK), which involved working with the body's energy meridian system, first discovered by the Chinese five thousand years earlier.

Callahan treated his first TFT case in 1980 when he was working with a middle-aged lady called Mary Ford, who had a phobia of water. This phobia was so severe that she could not take anything other than a very shallow bath and so had to avoid swimming pools and beaches. For eighteen months Callahan treated her with conventional therapies without much effect. Then one day he made an amazing discovery.

Callahan was working with Mary as she focused on her fear of water. He asked her where in her body she felt her anxiety, and she said she felt it in her stomach. Suddenly Callahan had a brainwave. He knew that the body's stomach energy meridian passed under both eyes so, as Mary thought of the fear, he tapped under both her eyes a few times. Instantly Mary's fear of water vanished and has stayed away to this day, more than thirty-five years on.

Callahan repeated this simple technique of tapping under the eyes with a large number of phobia sufferers and soon discovered that such a simple treatment worked with very few phobics. But he knew he was onto something, and many years of research and experimentation followed. Eventually Callahan found that many psychological problems such as phobias, anxieties, traumas, and depression could be treated by finger-tapping on the energy meridian points of the body. Although TFT was originally developed as a treatment for psychological problems, Callahan subsequently discovered that it helped many physical health problems as well.

Although most TFT treatments are carried out face-to-face with a trained therapist, some TFT practitioners can do 'remote healing' on patients from anywhere in the world using either a form of TFT or other healing methods.

So when Vivien suffered her stroke and it seemed that no medical treatment could help her, I decided to use every alternative healing technique that I thought might be of benefit. My own view was that the situation was so hopeless that it was worth trying anything. Even if there was only a one-in-a-million chance that she would get a 1 per cent improvement in her condition, I still thought it was worth trying because what did she have to lose? She had ended up in this terrible predicament as a result of a flawed investigation by NHS doctors, so I thought it was time to see what alternative medicine could do.

I had first requested remote healing from the TFT Internet discussion group the day after Vivien's stroke and was touched by the response. Scores of TFT practitioners from every corner of the globe – many of whom I had never met – were moved by news of Vivien's plight and emailed me offering to do distant healing for her. Others said they would say prayers for her. One practitioner even volunteered to travel hundreds of miles to give her Reiki healing in her hospital bed. I was overwhelmed by all the messages of support. If nothing else, it made me realize just how much love there is in the world.

I wasn't bothered by the apparent craziness of some of these healing methods. I just wanted to do everything I could for my wife. In addition to the healing that was being offered by members of the TFT community, I also found numerous websites which offered free remote healing for people with a variety of medical conditions, and I signed up to as many as I could. For example, I requested remote healing from practitioners of an American system called the Silva Method, which I had learned myself in 1996. It is essentially a technique in which you put yourself into deep meditation, known as the alpha level (so-called because the brain produces alpha waves in this state), visualize the person who is ill, and then imagine them getting better.

To give Vivien every possible chance, I decided that I would treat her myself using the Silva Method three times a day, every single day, while she was in hospital. To brush up on my technique, I read through all my lecture notes again, listened to all the Silva Method audiocassettes and CDs I possessed, and read several books on the method. Three times a day I would close my eyes, go to the alpha level state, and visualize Vivien's brain healing and making new neural connections. I also imagined her heart tumour shrinking under the influence of a healing white light.

I also used my TFT and hypnosis skills to help her. Back in 2008 I had removed a wart under Vivien's right eye by using hypnotic suggestion, so Vivien already knew that her own subconscious mind could bring about healing. By this time she was in her own single room in the new Scottish General Hospital, so it was relatively easy to give her a hypnotherapy session while I was visiting.

I also recorded a self-hypnosis CD for her featuring various techniques such as hypnohealing (similar to the Silva Method) in which Vivien was asked to imagine her brain healing and creating new neural connections. I also used carefully constructed metaphors, since it is known these have a powerful effect on the unconscious mind. One I used was a tale I created about a telephone exchange that had been damaged by an explosion and was now being repaired. I suggested that hundreds of telephone engineers were scurrying about laying new cables and soldering connections. I knew Vivien's unconscious mind would interpret this as instructions to bring about healing. I also employed some hypnotic suggestions from D. Corydon Hammond's book Hypnotic Suggestions and Metaphors, which were carefully designed to help stroke survivors.

I also decided that Vivien should receive some homeopathic treatment. Although I am not a qualified homeopathic practitioner, I was very familiar with an offshoot of homeopathy called psionic medicine, in which a hair sample from the patient is dowsed with a pendulum in order to provide an accurate homeopathic diagnosis.

As someone with an orthodox scientific background, I am familiar with all the objections to homeopathy from the medical profession, particularly the view that homeopathic remedies are so dilute that there can be no active molecules in them. On the other hand, my own view was that homeopathy did work for some people, and the situation was so desperate that it was worth trying anything, so the next time I was visiting Vivien in hospital, I pulled the curtain round her bed for a couple of minutes, clipped off a small hair sample, and popped it into an envelope which I posted to a psionic medicine practitioner. Within a few days I had received a psionic diagnosis and details of the homeopathic remedies I had to give to Vivien.

I also asked an old friend, Dr Susan White, who is a fellow member of the British Society of Medical and Dental Hypnosis (Scotland), to give Vivien remote healing using a device called a Lybra machine.

What difference did all these alternative treatments make to Vivien's condition? Well, the simple answer is that I don't know, and I don't think anyone could say whether they really helped or not. But at the very least, they boosted my morale at a time when there didn't seem to be any good news. It was very comforting to come home after another harrowing day at the hospital, look at my emails, and discover that someone was doing some remote healing for Vivien. It gave me such a lift because when you are in a hopeless situation, just the fact that someone is doing something can make you feel much stronger.

Back in early 1942 the British forces in Malta were in a desperate situation. Short of fuel, food, and ammunition, soldiers and airmen cowered in slit trenches as scores of German and Italian planes flew over, opposed only by a small force of obsolete Hawker Hurricane Mark II fighters. Malta had become the most bombed place on Earth, and morale was at rock bottom.

Then one of the RAF station commanders had a brilliant idea. He got hold of all the spare machine guns he could find and set them up around the perimeter of the airfield close to the slit trenches. He then announced that, during air raids, RAF personnel had the option of manning machine guns and hitting back at the enemy instead of just lying passively in their slit trenches.

Soon scores of RAF personnel could be seen blazing away at Axis aircraft during air raids. There is no evidence that this new policy resulted in more enemy aircraft being shot down, but it did have one big effect: it raised morale. In fact, the RAF commander's decision probably prevented many of his men from developing post-traumatic stress disorder (PTSD). When you are in a seemingly hopeless situation, then doing something – anything – that might possibly change things can make you feel so much better.

I will always be eternally grateful to all these healers who did everything they could for Vivien without thought of recompense, and if I were in the same situation again, I would do exactly the same thing. Alternative healers around the world, I salute you for your compassion and dedication.

CHAPTER 8

THE ACCOUNTANT WHO BECAME A TEACHER

In 1951 May Malcolmson, a GPO telephonist from the Maryhill area of Glasgow, was introduced to Andrew Thompson, a BP marine engineer who was on shore leave from the Merchant Navy. They had a whirlwind romance, and three years later they were married in a church in Maryhill. Afterwards they had a wedding reception in Colqhouns, a popular tearoom in Byres Road.

After they were married, they lived in a flat in a large tenement on Woodlands Road near Charing Cross and then moved in with May's mother in Drumchapel for a short while.

In 1956 May gave birth to her first daughter, Vivien. The following year she had a son, Andrew, and in 1960 the family moved into a large three-bedroom semi-detached 1930s house in Larchfield Road, Bearsden. Eight years later their second daughter, Margaret, was born.

In August 1961 Vivien started her primary education at Westerton Primary School, Bearsden. She remembers being a shy and timid child who liked English and reading but who had a great dislike of sports and gymnastics. In her spare time she liked going cycling and swimming.

Seven years later Vivien started Secondary One at the Glasgow High School for girls in Cleveden Road in Glasgow's West End. This school still exists but is now called Cleveden High and is only 150 yards from the Glasgow Nuffield Hospital where I saw hypnotherapy patients between 2000 and 2014.

Vivien's best subjects at secondary school were English, history, and chemistry, and like her future (second) husband, she disliked mathematics and physical education. At that time her school was for girls only, but she was still able to meet boys at youth club discos. When she was fourteen she started smoking, a behaviour which was virtually the norm in those days although she gave it up fourteen years later at the request of her first husband, Peter.

In May 1973 Vivien suffered the greatest trauma of her life to date when her father Andrew developed pancreatic cancer and died soon afterwards (by a curious coincidence my own Uncle George died from the same cause in 1988). The whole family was devastated by this tragedy, though it particularly affected Vivien, who was very close to her father.

In the summer of 1973 Vivien made the decision to train as an accountant, and in October that year she started a three-year B.A. course in Glasgow University. As she recounted to me many years later she wasn't really interested in the subject but had made a career choice at a time when she was still reeling from the unexpected death of her father. Vivien was supposed to graduate in 1976 but did not do so until 1977, as she had to resit some subjects.

After graduating, Vivien started work with a firm of accountants in Glasgow called Binder Hamlyn. She stayed with them for three years and then moved to London, where she lived in a flat in Upper Montagu Street, quite close to Baker Street tube station. The following year she moved to Walton-on-Thames in order to start work for Thursung Winthrop Auditors who were based in nearby Guildford.

In the early 1980s Vivien had a steady boyfriend called Howard, who was a chemical engineer. The relationship ended when Howard went to Canada to work. Soon after this Vivien met English chartered accountant Peter Smiley in a pub and they started going out together. Eventually they became engaged, but at this point Howard suddenly arrived back on the scene. He tried to win back Vivien by putting notes through her letterbox (which on one occasion included an engagement ring). By now, however, Vivien had decided that her future lay with Peter, so she told Howard to get lost.

In 1984 Vivien and Peter got married. It was a small registry office wedding, and afterwards the couple moved into a house in Godalming. Three years later they moved to East Grinstead, a town which is best known for the Royal Victoria Hospital where plastic surgeon Sir Archibald McIndoe carried out his pioneering plastic surgery on burned RAF airmen during WW2. These injured pilots eventually went on to form the Guinea Pig Club.

In 1985 Vivien gave birth to her first child, David. Two years later a daughter, Gillian, followed. Unfortunately, by this time the marriage was in trouble, and a few weeks after Gillian's birth, Vivien left Peter and – with her two young children – went to live with her mother in Bearsden. As Vivien told me in 1999, the marriage only lasted just long enough to produce two children.

Vivien was now a single parent with all the problems this entailed and now had to rebuild her whole life. She decided to retrain as a teacher, since the reasonable hours of work and long holidays would make it easier for her to bring up two children while earning an income. She had never been that interested in accountancy anyway as it involved nothing more than adding up figures. She found it extremely boring, which was probably why she never went on to become a chartered accountant. (Author's note: any readers who want further confirmation that accountancy isn't the most interesting profession in the world should read the short article entitled 'Why accountancy isn't boring' by Mr Eric Putey, which can be found in Monty Python's Big Red Book [Methuen,1971].)

With her background in accountancy, Vivien was able to retrain as a business studies teacher and only had to do a one-year course at Jordanhill College, which was quite close to her mother's house.

In 1990 Vivien started work as a supply teacher, going wherever her services were required, and she taught at a number of educational establishments including my former school, Greenock Academy.

Eventually she became a learning support teacher, working with pupils with special needs, and got a job at St Ambrose in Coatbridge. By this time, her divorce had come through, and she bought a property in Campsie Drive, Bearsden, about two miles from her mother's house.

In the mid-1990s, she joined a social club called Club 30+ which held regular meetings in Glasgow city centre, usually at a pub called the Lemon Tree. In 1995 she met Tony, who worked as the caretaker for a large block of flats in Glasgow, and they embarked on a three-year relationship.

Tony had previously worked as an auto electrician and enjoyed tinkering with mechanical things. He owned a motorbike and a Fiat 126 car and was also interested in cycling.

Vivien decided to take up this hobby as well and bought a blue Raleigh hybrid bike, and the couple enjoyed many cycling trips together, including a three-day cycling holiday in Arran which involved overnight stays at bed and breakfasts.

However, there were problems with the relationship, with many breakups and reconciliations. In addition, Vivien's children disliked Tony, and the fact that he smoked did not help matters. Vivien's mother also disapproved of Tony even though she never met him.

In the autumn of 1998 the couple finally split up for good, and Vivien sent Tony a letter stating that she never wanted to see him again. They had thought of getting married at one point and had even put their names down for a new-built house in Lenzie. However, that was now all history, and in late 1998 Vivien moved into a large four-bedroom 1970s split-level bungalow in Montrose Drive, Bearsden.

She was saddened by the breakup of her relationship but wanted to rebuild her social life and hopefully meet someone else. So she joined a Glasgow social club called IVC (Inter-Varsity Club), which held regular meetings at various venues throughout Glasgow. And it was at the annual IVC Christmas dinner dance on 19 December 1998 that she was to meet the man who was to sweep her off her feet and change her life completely!

CHAPTER 9

AN INTERESTING LIFE

Like Vivien I have had an interesting and unusual life. My father, Peter Barron, was born in Glasgow in 1918 and studied medicine at Glasgow University, graduating in 1941. He had originally intended to graduate in July 1940 but took a year out to join the Home Guard. Being Jewish, he was especially fearful of the possibility of a German invasion, as he might have ended up in a concentration camp, so he elected to join the Home Guard so that he would have access to firearms. As he told me some decades later, he decided that if the Germans ever came for him, he would die a soldier's death with a gun in his hand and take as many Nazis with him as he could.

Fortunately, the German invasion never happened, but my father remained in the Home Guard for some months, eventually becoming an instructor on the Bren gun (the British Army's standard light machine gun in WW2). After graduating in 1941, he spent several months in general practice in Wales before being called up in early 1942. With his medical qualification my father became a captain in the Royal Army Medical Corps and was sent to North Africa in the summer of 1942 where he served with a field ambulance unit attached to the 51st Highland Division, part of General Bernard Law Montgomery's Eighth Army.

This was a very exciting and dangerous time for my father, and as a child, I was fascinated by his tales of sleeping in tents, washing in canvas basins, and living on a diet of bully beef, tea and hard tack biscuits. Thanks to him, I soon became an expert on the inadequacies of wartime British tanks and the effectiveness of the various British anti-tank guns (the two-pounder was useless; the six-pounder was good but couldn't penetrate the frontal armour of a Tiger or Panther, while the seventeen pounder could knock out any German tank).

After serving in the North African campaign and North-West Europe, my father was demobbed in 1945 and eventually ended up working at the Southern General Hospital in Glasgow where he met my mother, Agnes.

My mother was born in Eastercraigs, Glasgow, in 1920 and went to Hutcheson's Grammar School for Girls, where she eventually became the dux. In 1938 she went to Glasgow University to study medicine, graduating in 1944.

My parents got married in Glasgow in 1949, and the following year – following a move to Greenock – my mother gave birth to my sister, Sally. Two years later she had a son, Alastair, and then in 1956 I was born. I should have been born in December but was six weeks premature. I have often wondered if this was responsible for my well-known habit of always being early for everything: 'I was born six weeks prematurely and have been early for everything ever since!'

My mother had stopped work in 1950 to bring up her family, but in 1960 she started a new job as a clinical assistant in ophthalmology at Greenock Eye Infirmary, while my father had a GP practice in nearby Port Glasgow.

In August 1961 I started school at the original Greenock Academy, dating back to 1855, which was situated in Nelson Street on the site of what is now the West College. In June 1964, when I was in primary three, the school moved to a new building in Madeira Street. Greenock Academy closed its doors for good in June 2011 and was then used as the set for the popular BBC school drama Waterloo Road between 2012 and 2014 before being demolished in 2015.

My best subjects at school were physics and chemistry. I was also very good at art, and one of the greatest regrets of my life was that I was persuaded to give up art at the end of secondary two in order to do German, which at that time was thought to be advisable for anyone who was thinking of doing physics at university, as many of the classic physics papers were written originally in that language. I wasn't very good at German, partly because I wasn't really interested in learning it and also because my teachers were poor, and it was no surprise when I failed my 'O' Grade German in the summer of 1972.

Although I was good at science subjects, I didn't seem to be doing very well at modern languages and English, and my parents wondered if I would ever go to university and get a decent job. I believe I was good at English, in the sense that I liked writing things and enjoyed reading. What I didn't like was the emphasis on analysis of plays and poems which played such an important part in 'O' Grade and Higher English at that time. I found this to be boring, tedious, and pointless.

One play I particularly loathed was The Winslow Boy by Terence Rattigan. Set in pre–WW1 England, it dealt with the true story of a boy who was expelled from a naval college for allegedly stealing a five shilling postal order and his family's efforts to clear his name. As you can see, the plot wasn't exactly Die Hard, and I couldn't see the point of analysing every word of Terence Rattigan's rather leaden prose. I am sure that if he had written the screenplay for Where Eagles Dare, it would have consisted of three hours of Richard Burton and Clint Eastwood agonising about their personal problems, in a Bavarian bothy!

In the nick of time I pulled my socks up and realized what I had to do to pass exams in subjects I disliked. In the summer of 1973 I passed my Highers with flying colours. I got As in physics, chemistry, English, and geography, a B in maths, and a C in French.

The story of my B Higher in maths is quite interesting. I had always struggled with this subject, but when I was in my fifth year, I studied hard and thought I might possibly get an A. Unfortunately, I was very anxious the night before my maths Higher exam, and seeing my anxiety, my father gave me a sleeping pill known as Mogadon (nitrazepam). This drug is similar to Valium, except that it is longer acting with a half-life of twenty-four hours.

Of course, back in May 1973 I didn't know all this. I presumed the Mogadon would give me a full night's sleep, and I would wake up feeling refreshed. Unfortunately, the next day I was very drowsy, and when I came home at lunchtime, I fell asleep in an armchair for fifteen minutes.

The fact that I managed to complete the maths exam, let alone get a B, was itself a great achievement, and to this day I'm convinced that if I had not been given that Mogadon, I might have got an A – not that it would have made any difference to my subsequent career. However, this episode was probably the genesis of my view that the medical profession's belief that every problem can be sorted with a drug is fallacious and, at times, extremely harmful.

Up until the summer of 1973 I had assumed that when I left school I would go to university and study science subjects such as physics, chemistry, or electrical engineering, particularly as one of my hobbies in the early 1970s was building my own radios and other electronic devices. But as I had got exam results which were far better than I'd expected, I began to wonder if I should consider becoming a doctor. In the autumn of 1972 – in common with other pupils about to sit their Highers – I had an interview with the rector of Greenock Academy, Mr Robert K. Campbell, and he recommended that I should go into medicine. My doctor parents were also very keen that I should continue the family tradition, since my sister had already graduated in medicine, and my uncle was a GP.

I'd never seriously considered being a doctor because I realized that it involved long hours of work with little sleep and dealing with some gruesome situations. But I had got a really good set of Higher results, and the fact that the medical course was very difficult to get into seemed to attract me in a perverse way. So in the autumn of 1973 I applied to study medicine at Glasgow University.

Initially I thought I would probably end up as a psychiatrist because I've always had an interest in the workings of the human mind, and this was partly due to psychological problems I'd experienced during my teenage years. It is often said that some people become psychiatrists or psychologists because they want to find out what's wrong with themselves. I think there is a grain of truth in this, and it was certainly true in my case.

Although I had enjoyed a reasonably happy childhood without suffering any great traumas, I had had my problems. I had always been a shy, timid child, and when I was twelve, something happened that was to affect me for many years afterwards. I was in the science class, and the female teacher was discussing the facts of life. Suddenly she stopped talking, looked at me, and said, 'Colin, am I embarrassing you?' She had noticed that I was blushing, and unfortunately, without realizing it, she had done the very worst thing she could possibly do: pointing it out to everyone in the class. Immediately everyone in the class turned round, looked at me, and laughed.

From that point on I was constantly teased about my blushing. People would say things to me just to get me to blush, and one consequence of this was that I developed a social phobia. I didn't want to go to parties or discos or social events. Fortunately, my blushing problem seemed to fade away by the time I was seventeen, but I still had a lot of social anxieties, in particular a fear of discos. I was afraid that if I went to such events, I wouldn't know what to do or how to behave, people would laugh at me, and I would start blushing. This probably would have happened if I had gone to a disco when I was twelve years old, but it's unlikely it would have happened when I was seventeen, as my classmates had by then become a little more mature, with better social skills.

My fear of discos didn't really end till I was twenty-one years old when I cured myself by accident. What happened was that I got myself drunk and then went to a disco, and once I had been to a disco drunk, I could then go sober. I have never had a problem with this particular scenario ever since, although of course now that I'm sixty –one, I have no desire whatsoever to go to a disco again!

One consequence of all the problems I experienced in my teenage years was that I became very interested in the workings of the human mind. Every Saturday morning, my school friends were playing football or rugby, or smoking, drinking, or sniffing glue, or whatever it was they liked to do. Meantime, I walked to Greenock's public library and read all the books I could find about psychology in the hope that I would find an answer to my problems. I also studied my father's books on hypnosis and psychiatry.

My weekly trips to the library gave me a great understanding of the workings of the human mind, but I still had not discovered how to rid myself of my problems. All the same, by the time I started university in October 1974, I was a much more confident person than I had been a few years previously, although I still had my anxiety about discos. But there was a new problem. A more confident phoenix had emerged from the ashes of the old Colin Barron, but unfortunately it wasn't a very nice phoenix because – as a way of masking my own insecurities and anxieties – I became very selfish and self-centred and constantly boasted about my own achievements, even though I didn't really have anything to boast about! I believed that the way to make friends was to be 'interesting' – to brag about my accomplishments and to get other people to become interested in me. It was a set of beliefs which, with the benefit of hindsight, were totally wrong and could have led to long-term social disaster. Fortunately, in the spring of 1976, I came across a book that showed me what I was doing wrong and changed my life.

I had just completed the middle term of second-year medicine – probably the hardest part of the entire medical course – and had just passed exams in anatomy and biochemistry, when I came across a book called How to Win Friends and Influence People by Dale Carnegie. First published in 1937, it was one of the earliest books on personal development.

As I read this book, I had a kind of epiphany because Dale Carnegie pointed out all the things I'd been doing wrong in my dealings with other people. After finishing his book, I realized that instead of trying to get other people interested in me, I had to become interested in other people if I wanted to be liked. As Carnegie pointed out: 'People are not interested in you. They are not interested in me. They are interested in themselves- morning, noon and after dinner. People are more worried about a spot on their chin than in an earthquake in China that kills 3000 people.'

One person who was quoted frequently in this book was one of the fathers of modern psychology, Professor William James. One of his best quotations was this one: 'Even people you consider your friends get greater pleasure from your failures than they do from your achievements.' I know this to be true from personal experience. Back in 1990 I had my first book published (on running nursing homes), but – apart from my mother and father – hardly anyone I knew was pleased at my achievement or was even the least bit interested. Most people didn't even mention it.

Carnegie even provided this little bit of advice from one of America's greatest lovers – who had broken hundreds of women's hearts – on how he chatted up women so successfully. It consists of just six words: 'I talk to women about themselves.'

After reading Carnegie's book, my life went down a completely different path. It didn't bring about an instant personality change, but at least I realized all my past mistakes in dealing with people. My only regret was that I had not come across that book much sooner. Had I read it five years earlier, when I was fourteen, it could have made a tremendous difference to my teenage years.

Despite my epiphany, I had a new problem, which first started in 1975. After I'd been at university for a few months I realized I was feeling quite anxious a lot of the time and was also having episodes of low mood. By 1976 I was having daily episodes of what I would now describe as obsessive thoughts. I didn't have a full-blown obsessive-compulsive disorder in the sense that I didn't have any rituals or compulsions. For example, I didn't have an urge to wash my hands a hundred times a day or repeatedly check that the front door was locked (as many OCD sufferers are prone to do). Instead, my problem lay with intrusive thoughts.

A lot of these intrusive thoughts occurred while I was driving up to Glasgow University. I had made the decision to stay at home with my parents throughout my university years, and my parents bought me a Renault 5TL car for travelling to university. With the benefit of hindsight I realize this was a great mistake, and I think I would have developed more as a person and matured much earlier if I'd stayed in a student flat and gone to lots of wild parties.

As it was, I had a daily commute of fifty miles from Greenock to Glasgow University and back, and this proved to be a stressful experience. I would leave the house at 7.45 a.m. feeling quite relaxed, but during the drive up to university, I would have a number of intrusive thoughts, which raised my anxiety level. For example, if I went over a bump in the road, I would worry that I had accidentally run over someone. If I momentarily found myself exceeding the speed limit or committing some minor driving error, I would wonder if I was going to be reported to the police for careless driving. Particularly distressing were intrusive thoughts I started to get about the concept of God, which was rather odd because I was actually agnostic. I hadn't been to church (except for weddings and funerals) since 1968. And I've always joked that the last time I attended Sunday school, I was president of the escape committee!

I would tell myself, I must not think the words 'Fuck God', because if I did, then God would punish me. Of course if you try not to think of certain words, what happens is that you do think of them. I also started to feel intense guilt about the way I had treated various people when I was much younger and felt that I deserved to be punished for my 'crimes'.

For a year or two I endured this daily inner torment, and then in October 1976 my father put me on Ludiomil, a tetracyclic antidepressant, which was supposed to be an improvement on the earlier tricyclic drugs. This made no difference to my symptoms. All I got out of the medication was a lot of side effects, including horrendous constipation, a dry mouth, and slight drowsiness.

By March 1977 my mental pain was so great that I realized I had to do something about it, and one afternoon I skipped my lectures and went to see a man called Simon Munro at the Glasgow University student counselling service. Simon was very friendly and said he believed a lot of my problems were due to the fact that I didn't have a girlfriend. Even at the time, I thought that was a very strange thing to say.

On a more positive note he did arrange for me to see a consultant psychiatrist, Dr Chesterton, who told me to stop taking antidepressants and referred me to the Lansdowne Clinic in Great Western Road for some treatment from a clinical psychologist. The treatment consisted of relaxation exercises (similar to the first stage of a hypnosis session) and a daily diary, which I was to complete with details of all my obsessions. At each subsequent appointment the psychologist would read the diary out loud and laugh at all my ridiculous thoughts. I think the idea behind this was to make me realize just how daft they were.

Following this intervention my mental state did improve. Although I would now regard the treatments that were used as being not nearly as effective as other methods like hypnosis, NLP, and TFT, at least I did realize that my problems were not as severe as I thought. I had worried that I was developing a psychosis, but Dr Munro reassured me that the only thing wrong with me was stress caused by my lifestyle.

One thing I found that did help was to take some exercise. Cycling seemed to work best, followed by walking and then swimming. Gradually my anxiety and depression problems faded away, just as my blushing had done some years before, but in a way I am glad I had these negative experiences because they gave me an insight into some of the problems my hypnotherapy and TFT patients have faced.

Around this time I was appointed editor of Surgo (the Glasgow University Medical Journal), to which I had contributed to for many years. Ever since my teenage years I had been very interested in drawing cartoons and writing funny stories, and in my sixth year at Greenock Academy I even produced an underground school magazine which featured cartoons about teachers and satirical articles about school life.

I became very interested in editing, writing, and producing Surgo and enjoyed this far more than any other part of the medical course. In 1979 Surgo won a Glasgow Herald competition to find the best student magazine. If a millionaire publisher had offered me a large annual salary to produce Surgo for the rest of my life, I would have been quite happy to do so. I also found that creating the magazine greatly helped my mental state, as it was an excellent diversion from the stress of the medical course.

At that point I was still intent on becoming a consultant psychiatrist after I graduated, and in the summer of 1977 I spent four weeks attached to a large psychiatric hospital in southern Scotland. Unfortunately, this had unintended consequences for the rest of my life, because I discovered that being a psychiatrist was nothing like what I had imagined. I had always thought that psychiatrists would spend a relatively short time interviewing patients and then carry out a very short and highly effective intervention such as hypnotherapy, rather like what I later did. I found that what happens in a psychiatric consultation is that the psychiatrist spends literally hours going over every detail of a person's life and then, at the end of the session, the treatment is either a drug or else a not-very-effective treatment administered by someone else.

After I took this student elective in psychiatry, I wasn't so sure I really wanted to make it my career. A few months before I had done a single-term course in ophthalmology, which I found fascinating, and in 1978 I decided that, instead of becoming a psychiatrist, I would go in for ophthalmology.

After graduating in the summer of 1979, I did a six-month junior house officer post in general surgery at Law Hospital, Carluke, followed by six months in general medicine at Monklands Hospital in Airdrie. I liked Monklands Hospital so much that I then did a further six months in accident and emergency, followed by a six-month stint as a senior house officer in orthopaedic surgery.

By this point I had met the woman who was to be my first wife, and in June 1981 I got married to Alison Brown, a staff nurse I had met when we were both working in the Accident and Emergency Department at Monklands Hospital. Soon after that, we moved into a flat in the Kelvindale area of Glasgow and I started work as a senior house officer in ophthalmology at Glasgow Eye Infirmary and Gartnavel General Hospital.

To begin with, I enjoyed ophthalmology, and everything seemed to be going very well with my chosen career. I was surprised though, at how busy the ophthalmology casualty department at Glasgow Eye Infirmary could be. It had a huge catchment area covering the whole of the west of Scotland, so the number of patients attending on any given day could be enormous. On one occasion I saw sixty-four patients in four hours.

One day, as the eye infirmary was about to close its doors at 5 p.m., a young man walked into the building holding a bloodstained handkerchief to his right eyebrow. He explained that he had been walking along nearby Sauchiehall Street when he had unexpectedly walked into a scaffolding bar and had sustained a wound above his right eye.

'Of all the bars in all the towns, you had to walk into this one,' I quipped as I sutured his eyebrow.

Unfortunately, things did not go as I had planned in my chosen career. One of the most important skills an ophthalmologist must possess is the ability to do eye operations. Ophthalmic surgeons have to carry out delicate procedures, many of which involve a device called an operating microscope, which gives the surgeon a magnified view of the operating area. After I'd been doing ophthalmology for a while, I was given a few operations to do, and it soon became apparent that I didn't have the necessary manual dexterity to do these procedures. Ironically, much of the problem seemed to be related to my own eyesight. Since childhood I had suffered from an intermittent divergent squint, and this had affected my depth perception, which meant that when I was working using an operating microscope, I often had great difficulty in perceiving things in full 3D, making surgery very difficult.

I was quite surprised when this was pointed out to me in late 1983 because I had always enjoyed working with my hands, doing DIY, drawing, painting, and making Airfix models, and I never expected that I would have a problem in this area. But I had to face reality, which was that I would never become a consultant ophthalmologist because of my problems with the surgery.

I now had to choose a new career, but in what? Many people in my position would have simply retrained as a GP, but I didn't really fancy it. It's a well-paid job and a respected one, but it involves long hours doing work that at times can be highly unpleasant and stressful. If cleaning lavatories and being a GP paid the same money, I know what I'd rather do for a living! One of my friends works as a part-time GP and once told me about the misery of being a GP three days a week.

As mentioned earlier, I'd always been very interested in writing and producing magazines, so an obvious solution was to get a post in medical journalism. Unfortunately, such posts were few and far between, and many of them weren't all that interesting. I did go for an interview for a job as a medically qualified journalist at The Lancet, but I didn't really fancy it because it involved working in a grubby old office with worn furniture, reading hundreds of rather boring scientific papers that had been submitted by doctors. If you think the articles that get published in medical journals seem boring, you should read the ones that don't get accepted!

I also applied for a few jobs in the pharmaceutical industry as I thought my writing experience might get me a good position, but I didn't get anywhere with that either. By the summer of 1984 I had attended about ten unsuccessful interviews for various positions in medical journalism and the pharmaceutical industry, without a positive outcome. Then, out of the blue, my wife, Alison – who was a highly qualified and experienced nurse – told me that her friend Cathy Livingstone (who was a district nurse) was planning to open a private residential home for the elderly with her husband, Alan.

We went over to visit the Livingstones and viewed their property, a large Victorian villa in Neilston, Renfrewshire, which was being refurbished for its new role. I was thrilled by the idea of opening a residential home for the elderly because it was a way out of the NHS and would provide us with a much better lifestyle in which we were working for ourselves without the bureaucracy of the Health Service.

Within a few weeks we had purchased a former hotel in Callander, Perthshire, called Ashlea House, and six months later in January 1985 it opened its doors as a private residential home for the elderly. In July that year we re-registered it as a private nursing home, as we felt this was more appropriate for the sort of care we wanted to provide.

The first few months of running the business were extremely stressful as we only had a few residents and were borrowing up to the hilt. I'd also borrowed a large sum of money from my parents to enable us to make a sufficient deposit on our bank loan. Six months after opening we achieved full occupancy, and within a couple of years, the business was producing handsome profits which enabled us to have a good lifestyle and eventually buy a large modern house on the outskirts of Callander.

Unfortunately, my marriage to Alison eventually failed. In November 1989 we separated, and I moved to a house in Doune. We agreed that we would continue to run the business as before, and we remained business partners and good friends. We ran Ashlea Nursing Home for fifteen years until we agreed to sell the business in 1999. By this time Alison had had two children with her new partner Robert, whom she later married, and I had met Vivien, so we both realized that the time had come to close this chapter in our lives. Running the nursing home was a very challenging experience, but it gave me a lot of useful experience in various areas that I later used to advantage when I had to cope with Vivien's stroke.

CHAPTER 10

IMPOSSIBLE ODDS

We were devastated by the news that Vivien had a heart tumour that could not be removed for some months. But we agreed that we would not tell her about it as it would traumatize her, destroy her morale, and possibly even affect her will to live. I felt that she should not be told about the myxoma until just before her operation, which might be two or three months hence.

Vivien had a great fear of any kind of malignancy, and this was partly explained by the great trauma she had suffered when her father died of cancer when she was seventeen. Atrial myxoma was actually classified as a benign, non-cancerous tumour in the sense that it was not malignant; i.e., it did not spread to other organs, although it did have a tendency to produce emboli.

The whole family also made great efforts to remain cheery and positive when visiting Vivien, as we knew this would affect her morale and mood. It didn't matter how bad the news was or how devastated I felt inside; I always greeted her with a big smile, cracked a few jokes, and made her laugh. As far as Vivien was concerned, everything was fine, and she was going to make a great recovery.

I knew from my medical training (and also from my experiences as a hypnotherapist) that a positive mental attitude was very important in recovery from any kind of illness, so we ensured that she got only good news.

I knew that she could have another stroke – or even die – before she was fit for an operation, but I strove to put on a brave face and hope for the best. I kept reminding myself that as long as Vivien was alive, there was still hope. As the old saying goes, where there's life, there's hope.

By this time Vivien had been transferred to the Scottish General Hospital, in a new building which had not yet been officially opened. Although it was farther away from our home in Dunblane than Central General Hospital, it had a far larger car park and even had a few shops, including a Marks & Spencer food outlet and a Starbucks café.

Vivien now had her own single room with en suite bathroom and a small television set, so she enjoyed far greater privacy than she had at Central General Hospital. When we visited, we could take her down to Starbucks in her wheelchair. On fine days we all sat outside in the warm sunshine in the hospital gardens.

Much of my day was spent travelling to the hospital to see Vivien and then returning to Dunblane. But I decided that, when I was not visiting, I would have as normal a life as possible and do all the things that I would usually do. I went for walks and cycle runs, swam, watched DVDs, and read books. I even dined out on my own a few times.

Then on Thursday, 9 June, I received some dramatic news, which changed everything. At 11.30 a.m. I was cycling through Bridge of Allan in brilliant sunshine when my 633 Squadron ringtone told me I had a call on my mobile phone. I pulled to the roadside and unclipped my mobile from its handlebar-mounted holder. It was Gillian, and she had some important news.

Dr Brian Sutton, the stroke consultant at Scottish General Hospital, wanted to talk to us about Vivien's case at 2 p.m. that afternoon. I was planning to go to Stirling for a pub lunch, but I cancelled my plans and hurriedly cycled back to the house to have a shower and a quick snack. Just before 2 I met Gillian in the hospital car park, and we made our way up to the ward.

Dr Sutton showed us into a small room at the end of the ward and closed the door. He looked anxious. He started off by explaining that Vivien had suffered a very severe stroke and then went on to point out that she was at very high risk of having another, as it was extremely likely that the atrial myxoma would throw off another embolus. 'It could end up in her right hemisphere or her left hemisphere; in fact, it could end up almost anywhere in her body. She could have another stroke or even die!' he said.

We already knew that what he had said was true. Then Dr Sutton went on to explain what had happened in the last couple of days. Consultant Cardiologist Dr Patrick Camfield, who had diagnosed Vivien's myxoma on 25 May, had been in touch with Mr James Troughton, a cardiac surgeon at the Scottish Heart Hospital. Mr Troughton had viewed Vivien's ultrasound scans and believed that her myxoma should be excised as soon as possible in view of the high risk of another embolus.

Dr Sutton said he was unable to determine what the results of the surgery might be, as there wasn't much statistical information available on how people did after surgery, and there was a possibility that Vivien might have another stroke during the operation.

Gillian and I were both shocked by this news, but I felt that, although there was some risk involved in the surgical procedure, doing nothing would probably be even more dangerous. I was aware that there were problems in giving a general anaesthetic so soon after a stroke but felt sure that the team at the Scottish Heart Hospital – which was known as a centre of excellence – would be able to handle the situation.

All three of us then went through to Vivien's room so that we could explain things to her. Dr Sutton told Vivien that her stroke had been caused by a growth in her heart, which had to be removed. Vivien looked terrified. She couldn't say anything, so she burst into tears and sobbed uncontrollably for several minutes.

That evening I received phone calls from Vivien's sister, Margaret, and her mother. They were both concerned about this latest development because we had been previously told that it would be too dangerous to give Vivien an anaesthetic for two or three months. I had to reassure them that – despite what we had previously been told – it was still in Vivien's best interest to have the operation as soon as possible.

The following day Vivien was transferred to the Scottish Heart Hospital. All the nursing staff were very skilled and competent, and one of the staff nurses seemed very distressed when she learned what had happened to Vivien over the last few weeks. She also told us that Mr James Troughton was regarded as the finest cardiac surgeon in Scotland.

Late on the afternoon of Friday, 10 June, we met the great man himself. He sat down on an empty bed in the ward and spent a few moments telling us what was going to happen on Monday morning. He was going to operate to remove the myxoma, something that he had done many times before without any problems.

He reassured us about the challenges involved in giving Vivien a general anaesthetic so soon after her stroke. He explained that the main problem in such cases was that there was a risk of cerebral oedema (swelling of the brain). However, he felt sure that if this developed, the anaesthetist would be able to treat this using intravenous drugs such as Mannitol. As far as Mr Troughton was concerned, this was a fairly unremarkable operation.

He exuded great confidence, and I knew straight away that Vivien was in good hands. She was going to be anaesthetized for some hours, her chest was going to be cut open, and her heart was going to be stopped while the tumour was cut out. Still, as far as Mr Troughton was concerned, it was a routine procedure. I got the impression that to him it was as simple a job as changing a car exhaust would be to a Kwik Fit technician. We both came away from the meeting with Mr Troughton feeling very buoyed up and confident that everything was going to be all right.

Unfortunately, as I was travelling home that evening, I started to worry again about what might go wrong. I wasn't too concerned about what might happen during the operation; it was just that it was almost 72 hours away and I feared that the myxoma might fire off another embolus in the next two or three days. I prayed that the myxoma would behave itself until it could be removed.

That night I had a terrible nightmare and woke up in a cold sweat with a feeling of panic. I had dreamt that Vivien had suffered a number of further emboli. Both her arms had fallen off, and she was left with tiny stumps protruding from her shoulders, like chipolata sausages.

The next day I visited Vivien as usual, and although I was quite anxious, I put on my usual cheery face. On the Sunday afternoon Dr Smith, the anaesthetist, called round to see Vivien. He apologized for the fact that he was wearing motorcycle clothing, as he had travelled in on his bike to see the patients on his operating list for the next day. I couldn't care less what he wore. If he was going to help Vivien, he could wear a Mr Blobby outfit as far as I was concerned.

Although the Scottish Heart Hospital was seventy minutes from Dunblane by car and even longer by train, it did at least have excellent catering facilities. The restaurant offered wonderful food, which was all freshly prepared on the premises (in contrast to most NHS hospitals, where the food was often made elsewhere), and the patients ate the same meals that were offered in the canteen. Vivien had always been notoriously fussy about her food, but she enjoyed the food in the Scottish Heart Hospital much better than anything she had been served in the Scottish General Hospital.

On Monday, 13 June, Vivien went into the operating theatre at 7.45 a.m., and the long, complicated operation to remove her tumour began. After Mr Troughton cut open her chest, Vivien's heart was stopped to enable the myxoma to be excised. A heart-lung machine took over the role of oxygenating her blood and pumping it around her body.

At that moment Vivien's consciousness floated out of her body and travelled to another nonphysical realm of existence where she met her father, Andrew, thirty-eight years after he had died. Andrew was bathed in a brilliant white light, and the most beautiful music Vivien had ever heard was playing gently in the background. As her father held her hand, she felt tremendous love flowing through her, coming not just from him but from the Creator of everything. In this plane of existence, the discomforts and concerns of the physical world did not exist, and past, present, and future merged into one.

For what could have been a moment or an hour – as time did not exist as such in this place – she felt the presence of her father and his great love for her. Then he spoke just a few words: 'Your time has not come yet, Vivien; you have to go back.' In an instant she returned to her physical body, coughing and spluttering, her chest aching as she came round from the anaesthetic.

I knew her operation wouldn't be over till lunchtime, so I didn't think there was any point in phoning the hospital to find out how things were going until at least 1 p.m. As it happened, Mr Troughton very thoughtfully phoned me on my landline phone while I was in the Dunblane branch of Tesco, and when I returned home at 11.35 a.m. I found a voicemail message from him which said that everything had gone well with the operation.

I did not visit Vivien that day because she was in intensive care following the operation, and this was the only day between the time of her stroke and her discharge home when I did not see her. I felt a great sense of relief that she had survived the operation, but my new worry was that she might get a wound infection such as MRSA. Fortunately, her wound healed up beautifully, and by late June the crisis had passed. The doctors were so pleased with her recovery that on Tuesday, 21 June – just eight days after her operation – she was transferred to Ward 16 at Central General Hospital, and two days later on Thursday 23 June she was moved back to Ward A22 at Scottish General Hospital. The staff were very pleased to see Vivien back, and one of them told me they had feared she might die during the operation because of the severity of her stroke and the risk of cerebral oedema.

I felt elated that Vivien had survived. Despite my fears – and those of other family members – Vivien had pulled through the operation unscathed. The only question now was how good a recovery she was going to make. Unfortunately, in late July there was further bad news.

CHAPTER 11

WHAT IS MEDICAL NEGLIGENCE?

Vivien had survived against all the odds. For the first time since she collapsed at home, I was confident she was going to live. The only question now was how good a recovery she was going to make.

Now that the immediate crisis had passed, I turned my attention to something that had been bothering me for weeks: the terrible diagnostic error that had been made by the NHS and what I was going to do about it.

I had already phoned a few Scottish legal firms that dealt with compensation claims and had found only two that specialized in medical litigation. They provided me with a lot of useful information on what was involved in suing the NHS but said that they would be unable to do this work on a conditional fee basis (no win–no fee) as the outcome was so uncertain.

When I was a medical student at Glasgow University, I had done two terms of a subject called medical jurisprudence, which dealt with the legal aspects of medical practice, and so had a vague recollection of what was involved in negligence actions. I now updated my knowledge by reading a few articles on the Internet that explained all the difficulties involved in claiming compensation. I also got a lot of useful information from a charity called AvMA (Action Against Medical Accidents), which provided free advice to anyone contemplating litigation.

There were two main legal hurdles to be overcome in making a claim for negligence. First of all, you had to prove that the medical practitioner in question had done something that no other competent doctor in the same specialty would have done. In other words, there was some kind of standard procedure involved, and this doctor had deviated from this protocol (in Scotland this is known as the Hunter v Hanley test; in England the similar Bolam test is used). Second, you had to prove causation: you had to show that even if the doctor's mistakes – or substandard care – had directly led to the patient suffering injury or disability. This is because in some cases it could be shown that the unfortunate outcome would have happened anyway.

I was reluctant to commence legal action against the NHS unless it could be funded on a conditional fee basis. I didn't want to end up like the late Dorothy Squires (Roger Moore's second wife), a highly successful singer who made a fortune and then lost all her money through a series of unsuccessful lawsuits. I could see that if the case went on for years – involving hundreds of hours of legal work – and ended with a court case that we lost, then the costs could ruin us financially, and we could even end up losing our house. According to Scottish government statistics, the average time for settlement in a medical negligence case was 3.5 years. The record was twenty-one years for a case in the greater Glasgow area. There was also a case in the Forth Valley NHS region which took sixteen years to settle.

However, I concluded that I should at least make a complaint against the NHS. As I was very worried about our finances (as Vivien would soon lose her job and I was not earning much), I decided to get some free legal advice from the Citizens Advice Bureau.

So on Thursday, 30 June 2011, I cycled into Stirling and arrived at the Citizens Advice Bureau just as it was opening at 10 a.m. After filling in a couple of forms and waiting for a few minutes, I was seen by a retired solicitor called Susan and one of her colleagues, who explained that the service provided by the CAB was both free and completely impartial. They listened patiently as I explained what had happened to Vivien and how I felt that there were grounds for a serious complaint to be made, possibly leading to litigation at a later date.

Susan said that the very first thing I must do was request copies of all the case notes from both the GP practice involved and the two NHS hospitals that had looked after Vivien. She gave me some specimen letters which explained exactly how I should do this. Once I had obtained all the relevant case notes, I needed to study them very carefully and then use them as a basis for a formal complaint against the NHS. If I did not get a satisfactory response from the local NHS, I then had the option of taking my complaint to the NHS Scotland Ombudsman, who was completely independent.

She also said that she could arrange for me to see one of her colleagues, Douglas White, who worked in the Alloa branch but who had previously been employed by the NHS and was regarded as an expert on complaints against the Health Service. A very friendly middle-aged man with grey hair and spectacles, Mr White was very helpful.

Later that day I phoned our GP practice and the local Medical Records Department and requested the appropriate forms for obtaining copies of medical records. The only problem was that the request had to come from the patient, rather than a spouse, and as Vivien could not yet speak and was unable to write, I had to get her to make a cross in the signature box on the form. I then had to write a note explaining that this was all she could do for the signature and then countersign it.

The GP case notes arrived within two weeks while the hospital records didn't drop through my letterbox till early September. I was told that this was because all the different consultants who had treated Vivien had to give their written permission for the case notes to be released.

On Thursday, 11 August, I went to the Stirling branch of the Citizens Advice Bureau for the second time to meet Douglas White. I showed him a rough draft of a complaint I was planning to submit to the NHS. Douglas said that this was fine but pointed out that I should make no mention of any financial loss that we had suffered as a result of Vivien's misdiagnosis. Nor should we state at any point that we were considering legal action. The reason for this was that if you mentioned in your complaint that you were contemplating legal action or had suffered financial loss, the NHS were then entitled to say that they would not investigate the complaint until all legal proceedings were concluded.

In early September I received copies of Vivien's hospital case notes covering the period from the spring of 2010 up until the middle of June 2011 and spent some hours studying them.

I had also acquired a lot of information about atrial myxoma and vasculitis. My old friend Ian Graham, who had originally trained me in TFT back in 2000, had sent me an article entitled 'Cardiac Tumours simulating Collagen Vascular Disease,' which had been published in the British Heart Journal in 1986.[1]

The authors explained that the early diagnosis of cardiac tumours was important because most were benign and could usually be surgically excised. Atrial myxoma, I discovered, could present with the signs and symptoms of vasculitis for two distinct reasons. First, the myxoma often secreted an inflammatory substance (a cytokine) that could cause vasculitis and a systemic disturbance with symptoms such as fever. Second, and more commonly, because they consisted of friable tissue, myxomas often released small emboli, which could block small blood vessels in the fingertips and toes (as well as other parts of the body), making them red and painful and simulating the appearance of vasculitis (known as pseudovasculitis). The article specifically warned doctors to consider atrial myxoma in the differential diagnosis of vasculitis, and it was truly astonishing that none of the doctors who treated Vivien thought of this possibility.

When I discussed Vivien's case over the telephone with one of the GPs in August 2011, he was unaware that there was any connection between vasculitis and atrial myxoma. In mitigation it should be pointed out that this was a highly specialized area, and atrial myxomas were rare with an incidence of just one new case per 2 million population per year. But although I would not expect the average GP to know this, a consultant rheumatologist or dermatologist should have been aware of atrial myxoma as a possible cause of Vivien's symptoms.

The GPs had diagnosed Vivien as suffering from vasculitis. On the first occasion this had happened in August 2009, no investigations apart from an ECG had been carried out, and when the problem recurred the following spring, Vivien had had a few blood tests and was then referred to Dr Brown, a consultant dermatologist at the Scottish General Hospital.

Clearly the GPs had made an incorrect diagnosis, but to their credit they had at least referred Vivien to a consultant who really should have got to the bottom of things. Dr Brown had seen Vivien twice and was unsure about the diagnosis, particularly as he had not seen the skin lesions for himself (they had cleared up by the time he saw her). He had then referred Vivien to Dr Green for further investigation.

Unfortunately, Dr Green had not considered atrial myxoma in the differential diagnosis of Vivien's condition. Nor had he considered that the suspect lesions might be caused by emboli from other causes. Had he done so, and had he ordered an echocardiogram in late 2010, then it is likely that Vivien's atrial myxoma would have been discovered within a few weeks. She could then have had had emergency surgery, thus preventing her stroke, and (after recovery from surgery) she would have lived a perfectly normal and healthy life.

I had originally considered making a complaint to the GP practice, but on calm reflection I realized that, to their credit, they had eventually referred Vivien to a consultant dermatologist and by doing so had passed responsibility on to him. Dr Brown had then referred Vivien to Dr Green because of the unusual presentation and also because Dr Green had a special interest in vasculitis. Regrettably, Dr Green had failed to diagnose the very serious underlying condition causing my wife's vasculitis with resulting tragic consequences, so I felt that any litigation should focus on him.

I also realized there were a number of other occasions when the atrial myxoma might have been picked up if things had happened differently. On 31 May 2010, Vivien had a sudden attack of dizziness, vertigo, nausea, and vomiting. (By the way the word vertigo means a sensation of spinning when the head is stationary; it doesn't mean a 'fear of heights' as many people think. This popular misconception may date back to the 1958 Hitchcock film Vertigo, about a policeman who develops a fear of heights after a fall at work. A fear of heights is more correctly termed acrophobia. Curiously, acrophobia is often accompanied by a spinning sensation in the head, which probably explains why the word vertigo often occurs in this context.)

At the time I thought that she was suffering from acute viral labyrinthitis, and the NHS emergency GP who came to see her that afternoon thought the same. With the benefit of hindsight, I wondered if this episode had actually been a transient ischaemic attack (TIA), often called a mini-stroke, caused by an embolus from her atrial myxoma. What made me suspicious was the fact that her attack of dizziness had only lasted a few hours and by the next day she was able to return to work and drive her car. The emergency GP had given her an intramuscular injection of Stemetil and a prescription for five days' supply of the same medication in tablet form, but she never really needed them as she was symptom-free by the next day.

From what I have read, viral labyrinthitis lasts at least seven days, and in some cases goes on for six weeks. Vivien was symptom-free within a few hours, which is exactly what you would have expected if she had suffered a transient ischaemic attack. She also returned to work the next day and drove her car, two things you wouldn't expect someone to be able to do if they were suffering from acute labyrinthitis. I also discovered from reading scientific papers that dizzy turns and TIAs are a recognized symptom of atrial myxomas.

I had wondered what might have happened if this episode had been treated as a suspected transient ischaemic attack. Vivien would have been referred to hospital for further investigations, including an ultrasound scan of her carotid arteries. However, I have since been told that echocardiograms are not routinely carried out in all cases of suspected transient ischaemic attacks (for reasons of cost), so it is possible that, even if she had been referred to hospital for investigation following that episode, the atrial myxoma might still have remained undetected.

In the two years leading up to her stroke, Vivien had a number of very strange symptoms and signs. For example, on 4 September 2009, she had an attack of 'gout' in her left big toe and also had a number of episodes of pain and swelling in different parts of her body, which were diagnosed as things like muscle strain, bursitis, and viral myalgia. I think it was likely that most of her symptoms in the two years leading up to her stroke had actually been caused by embolic episodes, and it was regrettable that this had not been realized at the time. Some symptoms were also attributed to the side effects of the medications she was taking – originally corticosteroids and then azathioprine.

On 4 September 2011, I made a formal written complaint to the NHS about Consultant Rheumatologist Dr Green. I briefly summarized Vivien's case and then said that – in my opinion – Dr Green should have considered atrial myxoma in his differential diagnosis and should have ordered an echocardiogram. Had he done so, then the myxoma could have been surgically excised long before it caused the stroke. I also asked if the Department of Rheumatology at Scottish General Hospital had a protocol for the investigation of vasculitis and – in view of what happened – if they were now going to order an echocardiogram in every case of vasculitis or suspected vasculitis as – in my opinion – this would be the only way of ensuring this tragedy was not repeated. Two months passed before I received a reply, and in the meantime a lot of dramatic things were happening.

CHAPTER 12

COMING HOME

On 23 June Vivien was transferred back to the Scottish General Hospital, and her rehabilitation started. Immediately after her stroke she couldn't even say yes or no, but within a few weeks, she was able to say several words. She still needed a wheelchair to get about, though by mid-July she could walk a few yards with a Zimmer (walking frame) and eventually managed to reach her en -suite toilet without any walking aids.

She was now receiving treatment from speech therapists, physiotherapists, and occupational therapists. At that time, we had no idea when she would be discharged home, although we thought it would probably be sometime in mid-September.

In mid-July Vivien started to do something very strange. Every time I visited her, she would motion with her left hand towards her left eye and say one word – 'nose'. Eventually I realized what the problem was: there must be something wrong with the vision in her left eye. I should explain that if you have two healthy eyes you cannot usually see your own nose unless you look in a mirror and the reason for this is that the visual fields of your two eyes overlap. However, if you cover or close one eye, you will immediately be aware of one side of your nose because you now only have a single visual field, rather than two overlapping ones.

On 18 July, I brought in my pen torch and did a visual assessment on Vivien. For some time I had noticed that her left eye was divergent (i.e., it pointed outwards). The doctors had recorded this in the case notes but didn't seem to know what was causing it. Perhaps they thought it was due to brain damage caused by the stroke or a cranial nerve palsy.

I carried out an eye examination and quickly discovered that Vivien was blind in her left eye, with her visual acuity being just perception of light.

This was the explanation for her diverging eyeball, because a blind eye tends to turn either outwards or inwards as it has nothing to fix on. These findings, plus an absent pupil reaction in the left eye, led me to suspect that she had suffered a central retinal artery occlusion, caused by a small embolus from the atrial myxoma, which probably occurred at the same time as the stroke. Unfortunately, I no longer possessed an ophthalmoscope to look at Vivien's retina, but I was sure that was the diagnosis.

I told the nursing staff what I had found, and they asked one of the junior doctors in the ward to check my findings. He agreed with my assessment, and arrangements were made for Vivien to be seen by a consultant ophthalmologist as soon as possible. A few days later, on 26 July, Consultant Ophthalmologist Dr Patrick Russell saw Vivien at the ophthalmology clinic and confirmed that the diagnosis was indeed a central retinal artery occlusion, for which no treatment was possible. What had happened was that the retina in Vivien's left eye had died from lack of blood and oxygen.

It was yet another blow. Not only was Vivien affected by a very severe stroke which had left her semi-paralyzed and unable to speak, read, or write, but she also could not see out her left eye. If anything happened to her right eye, she would be completely blind.

This partial blindness could also make her rehabilitation more difficult. It is possible to drive a motorcar safely and legally with only one eye, and it is also feasible to drive a car after a stroke – even one as severe as Vivien's – if sufficient modifications are made to the vehicle. But I felt that the combination of her severe stroke and the blindness in her left eye meant that it would be too difficult for her to learn to drive again.

The only positive aspect of all this was that at least she didn't have a homonymous hemianopia (aka heminanopsia). To explain further – some stroke survivors are left with a defect in vision caused by brain damage, rather than a problem with the eye itself. Such individuals only have half a visual field in each eye. Most strokes affect the left hemisphere of the brain, so homonymous hemianopias usually affect the right half of the visual field of both eyes.

To understand what this is like – if you put on a pair of spectacles and covered the right half of each lens with a piece of duct tape, then that simulates the visual loss in a hemianopia quite well.

It is a far more disabling condition than blindness in one eye. People who are blind in one eye can still legally drive a motor vehicle in complete safety, providing that they remember to move their head around to maintain a reasonable field of vision. But people who develop a hemianopia cannot retain their driving licence for obvious reasons.

Dr Brian Sutton, the stroke consultant who was looking after Vivien, had told me some weeks earlier that he believed that Vivien was suffering from a right homonymous hemianopia but this had apparently recovered in the first few weeks after her stroke.

In early August the rehabilitation team said that they were now considering setting a date for Vivien to return home, and June, the occupational therapist, suggested that Vivien should make a brief home visit so that the team could assess whether any modifications would be required to our house. So on Monday, 8 August, at 10 a.m., Vivien returned to our house for the first time since her stroke, accompanied by June and her assistant.

I was worried that Vivien would be unable to manage the stairs and that this would cause problems, as all our bedrooms were on the first floor. The rehabilitation team had suggested that she might have to sleep in the lounge on the ground floor if she was unable to climb the stairs. Fortunately, June established that Vivien could walk up the stairs provided an additional banister was fitted. The team also identified a need for additional handrails, grab rails, raised toilet seats, and non-slip shower mats, which would have to be installed before she could come home. I was also advised to bin all our rugs, as she might trip on them.

I felt rather anxious at the thought of Vivien coming home. Although it would be good to have her around again, I was worried that I wouldn't be able to cope. I would need to do all the washing and ironing, clean the house, go food shopping, and make all the meals in addition to looking after all her care needs.

I also wondered if I could handle the physical demands of being a carer as, at that time, I thought I might need to lift her on and off the toilet, bathe her, help her get dressed, and maybe even turn her over in her bed at night to stop her getting bed sores.

On 17 August, almost three months after Vivien had been rushed to hospital, the NHS joiner turned up at 8.45 a.m. to fit a second handrail to our main staircase. This was cutting things a bit fine, as I had to collect Vivien from the hospital at 11 a.m. The joiner had the job done in an hour, and I just had time to paint the new handrail with its first coat of coloured acrylic varnish before I dashed off to the hospital.

By 11.45 a.m. we were home. I helped Vivien out the car and held her left arm as we walked up the front path to our door. I turned the key in the lock and swung the door open. Oscar and Kiki were there to meet us. I'm not sure whether they were genuinely pleased to see us or whether they were just angling for another helping of cat food!

'That's Mummy home again,' I said to the cats as I closed the front door behind me.

For that first lunch together I had bought in some Marks & Spencer salads, which only had to be unwrapped, but I knew I had a number of challenges ahead of me, one of which was that I would have to cook nutritious meals for my wife. Very early on in our marriage, I had made a chicken curry for our dinner. Vivien was quite scathing about this meal, particularly as I had used pre-diced chicken which, she pointed out, was usually of poor quality, and I had also added chopped banana which appalled her. I was so hurt by her comments that I never made dinner again for years afterwards!

I had been very interested in cooking when I was at primary school and used to do baking. I clearly remember making my own tablet, toffee, and fudge at the age of eleven and also recall baking sponge cakes and 'melting moments', a form of shortbread. Now, at the age of fifty-four, I would have to become a cook once more and make an effort to provide my wife with tasty and nutritious meals.

I soon found that cooking was much easier than it had ever been. A large Marks & Spencer food store had opened in Dunblane a couple of years before, and there was also a Tesco. I already knew how to make curries, stir-fries, and pasta dishes, and I rapidly learned how to make roast dinners. Back in the nineties I had bought a two-tier aluminium steamer from a Chinese supermarket, specifically for heating up dim sum. I now brought this out of storage and used it for steaming vegetables. I also studied a number of Vivien's cookery books, bought a couple of my own, and downloaded a few recipes from the Internet. One day I made my own Irish stew from scratch (which Vivien enjoyed very much) and I also learned how to make home-made baked sweet potato chips, which were a far healthier and tastier alternative to conventional chips.

Vivien had always hated packet and tinned soup, but we both loved the plastic beakers of chilled gourmet soups which could be purchased in any supermarket. In the same way I soon found there was little point in making my own custard with Bird's custard powder, since the ready-made versions were far superior.

I also learned a few tips about cooking from YouTube videos, such as the best way to make scrambled eggs and boil pasta. Within a matter of weeks my culinary ability had soared, and Vivien even said that she thought I was a good cook, something I thought I would never hear her say.

The only thing I didn't seem to be very good at was managing frozen food. We had two freezers in the kitchen, a small two-drawer freezer which was part of the main fridge and a large chest freezer in a cupboard. Originally I had intended to buy in a large stock of frozen food, enabling me to shop only once a week, but I soon found that I couldn't handle this. What kept happening was that I would keep food frozen way beyond its safe limit and then have to throw it out, so I eventually decided that I would go shopping almost every day and just buy in one or two days' supply of food at a time, as this avoided wastage.

The next problem that had to be overcome was laundry and ironing. In an earlier chapter I mentioned a number of anxious thoughts that were going through my mind as I followed Vivien's ambulance to Central General Hospital. Another one was 'Oh, shit, this means I'll have to do the ironing!' Like most people, I have always found ironing to be a chore. My mother showed me how to do it when I first left home, but I had never had to do it very often. Both Vivien and my first wife had very kindly done all my ironing for me, and during my bachelor years, when I lived on my own in my bungalow in Doune, I had employed a cleaning lady twice a week who used to do all the laundry and ironing for me.

Obviously I could have used an ironing service. There were a number of such businesses in the area, including one called The Ironing Station which had premises at Dunblane railway station. However, I was very concerned about our finances, as I was not getting much work. Vivien was already on half pay as she had been off sick for a few months, and I knew that she would eventually lose her job. I decided the best option would be for me to do all the laundry and ironing myself.

One thing I thought would help would be a much more effective steam iron, so I bought a Philips steam generator iron from Argos. As expected, this greatly speeded up the ironing process, as the Philips proved to be the .44 Magnum of irons with its powerful steam jets! With certain garments it wasn't even necessary to iron them as I could simply put them on a clothes hanger and then blast them with steam from the base plate. I also decided to do all the washing and ironing almost every day since I found that a small ironing each day was a much less onerous task than a large one once or twice a week.

Cleaning the house was no problem because I had always done this since the start of our marriage. Vivien had always disliked housework. Although she was quite happy to do all the food shopping, cooking, washing, and ironing, she didn't like cleaning. She told me that she believed this stemmed from her childhood, as she was required to do housework every day, including dusting a large number of ornaments. This gave her an aversion to cleaning which had persisted to this day.

Vivien's childhood experiences had put her off housecleaning, but my own experiences as a teenager had the reverse effect. In early 1971 my father had bought a brand-new teal blue Austin Maxi 1750, and one Saturday afternoon, in an effort to relieve my boredom while waiting for the latest episode of Doctor Who, I had offered to wash and polish his car. I'd never cleaned a motor vehicle before, but I found that I really enjoyed it and soon developed great skill at the task. I got great satisfaction from taking a dusty, dirty motor vehicle and, within an hour, turning it into a car that gleamed like new.

Ever since then I have always derived great enjoyment from cleaning my own car. If I was ever stuck for a job, I could probably start up my own car valeting business. So I've always enjoyed cleaning motorcars, and when I was in my late twenties I found that I also enjoyed housecleaning, so it was no bother for me to do all the domestic work around the house.

One problem that had to be solved though was how Vivien was going to bathe herself now she was home. She had usually preferred to shower but occasionally liked to soak in a deep bath in the evenings for relaxation. Since her stroke she had indicated that she didn't want to have another bath and particularly didn't want to use the one in which she had suffered her cerebral infarct, so I had to find a way for her to shower safely.

The NHS joiner had been instructed to fit a grab rail in the shower cubicle in Vivien's en suite bathroom but had refused to do so (for health and safety reasons) when he discovered the wall was only a stud partition as is the norm in most modern houses. I solved this problem by fitting the grab rail myself using heavy-duty metal Rawlplugs designed for plasterboard walls. I also fitted a second grab rail which was attached to the tiles by suction and installed a non-slip mat in the base of the shower cubicle.

On 18 August Vivien had her first shower since she had come home from hospital. As expected, she had difficulty opening the shower cabinet door, closing it, turning on the shower, and using shower gel as all these functions had to be carried out with just one hand. I soon realized the only way to help her overcome these hurdles was for me to get into the shower with her, so I took off my clothes and squeezed into the cabinet behind her.

For the next few days I repeated this process of showering with her, standing behind her and guiding her through all the different motions she needed to do in order to bathe with just one good hand. Although her right hand and arm were semi-paralyzed, she could just about hold the bottle of shower gel, and I made things easier for her by decanting her shower gel into a large plastic travel bottle.

After we had gone through this routine for a few days, Vivien was able to bathe on her own with me standing immediately outside the shower cabinet giving her directions. Within a few weeks she was able to shower unaided, though I needed to be within earshot.

Another problem was eating meals. Vivien had little function in her right hand, so she had to eat all her meals using just a fork held in the left hand. This meant that I had to chop up all her food into small pieces. For this reason pasta dishes, curries, and stir-fries were popular meal choices, as they required no further dicing.

She also had a tendency to spill food onto her clothing. One solution would have been to get her a plastic bib which went all the way up to her neck, but I didn't want to use such a garment as I felt it would be very degrading; even with her communication difficulties she confirmed this herself! The answer I came up with was for both of us to wear matching aprons. Before each meal I would put on my red-and-white striped cook's apron and then invite Vivien to do the same. As we were both wearing identical garments while we ate our meals, she did not feel embarrassed or humiliated.

She also had another problem as she tended to get bits of food on the right side of her face, particularly around the corner of her mouth. This was because the right side of her face was both paralyzed and numb.

When I was very young, my elderly grandfather had stayed with us for the last few years of his life. Although I loved him dearly, one thing that used to horrify me was that, when he ate his meals, he would always get food stuck on his face which someone had to wipe off.

Now my fifty-five-year-old wife had the same problem. She became very upset if I attempted to wipe her face myself. So I solved the problem using a similar strategy to the apron issue. I always made sure that there were plenty of paper napkins on the table, and any time Vivien got food on her face, I would pick up a napkin and wipe my own face. Vivien would see me doing this and copy me without me having to say a word. What I was doing was what psychologists would term a 'mirroring' technique which avoided humiliating her. By the end of August Vivien had overcome many obstacles, but many more difficulties lay ahead as I was soon to discover.

CHAPTER 13

SUPERNATURAL EVENTS

I'm a rather odd beast. I've had a very orthodox scientific and medical training but have always been interested in alternative therapies and the unexplained, believing that so-called paranormal phenomena will one day be explained by an expanded version of mainstream science.

I also believe that if you think the paranormal is a load of bunk, it means you have been living your life with your eyes closed. Have you never had the feeling something bad is going to happen and it does? Or had a dream that has come true? Or had the almost universal experience of thinking of someone you haven't seen for some time and then answered a ringing phone and discovered it was that person calling? Before Vivien had her stroke, we shared a common interest in such things and often went to the Thursday evening lectures at Glasgow University arranged by the Scottish Society for Psychical Research (SSPR). Like me, Vivien believed there was more to life than chips and beans and Coronation Street.

There were some paranormal events before and after Vivien's stroke – as I shall shortly relate – but first I'd like to describe some very odd experiences I've had which have made me so interested in this topic.

My interest in the paranormal goes back decades. When I was a toddler, my elderly grandfather took me out in my pushchair. One summer's day, while he was pushing me along the Greenock Esplanade, we both looked up at the heavens and spotted a thin white streak high in the azure blue sky. 'It's a vapour trail,' I said. My grandfather was astonished at how a young child – who only spoke a few words – knew the term vapour trail.

By the time I was at primary school I had developed a fascination with aircraft, particularly those of the Second World War RAF. My favourite was the Avro Lancaster bomber, and the film I liked best was The Dam Busters. But where did this interest come from?

Many decades later, while doing a hypnotherapy course in Birmingham in 1998, I had a very odd experience that suggested an explanation. During one module we had to do something called automatic writing, where we held a pencil in our right hand, went into hypnotic trance, and allowed the pencil to write whatever it wished. The idea was that this technique could be used to get information from a person's subconscious to help them overcome problems.

I had known for years that I was a very good hypnotic subject, so I was not surprised when something spectacular happened. Most of the course delegates who did this exercise only scribbled a few words on their notepad, but my right hand seemed to go crazy – as though it had a life of its own – and wrote several pages describing life on an RAF bomber station during the Second World War, in great detail. It was as if my right hand was reproducing an airman's diary from 1944.

According to this subconsciously generated scroll, I had originally flown Bristol Beaufighters but had been transferred to heavy bombers against my wishes, and many other details of missions I had flown were given.

Geoff Brooks, one of the students on the course, was a clairvoyant and was fascinated by what had happened, so he put me back into hypnotic trance and asked my subconscious to take me back in time to when I had lived before. Instantly I got the most amazing Technicolor vision of Lancaster bombers parked on an airfield, silhouetted against the orange glow of the setting sun. I was enjoying a mug of tea and a bun from a NAAFI van. Then an RAF-blue Bedford MWD truck took me out to my aircraft. As my fellow crew members had a last cigarette outside the plane and urinated on the tailwheel for good luck, I climbed through the aircraft's main door, just in front of the starboard tailplane.

The interior of the bomber was still hot from that day's sunshine and smelled of high-octane petrol, rubber, metal, and leather as I struggled over the main spar in my heavy flying clothing and made my way to the cockpit, where I strapped myself into the pilot's seat.

Geoff then told my subconscious to take me forward in time a few hours. Now I was flying my 'Lanc' over Berlin at an altitude of eighteen thousand feet. I kept my aircraft straight and level while 88mm flak shells were bursting all around me and the bomb aimer prepared to drop his ordnance.

I could hear his voice in my headphones, 'Steady, steady, steady, Skipper.' And then came the words I was waiting to hear: 'Bombs gone!' Freed of its load of almost seven tons of bombs the Lancaster soared upwards, its four Rolls-Royce Merlin engines screaming. I pulled the lever that closed the bomb doors and started to turn the giant aircraft round, heading for England and safety.

Suddenly the plane shook as though it had been hit repeatedly by a giant sledgehammer. The thin aluminium skin of the port wing was being torn apart by 20mm cannon shells. The Perspex canopy shattered and I felt hot blood on my left cheek. Immediately both port engines burst into flames and, as I looked round to my left, I saw a Junkers 88 night fighter, painted in mottled grey camouflage, shooting past. The port wing of my aircraft was now ablaze and I knew I had to get out fast if I was to survive. Using the intercom, I told the crew to bail out and then set 'George', the automatic pilot, to keep the plane steady while I made my exit. The cockpit filled with smoke as I struggled to unfasten my Sutton harness and – as I was crawling down to the forward escape hatch behind the Perspex nose blister – the aircraft exploded in a huge fireball. Then everything went black.

Some weeks later another student regressed me, and this time I went back to 1942 and recalled flying an Armstrong -Whitworth Whitley bomber from an operational training unit in Wales.

So what was the explanation for all this? Was it a genuine past-life regression, or was it just some fantasy produced by my subconscious? To be honest, I don't really know. It is possible that I had lived before as a Second World War combat pilot, but I could never prove it. My experience could just have been a fantasy, but on the other hand it could have been true.

I have also had dreams that came true a few times, although they have tended to be about fairly trivial events. One of the most striking was this one. Back in the mid-1990s (before I met Vivien) I tried blind dating for a while, usually without any lasting positive result.

Nonetheless, on one occasion I met a young lady doctor. The first meeting seemed to go reasonably well, and we made arrangements to meet up again in a few days.

Then three days later, I had a strange dream about a letter arriving in the post. It was from this woman and stated that she did not want to see me again. Suddenly I was awakened by the noise of the postman putting something through my letterbox. I looked at my bedside clock; it was 7 a.m. Padding through to the front hall, I found a single letter lying on the carpet by the front door. I tore open the envelope and started to read it. I am sure you can guess what it said; it was the same letter I had dreamt about only a few minutes before. The only difference between my dream and reality was that the colour of the paper was different.

I have had premonitions on other occasions. In the spring of 1975, during the Easter break, I was studying anatomy in preparation for my first-class exam in the subject which was to be held after the holidays. After studying for a few hours, I went into what I would now recognize as a hypnotic trance and saw a vision of the exam paper in a few weeks' time. I now knew what the questions were going to be and committed the appropriate sections of the anatomy textbook to rote memory as though I was learning a poem. When I took the exam a few weeks later the questions I had visualized came up as expected, and I got an A grade in that exam. Unfortunately, I never repeated this feat, and when I sat my next anatomy class exam in the autumn of 1975 I only got a C.

I had another strange premonition in January 1978. At that time I regularly contributed cartoons to student publications such as Surgo (Glasgow University Medical Journal) and the Glasgow University Guardian. I would often get my ideas for cartoons during boring lectures (of which there was no shortage at Glasgow University) and would sketch my rough ideas in my lecture notes. One day, during a particularly tedious lecture on headaches, I got an idea for a cartoon (Fig. 1). A man with an axe stuck in

My rough sketch for a cartoon idea (Fig 1) looked very like this cartoon
by Pete Williams (Fig 2) which appeared in TV Times a week later.

(Fig. 2)

HOSPITAL DOCTOR

My SURGO cover for the December 1976 issue (Fig 3) looked very much like Norman Cookson's cartoon for Hospital Doctor (Fig 4) and Malcolm Campbell's rough sketch for a suggested cover for Scottish Medicine (Fig 5) resembles both of them.

I accidentally came across one of my cartoons in Scottish Medicine (Fig6) the day before Vivien had her stroke.

Vivien wearing her 'I am Sorry I was such a Cow' T-shirt.

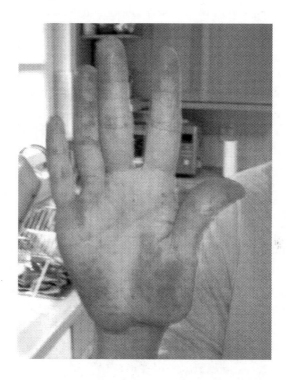

This photo taken by the author shows 'vasculitis' in one of Vivien's hands. We now know this was 'pseudo vasculitis ' caused by an atrial myxoma.

the back of his head is sitting opposite his GP. The caption reads, 'From the description of your symptoms I'd say it was a typical migraine headache.' Imagine my surprise when a week later the latest edition of TV Times arrived, and inside was an almost identical cartoon (Fig. 2).

Astonishingly, the same thing happened a second time. I did a cover illustration for Surgo showing a flying saucer landing in front of the Glasgow University buildings. Two aliens emerge and are immediately booked by a traffic warden (Fig. 3). Some time later an almost identical cartoon appeared in Hospital Doctor magazine (Fig. 4). The coincidence didn't even end there. In 1985 I was writing an article for Glasgow Medicine magazine about coincidences, which mentioned these incidents with cartoons. As I was writing it, a letter arrived in the post. It was a handwritten note and sketch from Dr Malcolm Campbell, then editor of the journal Scottish Medicine. He had just had an idea for a cover illustration that he wanted me to turn into finished artwork. His rough sketch showed two aliens emerging from a flying saucer in front of a hospital (Fig. 5).

There was one more strange occurrence related to cartoons, and it was connected with Vivien's stroke. The day before she had her cerebral infarct, I was sorting some old magazine files. Suddenly an old copy of *Scottish Medicine* landed on the floor. When I picked it up, I accidentally opened it at a particular page and noticed one of my old cartoons from the mid-eighties showing a disembodied brain in a tank. A man from the DHSS is taking some notes, and the caption reads, 'Of course we will have to have written proof of your disability before we can pay you your benefit' (Fig. 6).When I looked at this cartoon, a chill ran down my spine. Somehow I knew it was important, and I had the feeling that I had to show it to Vivien for some reason. Was it some kind of premonition?

Curiously, when I looked at this cartoon, I remembered something that I had written in a spoof newsletter (*Colin Barron News*) I had sent out with my Christmas cards in 1999. The newsletter featured a fake doctor's advice column by a fictional Dr Ivan Strukoffalot (get it?). One of the questions to the good doctor was the following:

Dear Doctor,

I went into hospital last April for the removal of an ingrowing toenail. There were some unspecified problems during the op and I am now a disembodied brain in a tank. I communicate by flashing a light bulb on and off (this letter took 4 months to write). Could I sue the doctors for negligence?

The Doctor replies,

Absolutely not. Doctors never get it wrong. What you are suffering from is a perfectly normal complication of ingrowing toenail surgery. Think of all the advantages of your present situation. You will never have to watch Eastenders, *and think of all the money you are saving on haircuts!*

(When I wrote these lines, I was perhaps subconsciously influenced by a two-part Star Trek story from 1966 called The Menagerie in which the very first commander of the USS Enterprise, Captain Christopher Pike, has ended up in an electric wheelchair, paralyzed and unable to speak and only able to communicate by flashing a light on and off.)

So when I wrote that little piece, and when I drew that cartoon, was my subconscious somehow accessing information from the future without me realizing it? I think that is perfectly possible.

In 1927 British aircraft designer J. W. Dunne published a book called An Experiment with Time1 in which he proposed that when we dream, our unconscious minds 'shift in time,' and we access information from the future. As most people don't remember their dreams, Dunne suggested keeping a pencil and notepad by our beds, so that we can jot down details of any dreams we can just remember as soon as we wake up. Dunne said that if you did this on a regular basis, you would soon find that at least some of your dreams contained information from the future. This would also explain the phenomenon of déjà vu, which Dunne suggested was due to us momentarily realizing that an event in the present moment had been dreamt about some time before.

In more recent times the respected British biologist Dr Rupert Sheldrake has written several books about his theory of 'morphic resonance' and 'morphogenetic fields'.2 Sheldrake believes that a 'morphogenetic field' surrounds all living creatures. Furthermore, he believes that all living things in the universe are connected through this field, and this is the keystone of his theory of 'morphic resonance'. This explains the phenomenon, which I briefly described earlier, of 'telephone telepathy' in which we think of someone and then the phone rings and that person is on the line. It also explains how pets know when their owners are coming home, and the well-known experience of realizing that someone is staring at you.

The latter is an extremely common phenomenon, and scientific experiments have been carried out to prove its existence. If you stare at the back of someone's head, after a short time they will very often get the feeling that they're being stared at and turn round. It is such a well-known and accepted occurrence that private detectives in training are told that they should always look at people's feet when they are following them and not the back of their heads, in case their targets get a feeling that they are being followed and turn round. SAS soldiers are also taught something similar – when they are in a concealed observation post spying on troops, they should not look directly at enemy soldiers' heads lest they realize they are being spied on.

Recently Dr Sheldrake has pointed out that we all have a certain ability to see into the future but that this usually happens without conscious awareness. Some years ago psychologists carried out a laboratory experiment to test this hypothesis. A group of people were shown a series of random images. Some of these images were of pleasant scenes, such as a sunset or kittens playing, but now and again an unpleasant picture would be inserted, such as the face of a road accident victim who had gone through a windscreen.

The subjects were wired up to sensors which detected any signs of stress in their body. As expected, the subjects showed signs of anxiety when viewing unpleasant images but were much more relaxed while seeing pleasant scenes. However, it was noted that the subjects showed some signs of physical stress when they were shown a pleasant picture which preceded a gruesome one, even though the subjects did not know that the next picture was to be unpleasant. The psychologists concluded that human beings seem to have some ability to access information from the future, though this tends to remain at an unconscious level.

This coincides with my own personal views on the subject. I believe we all access information from the future via our unconscious minds but cannot usually bring it to conscious awareness. The only difference between a clairvoyant and an ordinary member of the public is that such psychics have developed the ability to bring such information into consciousness.

Many years ago when I worked at Monklands Hospital in Airdrie, near Glasgow, I became very friendly with one of my fellow junior house officers, Tommy who shared a flat with me. Shortly before he finished his six-month job at Monklands, we held a party with a science-fiction fancy-dress theme. Tommy turned up wearing a costume that looked a bit like a spacesuit. It was a one-piece white disposable boiler suit which he had dyed black, and he also wore an oxygen mask and ribbed plastic tubing of the sort used in hospital ventilator machines.

Some of the people at the party thought he looked like a patient in an intensive care unit. A few weeks later he collapsed unconscious while playing rugby and was rushed to hospital, where it was discovered that he had suffered massive brain damage from a cerebral haemorrhage. He ended up in the intensive care unit and did survive, although he was left severely disabled. Is it possible that at a subconscious level he somehow knew his own future and that this influenced his choice of costume for the fancy-dress party? (By the way, I wore an identical costume to Tommy at the same party, and I also ended up on a ventilator in an intensive care unit thirty-five years later, as I recount in the second half of this book.)

So did Vivien have any inkling of what was going to happen to her at an unconscious level? Well, there was one event which I have found very curious. When we went on our first holiday together (to Portugal) in July 1999, I took Thomas Harris's recently –published book Hannibal with me. After I'd finished with it, I passed it to Vivien, who read it avidly.

From that point on Vivien became obsessed with the book and constantly read passages from it particularly when she was in bed at night. She felt that it somehow related to her and her role in life. What's this got to do with the stroke? Well if you have ever read Hannibal or seen the 2000 film adaptation directed by Ridley Scott, you will know that one of the main plot threads concerns a man called Mason Verger who is attacked by Dr Hannibal Lecter and ends up paralyzed, blind in one eye, and disfigured. He then plans to get his revenge on Lecter.

So Vivien became obsessed by a book in which a person ends up paralyzed, disfigured, and blind in one eye following an encounter with a doctor. Is that not spooky? Sometimes it seems that dramatic events in the future can cast their shadow in the present.

I have already mentioned Vivien's out-of-body experience in a previous chapter, but there was one other supernatural event which happened a week after a stroke. Gillian was driving me back from a hospital visiting session. As we pulled into the front drive of our house, one of our neighbour's dogs, who had somehow got free, ran up to us as we opened the doors of the car. We grabbed the dog's collar and took him to our neighbour's front door. They invited us in for a drink and to find out how we were getting on. Then, during the course of this evening, my left index finger started to become stiff, and within fifteen minutes it was absolutely rigid and unbendable.

By the time we got back to the house, it was quite late, and I didn't fancy going to the casualty department at Central General Hospital to get my finger checked out, as that would involve sitting in a waiting room for hours with a lot of very drunk people. I wasn't even sure what was wrong with it anyway. The next morning, when I woke up, my finger had returned to normal, and it was only then – when I thought about it – that I realized that the stiffness had come on at exactly 8.30 p.m., one week from the precise moment I had found Vivien semiconscious in her bath. Could it have been some kind of sign from a higher power? Perhaps it was an indication that she was going to live, because there was then a very strong chance that she would die before she could have cardiac surgery.

Certainly I cannot explain what happened to my finger according to anything I know about orthodox medicine, especially as the problem had not happened before and has not recurred.

It was a very strange episode, but there were to be even more dramatic events in the weeks to come.

CHAPTER 14

A LIFE CHANGED BEYOND RECOGNITION

By September 2011 I had adapted to my new life as Vivien's carer. Every day had a similar structure. We would rise at 6.45 a.m., and I would help Vivien with her breakfast and her medications. As she could only use her left hand – and so couldn't open bottles or bubble packs – I bought a drug administration system from the chemist. This consisted of a plastic cassette with twenty-eight compartments, four for each day of the week, each with a snap-shut lid which enabled me to make up a week's supply of drugs in advance. All Vivien had to do was open the appropriate lid at the right time of the day and take whatever was in that compartment.

After breakfast we showered and dressed, and I would start all my household tasks. I usually did a washing and ironing every single day, vacuumed the entire house every two days, cleaned the WCs and basins daily, and dusted about twice a week. Most days I also did a food shopping in the local Marks & Spencer or Tesco. Much of my day was spent helping Vivien with her exercises, cooking, cleaning and food shopping. At noon we would have lunch – usually soup and sandwiches, though occasionally we would have Nairn's oatcakes with cheese slices and cold cuts instead.

Dinner was at 4.45 p.m., and after I had done the dishes, we would go upstairs, lie on the double bed in the master bedroom, and watch a DVD together. This was my favourite part of the day because when we were lying together on the bed watching a movie, with Oscar snuggling up to us and Kiki sometimes joining us as well, I could almost forget what had happened and pretend everything was as before.

I owned hundreds of DVDs, but hardly any were what might be described as chick flicks. Much to my surprise, though, Vivien enjoyed films and TV series which she would never have considered before, such as British and American WW2 movies and box sets of series like The Professionals,

Secret Army, and Colditz. I was very keen that she should watch Reach for the Sky, the story of legless flying ace Douglas Bader, since I felt she might be inspired by his tale of incredible recovery against the odds.

It is accepted that films can affect your mood and personality since we all go into a hypnotic trance while watching them, and our unconscious minds accept suggestions from them without our realizing it. When I first started dating again in the early nineties, I watched all the Sean Connery Bond movies, since I knew they would make me feel more confident with women, which they did.

There is an American psychological treatment called movie therapy in which – after a lengthy telephone consultation – clients are advised to watch a carefully chosen selection of movies whose underlying story will be picked up by the unconscious to bring about the desired change.

I can understand how this would work. Back in the sixties I can remember watching The Saint or The Man from U.N.C.L.E. on TV. The next day at school I would be strutting around with a cocky manner pretending I was Simon Templar or Napoleon Solo.

Another movie which contains many great metaphors suitable for bringing about change is Ice Cold in Alex (1958). It is a tale about the crew of a British Army Austin K2 ambulance who make a long, hazardous journey across the Western Desert from Tobruk to Alexandria in June 1942. Along the way they encounter numerous dangers and obstacles such as minefields, Ju-87 'Stuka' dive-bomber attacks, and enemy armoured units.

The highlight of the film is the sequence where they try to drive the ambulance up a very steep hill of soft sand. The vehicle won't manage it, so they hit on the idea of taking the spark plugs out, putting the ambulance into reverse gear and slowly hand-cranking the engine to allow the vehicle to slowly ascend the hill backwards without slipping in the sand.

On their first attempt they almost get to the top, but then Sister Diana Murdoch (Sylvia Syms) accidentally lets the ambulance slip downhill and it careers down the steep slope out of control, only being saved from crashing when Captain Anson (James Mills) runs after it, jumps on board, and applies the brakes.

Anson doesn't explode with rage (as he would have earlier in the film) but takes the blame himself and calmly announces that they are going to do it all over again. At the second attempt they succeed and eventually make their way to a bar in Alexandria where they all have a glass of ice-cold Carlsberg lager to celebrate their achievement. The ambulance-pushing sequence is a wonderful metaphor because it gives a message to the unconscious mind that change can occur very slowly, and if we don't succeed at anything at the first attempt, we should do it again and again till we do. I think everyone recovering from a stroke should watch this film repeatedly.

The final scenes of the film also contain powerful messages of reconciliation and forgiveness. The ambulance crew discover that their passenger, Captain van der Poel, is not South African after all but a German, Hauptmann Otto Lutz, who has been working as a spy. To save him from being shot, they claim he was just an ordinary Afrika Korps soldier whom they captured. As he is led away by a military policeman, Lutz salutes the ambulance crew, saying that he has learned a lot about the English and that 'not everything we were told about them was correct'. It was probably the first war film to depict ordinary German soldiers as decent human beings who just happened to be on the wrong side rather than as Nazi brutes, and it was probably this which led to it receiving an award at the Berlin Film Festival in 1958.

In early September we started receiving visits from the local NHS stroke support service. They were to become very welcome visitors to our home over the next few months, and we were soon on first-name terms. There was Elaine the physiotherapist, Wilma the speech therapist, Julie the occupational therapist, and Tony, a multipurpose worker who could perform some of the tasks of the other three team members. Tony had previously been an electrician in the mining industry, but now in his later years he worked in the NHS.

I was particularly keen that Vivien should get speech therapy, as I felt her language problems were her greatest disability. I remembered seeing a speech therapist at work when I was a medical student. In the autumn of 1976 I had done a single-term course in geriatric medicine as part of my medical training and had seen a speech therapist working with an elderly patient at Lightburn Hospital, Glasgow. What happened was that she sat opposite the patient and encouraged her to speak. During this process, the therapist gave feedback on how she was doing and offered suggestions for improvements.

Vivien's speech therapy was completely different and was technology-based. The NHS supplied a small Dell laptop on loan which was preloaded with a computer program called React. This was a bit like a computer game – an audio track would tell a simple story, for example about a man driving a yellow car to the supermarket to buy certain items. Then there would be spoken questions based on that story, and Vivien had to select the appropriate box on the screen that contained the correct answer. The idea behind this programme was that it gradually stimulated the speech and language centres of the brain, thus bringing about recovery.

Vivien's speech and language centres had been totally destroyed by her stroke, but one of the main principles of stroke recovery is that – with appropriate and repetitive stimulation – other healthy parts of the brain can gradually learn to take over the role of the damaged or destroyed sections. What happens is that the brain learns to rewire itself and creates new connections and pathways around the damaged area, a phenomenon known as neuroplasticity.

Elaine, the physiotherapist, gave Vivien exercises to repeat every day to try and bring back some function in her right hand and arm and also improve her walking and balance. Julie focused on helping Vivien learn to do household tasks again. Under her guidance Vivien eventually made a sandwich for me and heated up a pot of soup.

Vivien had recovered a little since her stroke some months earlier, but it was clear that she was a completely different person, both physically and mentally. She could only say a few words and phrases, and when she did speak, her voice was different than it had been before. One thing I had always loved about her was her beautiful, cultured West of Scotland voice, something that I could now only hear by watching old home videos. Now when she did speak, she sounded like a different person. At times she sounded like a ninety-year-old woman with a weak, trembling voice. On other occasions she spoke like a very young child.

For decades it has been known that some people who recover their speech after strokes speak with a completely different voice. Sometimes they even develop a foreign accent, such as French or Italian, something that is known as the foreign accent syndrome. There was no indication Vivien was going to start speaking with a foreign accent, but the very small amount of improvement she had made in her speech over the last few months suggested that she would always have a problem with it.

Curiously, there was one time of the day when I would often hear her old voice speaking to me, and that was when I was drifting off to sleep or waking up. Often when I was in that curious twilight state between wakefulness and sleeping, I would hear her shouting the word Colin. In fact, what I was experiencing was what is known as a 'hypnagogic' or 'hypnopompic' hallucination.

When people fall asleep, or awaken from sleep, they pass through a state akin to a hypnotic trance and in this condition it is possible to experience visual, auditory, and olfactory (smell) hallucinations. Such phenomena experienced while falling asleep are known as 'hypnagogic' hallucinations, while 'hypnopompic' hallucinations are those encountered on waking. The first few times this happened, I thought that something terrible had happened and Vivien was calling to me, but eventually I realized what was really going on and ignored it.

Vivien's lack of speech (aphasia) distressed me greatly. My own father had suffered from this upsetting condition for a few years until he died in 1996. He had developed dementia, but in his case it was not the well-known Alzheimer's disease but the other main form of dementia, known as multi-infarct dementia, in which the intellect is gradually lost through a series of small strokes. One of these strokes had completely destroyed his speech centre, and like Vivien, he could only communicate with a few words. He did see an NHS speech therapist once, but they concluded that little could be done for him, as he also suffered from dementia and so would have difficulty participating in speech therapy sessions.

In the UK each year, 150,000 people have a stroke, and about a third of them are left with aphasia. I wondered why most people never seem to come across aphasics in everyday life, and I soon discovered this was because aphasics tend to become recluses and do not venture out into society, rather like many disfigured people.

Vivien had changed in many other ways. Before her stroke she was a chatty, outgoing, gregarious, humorous individual who enjoyed social events and going out. Now she had lost all her confidence and had a very small comfort zone. This problem even extended to her food and drink, as there were a large number of foods and beverages that she refused to consume as a result of the effects of her stroke.

Vivien now declined to eat apples, pears, tomatoes, carrots, broccoli, olives, cabbage, cauliflower, parsnips, peas, corn, onions, baked beans, runner beans, garlic bread, broad beans, and peppers – all of them foods that she had previously enjoyed. She used to like drinking wine in the evenings, especially when she had had a hard day at Central High School, and I often joined her to ensure that she didn't drink the whole bottle on her own! She enjoyed a glass of sparkling wine on the day she came home from hospital and also had a single glass at Christmas a few months later, but apart from these two isolated occasions, she now had no desire to drink any kind of alcoholic beverage. Her favourite tipple was now Diet Coke, a drink she didn't care for before.

She also disliked coffee, which she had previously loved. In the months following her stroke, she enjoyed an occasional latte in the Starbucks at the Scottish General Hospital and used to have coffee with me in the Marks & Spencer Café in Dunblane soon after coming home. But within a few months, she developed an aversion to coffee and would only drink tea. She also developed a distaste for any kind of pastry. On a couple of occasions when I made salmon-en-croute for dinner, she enjoyed eating the salmon but left the pastry behind! On a more positive note, she developed a great liking for supermarket ready-made custard, something she had previously avoided. She also enjoyed bananas and would eat three a day, along with the same number of clementines.

For some years we had gone into Stirling most Sundays for a pub lunch in an Australian bar known as Outback (now called The Kilted Kangaroo). I had always considered this to be one of the best places to eat in Stirling as it offered excellent food and chilled Australian beer in beautiful surroundings. (The fact that all the waitresses were young and gorgeous and looked like models did not in any way influence my judgement!)

Following Vivien's return home we started visiting The Kilted Kangaroo again, but it was soon apparent that her changed personality was now affecting her menu choices. Previously she would have chosen different things from the menu every time, but now she always had exactly the same thing every week – chicken and BLT sandwich on brown bread, washed down with a large glass of soda water and lime without ice.

The changes extended to other aspects of her personality as well. Prior to her stroke Vivien had been a very humorous person, and I think this was one of the things that originally attracted me to her, as we both enjoyed a good laugh. Now she seemed to have lost the ability to understand jokes or to laugh at funny films. As part of her rehabilitation I had intended to show her as many comedies and funny films as possible, as laughing and joking tend to put you into a positive state, which assists healing. Unfortunately, Vivien simply couldn't understand jokes anymore, and I think it was because she lacked the necessary brain centres to process them.

There were other changes in her behaviour. Prior to her stroke she could go for hours without having to go to the toilet, but now she visited the lavatory every half hour. She also went to bed early. Previously she had gone to bed at 11 p.m., but now her bedtime was 7.30 p.m. and she stayed there till she got up at 6.45 a.m. In order to make life easier for us both, I went to bed myself at the same time and usually read for an hour before I turned out the light at 8.30.

Her physical appearance had changed too. In the immediate aftermath of her stroke she looked much the same as she always had, except for her diverging left eye. Unfortunately, over the next few months her facial appearance started to alter. Her eyebrows thinned and became permanently arched like Mr Spock's. The right side of her face grew wasted and sunken, and most disturbing of all, her mouth developed a permanently downturned expression like an inverted U. She could return her mouth to a more normal expression by making an effort to smile, but most of the time she was left with this rather glum facial expression, which made her look very sad. The only time she looked like her old self was when she was lying in bed at night about to fall asleep. I think this was a combination of her facial muscles relaxing and the effects of gravity being neutralized by her horizontal position.

Vivien had been disfigured by the stroke, and this was one of the most upsetting aspects of her condition. I had always considered her to be a very beautiful woman with a lovely face. Now her appearance had been ruined by her extensive brain damage.

There was only one positive aspect of all this: I still loved her just as much as before, despite the changes in her personality and appearance. When you really love someone – and I mean really love them – as I love Vivien, then all these physical and mental changes don't affect the way you feel about them. The families of veterans who have returned, terribly injured, from Iraq and Afghanistan will testify to this. Even though their loved ones may have been horribly maimed and disfigured, perhaps lacking eyes, arms, or legs, their families still love them and cherish them just as much as they always did. When you really love someone, any degree of disability is still better than losing them, and I had to remember that.

Still, I was affected by what had happened to Vivien. Although on the surface I may have appeared relaxed and chatty and was sleeping well, deep down in the core of my being I was consumed with anger and anguish. The woman I loved, with whom I wanted to spend the rest of my life, had been left horrifically brain-damaged, disfigured, disabled, and half-blind as a result of poor standards of care in the NHS. All our hopes and dreams for the future were now in ruins.

We had planned to see more of the world – visit America, go back to the Middle East, see Australia. All these things were now impossible. Vivien had hoped to work at something else for a few years when she finally retired from teaching, perhaps private tutoring. That was now out of the question. She would never drive a car again. She would never go cycling with me on sunny days. She would never make me a delicious dinner, prepared with loving hands. She would never surprise me with some new clothes she had bought for me. We would never even have a proper conversation again! It looked as though she would spend the next thirty years of her life sitting in her special electric armchair, watching television with one eye, while I worked myself to a frazzle trying to look after her.

If she had had her stroke when she was seventy-five or eighty-five, then I would probably have accepted it a bit better. I could have taken the view that she had had a very good life and that this was the start of the final chapter of her existence, when she would not be able to do all the things that she had done when she was younger. But to end up living the life of a ninety-year-old when you were only fifty-five seemed to be a particularly cruel twist of fate.

Vivien's stroke had happened because none of the doctors who treated her had made the correct diagnosis or investigated her thoroughly enough. If just one of them had ordered an echocardiogram (an ultrasound scan of the heart) costing just £180, then this whole tragedy could have been avoided. On the surface I looked calm and functioned normally, but deep inside me was a burning volcano of anger and a feeling of injustice. How could all these doctors have failed to make the correct diagnosis?

From the moment I first discovered Vivien semiconscious in her bath on 20 May, I had experienced a constant feeling of horror at what had happened. This feeling has never really left me. They say that the average person has about 60,000 thoughts per day. In my case about 59,999 of them were about Vivien's stroke. Sometimes I could become engrossed in a particular task, like putting up a shelf or washing my car, for a few moments and momentarily forget my problems. Then I would remember what had happened, and the anguish would return. In this way I would be retraumatized hundreds of times a day.

Often I would wake up in the morning feeling quite good. Within seconds I would remember what had happened and feel awful again. There was a little voice deep inside my unconscious which kept saying the same thing: 'You can never be truly happy again, Colin, because you have a brain-damaged, half-blind, aphasic, semi-paralyzed wife, who is never going to recover.'

As Sarah Ockler wrote in Twenty Boy Summer: 'Every morning I wake and forget just for a second that it happened. But once my eyes open it buries me like a landslide of sharp, sad rocks. Once my eyes open I'm heavy like there's too much gravity in my heart.'

I can remember dreaming in past years that something awful had happened to me or Vivien. I would dream that one of us had cancer or that Vivien had died. Then I would wake up, realize it was all a dream, and feel a tremendous sense of relief and happiness. Now I could not wake up and discover that it was all a bad dream because all these terrible things really were happening! Our whole life was a nightmare, which would never end!

I also remembered how I used to worry when Vivien was visiting someone in her car and hadn't arrived home at the time she said she would. I would look at the clock and realize she was ten minutes late, then twenty minutes late, then thirty. I would ring her mobile and get voicemail. Then, as my anxiety level was rising, I would hear the welcome sound of her key turning in the front door lock, rush through to the front hall, put my arms round her, and realize that I had been worrying unnecessarily. Now all my worst fears had actually happened. She wasn't actually dead, which was one consolation, but at times I wondered if she sometimes felt her life wasn't worth living.

I even felt guilt that I was somehow responsible for her stroke, because if we had never met, she would have stayed in Glasgow. She would still have developed her 'vasculitis' but would have been referred to a top teaching hospital which would probably have carried out a more thorough investigation of her illness than she got at the Scottish General Hospital, which is a district general hospital, not a teaching hospital. I was determined to get compensation for her, but for the moment there was nothing I could do about it. I would have to be patient.

In the meantime, I was racking my brains to see if there was any alternative treatment that might help her. Many years before, I had known an alternative practitioner in Harley Street, Dr Michael Seear, a former GP who seemed to have the ability to heal people with his hands. Unfortunately, he had developed dementia a few years previously and had then died, so I made some enquiries to see if I could find someone else who could give Vivien some hands-on healing.

Eventually one of my friends told me about Mr James McManaway, who was a hands-on healer in Strathmiglo, Fife. James's father Bruce had been in the British army during WW2 and had been involved in the Dunkirk evacuation in 1940. While he was in France he was forced to care for large numbers of wounded soldiers without adequate medical equipment and supplies and had discovered that he had 'healing hands'. In 1959 he set up the West Bank Natural Health Centre in Strathmiglo, and eventually his son James took over the business. Two things that James specialized in were injured backs and helping animals, such as horses, but I felt that he might be able to help Vivien.

On Tuesday, 30 August, we drove to Strathmiglo to meet James for the first time. He was a friendly, quietly spoken man who looked in his early forties, very tall and thin with brown hair, who enjoyed skiing. He reminded me a bit of my late Uncle George, who looked rather like Roger Moore.

The healing itself was very simple. Vivien would sit on a wooden chair and then James would stand behind her and put both hands on her shoulders, applying considerable pressure. He would then focus on applying healing energy to Vivien's body for about a half hour. We saw James a few times over the next three months, and Vivien seemed to enjoy these visits and always came away from them feeling very relaxed; she would often fall asleep on the drive home.

During our last visit I experienced his healing for myself. I had had a bad back for some years and was very interested to find out if James might be able to help me. I also wanted to see what it was like to experience this form of healing. When James put his hands on my shoulders, he applied a lot of pressure, which felt almost painful, but within a few moments a tremendous feeling of calm and relaxation spread through my body and at the end of my half-hour session I walked away feeling invigorated. Since that single session my back has felt a lot better, so it is very likely that his treatment did something.

Around this time I started taking Vivien to a local organization in Bridge of Allan known as the Going Forward Stroke Group. This had not been established by the NHS or the local authorities but was an entirely private charitable venture set up by a local stroke survivor, Dot Collie, and her friend Jennifer Cameron.

I agreed to accompany Vivien to the stroke club for at least the first few weeks, and I must admit I went to the first meeting with a feeling of trepidation. What would this be like? I was rather afraid that it would just be a lot of people sitting around moaning about how awful it was to have a stroke, but it was nothing like that at all.

Some of the people who attended every week had clearly been very badly affected by their strokes, but despite this, the atmosphere at these meetings was very happy, positive, and cheerful. People were laughing and joking with each other, and I soon realized that this club was going to be a great help to Vivien. We played games like dominoes and enjoyed a form of indoor bowling with soft leather balls (called boccia, which is effectively bocce for the disabled), and then some weeks there would be live Scottish music and video presentations. Very often there was a quiz, which I greatly enjoyed because I have always been a bit of a know-all!

Each weekly meeting ran from 2 to 4 p.m., and halfway through we got a splendid afternoon tea with cakes and buns, etc. I got to know the people who attended these meetings and began to really enjoy them and look forward to them, contrary to my prior expectations, and I was quite peeved when – after I had been attending for a couple of months – Vivien told me that she would like to go on her own, and I was just to drop her off at 2 p.m. and collect her at 4. However, she did allow me to attend on the weeks when there was a particularly interesting topic.

Eventually I gave three presentations at these Thursday afternoon meetings. In the spring of 2012, I gave a one-hour talk and demonstration on hypnosis; in 2013 I gave one about Thought Field Therapy; and the following year I did one called 'The Power of the Subconscious Mind'. The Going Forward group was a wonderful resource, and the NHS should really hang its head in shame that it didn't provide something similar in the area.

CHAPTER 15

A NEW ROLE IN LIFE

By October 2011 I considered my main role in life to be Vivien's carer. Previously, when anyone asked me what I did for a living, I would say that I was a hypnotherapist or an alternative therapist or a medically qualified hypnotherapist. Now when people asked me about my job, I told them that I was my wife's carer.

A decade earlier I had a thriving hypnotherapy and TFT practice, but in the last few years my business had been in decline. Most people believe the economic recession started in the autumn of 2008, but in my case it began two years earlier. In the first seven years of my business I used to see between ten and twenty people each week, both at home and at the Glasgow Nuffield Hospital. Now I saw only one or two people a week and some weeks none at all. I also used to make a lot of money from training people in TFT, but the recession had hit this as well. In addition, changes in the way that TFT was being taught internationally meant there was now less demand for live trainings, as it was now possible to learn the first level of TFT through home study and online courses.

By the autumn of 2011 my business wasn't just down the toilet; it had arrived at the sewage works! But in a way this was a blessing in disguise because it meant that I had more time to look after Vivien. I was probably busier than at any time since I'd been a junior doctor. Laundry, ironing, cooking, cleaning, food shopping, filling in forms, writing letters and emails, taking Vivien to hospital and GP appointments, sitting in at appointments, helping her with her exercises – and the many other tasks involved in being a carer – filled my days. I had little time for anything else.

For years I had been a member of the local health club at the Dunblane Hydro Hotel (now called the Doubletree) and used to go to the swimming pool frequently. Now I was lucky if I even managed to get there once a fortnight, such were the demands on my time. Ever since my student days I had endeavoured to take some kind of exercise every day, and my favourites were walking, swimming, and cycling. Now I often had no time to take exercise, and my physical condition deteriorated.

I was quite slim until my late thirties but ever since then had struggled with my weight and had never been my ideal size since my early forties. The demands of being a carer and the resulting stress, combined with lack of exercise and eating comfort foods, meant that I became the heaviest I had ever been.

Curiously, Vivien had remained slim, contrary to my expectations. When she was first put on corticosteroids in 2009, I worried that this would make her a put on a lot of weight. Although Vivien did suffer a lot of serious side effects from her medication, weight gain was not one of them, and she actually lost weight, which is unusual; many people taking corticosteroids develop 'moon-faced adiposity'. She also did not put on weight while she was in hospital, probably because she didn't like the food at Scottish General Hospital and often left half her meals on the plate.

Now that she was home, and I was doing the cooking for both of us, she started to eat quite heartily, and I was afraid that she would put on a lot of weight, which would make her condition more difficult to manage. But she remained slim, much thinner than when I had first met her in 1998.

Now that we had settled into a new routine, I turned my attention once more to what I was going to do to obtain financial compensation for Vivien's horrific brain injuries. In early September I had made an official complaint to the NHS, focusing on Consultant Rheumatologist Dr Green's failure to investigate my wife's vasculitis symptoms thoroughly enough and was awaiting a reply.

I knew that any response I received from the NHS could never completely satisfy me because it was pretty obvious that – unless I applied legal pressure – they would never admit that they had made a mistake or offer financial compensation. So far all my efforts to find a legal firm willing to pursue a negligence claim against the NHS on a 'no win–no fee' basis (conditional fee) had come to naught. But in October 2011 there was a breakthrough.

So far I had contacted two legal firms in Scotland who specialized in medical litigation, but neither of them were willing to do the work on a conditional fee basis. However, they both suggested that I look through all my insurance policies as these sometimes included cover for medical negligence actions.

I did as they suggested but my search proved fruitless. My policies for both building and contents insurance didn't have any clauses covering medical negligence. But some years earlier I had taken out a subscription to a legal hotline service with a firm called DAS, as my insurance brokers had suggested that this would be a good thing to have. The DAS hotline policy did include cover for medical negligence but I noted that there was one exclusion mentioned on the documentation namely 'alleged failure to correctly diagnose a condition' which was exactly what this case involved. So although I did have an insurance policy which covered us for medical negligence it looked as though it didn't apply to the particular type of medical error that had caused Vivien's stroke.

Around that time, I happened to 'phone the DAS legal hotline service for some advice on Vivien's rights to severance pay and holiday pay, which she would be entitled to following her enforced retirement from her job as a teacher. During the call I mentioned the circumstances that led to Vivien's stroke and the advisor said that he thought that DAS might be able to help out with an action for damages. As I had already read the small print I knew that this wasn't possible but I said I was quite happy for him to check out the matter. A couple of weeks later I got a 'phone call from DAS which confirmed that (as expected) Vivien would not be covered for a medical negligence action. However, DAS then said that they would put me in touch with a Scottish legal firm which specialised in medical litigation on a 'conditional fee' (no win – no fee) basis.

Soon after that I received an information pack in the post from a legal firm called Bannisters, which had offices in Glasgow and Edinburgh. Their documents explained what was involved in such actions and included a lengthy form which I had to fill in if I wanted to go ahead. As far as I could see, Bannisters was the answer to my prayers. If they were successful in their legal action, then they would receive their own legal fees direct from the defenders; if the case failed, we wouldn't have to pay anything.

I emailed Bannisters and said that I would be very interested in using their services but would like to wait until I had received a response to my complaint from the NHS before I took things further. I didn't have to wait long because in early November 2011 I received a letter from the NHS Patient Relations and Complaint service which was written by Abigail Bamber, Director of Nursing at the Scottish General Hospital.

All my life I have enjoyed writing, and as a hypnotherapist I had used carefully chosen language to bring about change in my patients, so I had to admire the skill with which Ms Bamber drafted her reply. She had the unenviable task of attempting to answer my very serious complaints in an honest, open, and sympathetic way while, at the same time, not admitting liability or indeed even agreeing that anything had actually gone wrong.

Ms Bamber opened her letter by saying how very sorry she was to learn of what had happened. She then informed me that my complaint had been upheld but said that she felt that 'the rarity of the diagnosis has an effect on the outcome, and unfortunately means that it [i.e., the atrial myxoma] may not be diagnosed until severe complications develop'.

The letter went on to say how both Dr Green and Dr Brown had expressed how sorry they were to learn of Vivien's stroke and retinal artery occlusion. Ms Bamber then said that Dr Green had agreed that if Vivien had had an echocardiogram then 'the atrial myxoma would have been detected allowing it to be surgically removed before it could cause the stroke'. He then said that I was 'correct in thinking that he did not consider a diagnosis of atrial myxoma' and added that 'had he done so he would of course have arranged for an echocardiogram to be carried out'. He then expressed his 'profound regrets that he did not diagnose the atrial myxoma'.

Then came the most interesting part of the letter. As Ms Bamber related, 'Dr Green said that he had discussed Vivien's case with a very experienced consultant colleague in a teaching hospital who had a special interest in connective tissue disorders and vasculitis. He said that during his long career his colleague had seen one case of atrial myxoma causing vasculitis. In addition, he commented that it was "not the normal practice to do an echocardiogram on patients whose vasculitis was not severe enough to lead to inpatient admission unless there were cardiac murmurs", which Dr Green recorded Vivien did not have'.

The letter then went on to say that the Rheumatology Department (at Scottish General Hospital) currently 'did not have a departmental protocol for investigating vasculitis. Nevertheless, as is the way of learning from clinical experience, Dr Green would like to assure you that future patients who have vasculitis or suspected vasculitis will be referred for echocardiography. This approach goes further than what currently happens in the teaching hospital alluded to above. Additionally, Dr Green had discussed your wife's case and clinical outcome with the only other rheumatologist colleague within the department so that he is aware of this potential diagnosis in the circumstances. It is accepted that this will not benefit your wife but will act as a preventative measure for other patients'.

Ms Bamber also said that 'neither Dr Brown nor Dr Green actually saw the abnormal lesions in your wife's skin which left Dr Green with an uncertain diagnosis of something he had not witnessed. The photograph your wife gave Dr Green, which is filed in the medical records, does not show diagnostic features. Dr Green said that it is reasonable to describe the lesions as consistent with vasculitis though this is not the same as diagnosing vasculitis. Dr Green agrees with your point in paragraph 3, page 4 of your summary that micro-emboli were the likely causes of some of your wife's pre-clinical symptoms. It seems plausible that the peripheral symptoms were entirely embolic phenomena from the atrial myxoma.

'Dr Green explained that he was not entirely focused on considering connective disease only as a possible cause of vasculitis, highlighting the investigations that were also undertaken for hepatitis B, hepatitis C, and myeloma, and he also pursued the possibility of cervical ribs being relevant.'

On initial reading, Ms Bamber's letter appeared to be a very open and frank account of what had happened, but further review of what she said raised a number of important issues. Dr Green mentioned that he had 'phoned a consultant colleague in a teaching hospital to discuss Vivien's case, and specifically to enquire as to whether an echocardiogram should have been carried out'. This unnamed consultant had allegedly said that he would 'not normally order an echocardiogram in vasculitis cases and would only do so if the vasculitis was severe enough to cause hospital admission or if cardiac murmurs were present'. Although this might seem reasonable, it didn't really stand up to detailed analysis.

First of all, Dr Green had not mentioned the name of the consultant colleague or the hospital that he worked in, which meant that it would be impossible for me to contact this person directly to verify this information. Also, the protocol which (Dr Green claimed) existed in this hospital didn't really tally with what I had read about vasculitis and atrial myxoma. Where was the theoretical evidence which proved that severe vasculitis (i.e., requiring hospital admission) was likely to be due to atrial myxoma, whereas milder cases of vasculitis were not likely to be due to this cause? I don't think there was any, at least none that I could find. Also it must be noted that Vivien had what would be described as mild vasculitis – redness of some fingertips or toes. Yet the cause was eventually discovered to be atrial myxoma, rather casting doubt on this claim.

Dr Green then mentioned cardiac murmurs (abnormal heart sounds due to turbulence inside the heart caused by structural disorders such as damaged heart valves, a congenital defect, or a heart tumour), but I knew from my reading that in 36–37 per cent of atrial myxoma cases, no heart murmurs were present. And of course Vivien did not have a heart murmur but did have a myxoma. It should also be noted that it is possible for a murmur to be present which is not heard by the examining doctor. The fact that a murmur was not recorded does not prove that one was not present, merely that it was not heard, a very important fact which a consultant friend pointed out to me.

So the kindest thing I can say about this alleged protocol for the investigation of vasculitis used by this unidentified consultant in this unnamed teaching hospital was that if these guidelines really were being used in this establishment, then they might miss some cases of atrial myxoma and they would be advised to change their policy and carry out an echocardiogram on every single case of vasculitis or suspected vasculitis. I had learned from an old friend who was a consultant radiologist that the average cost of an NHS echocardiogram was just £180. Vivien's stroke had – by the autumn of 2011 – already cost the taxpayer tens of thousands of pounds, and over the course of the rest of her life the expense to the taxpayer could be a huge sum, even if our legal action was unsuccessful. So apart from all the distress and trauma caused by the stroke, on a purely cost-effectiveness basis it would have been a sound decision to carry out an echocardiogram.

Dr Green also mentioned that neither he nor Dr Brown had actually seen the skin lesions as they had always cleared up by the time Vivien was seen at the outpatient clinic. This was entirely true but – in my opinion – what either of them could have done was ask Vivien to return to the outpatient clinic or the wards (without a prearranged appointment) the moment the symptoms returned. This would have enabled them to see the lesions for themselves, have them photographed by the Medical Photography Department (if considered appropriate), and carry out a skin biopsy which might have revealed the presence of an atrial myxoma. From my reading I had learned that particles of myxoma can often be found in the 'pseudovasculitic' lesions which my wife had.

Many of my questions had been answered by the response I had received from the NHS, but I was far from completely satisfied. The NHS had explained how the error had happened, but they had not really admitted that mistakes had been made. Nor had they admitted liability or offered to pay financial compensation for their error.

In addition, I did not consider that we had received a proper apology from Dr Green. He had said that he 'profoundly regretted that he did not diagnose the myxoma', but to my ears this sounded like a lawyer's version of an apology, carefully worded to avoid an admission of liability. In my personal opinion 'failed to diagnose the myxoma' would be a more accurate description of what had happened.

Now that I had found a way to sue the NHS without risking our own personal finances, I was determined that this would be our goal. My complaint to the NHS was never intended to be the end of the matter; it was merely the preliminary artillery bombardment before the main assault.

I contacted Bannisters again and told them that I wished to go ahead with legal action against the NHS. On Wednesday, 16 November 2011, we travelled into Glasgow on a Citylink coach to deliver all the necessary documentation to the Glasgow branch of Bannisters. It was a lovely, sunny, crisp autumn day, and after handing in all the papers, we went for an early lunch at a nearby Mexican restaurant before returning home.

Around this time Vivien tried another form of alternative therapy which we hoped might improve the function of her right hand and arm. One of my TFT colleagues, Jo Cooper, had recommended a form of alternative physiotherapy called Trager (trager is the German word for 'carry') which she said had helped one of her colleagues who had suffered a severe stroke.

I made some enquiries and discovered that there was only one Trager practitioner in Scotland, and unfortunately she lived about ten miles from Dumfries, which meant we would have a round trip of 230 miles every time we wanted an appointment. On the other hand, I was determined that Vivien should have every possible treatment that might help, so on Thursday, 3 November, I took Vivien to meet Annie Kyle, the sole Scottish Trager practitioner. Annie was a slim, attractive blond lady who looked about forty and who had previously worked as a scientist in the NHS.

She lived in a little cottage in the countryside near Dumfries. As Annie worked with Vivien, I relaxed on a sofa in her lounge, enjoying the heat from a coal fire, and had a little nap.

Unfortunately, we only saw Annie three times over the next few weeks. The main problem was the length of time it took to travel to and from appointments, which meant that we had to give up a full day every time Vivien needed a treatment. By early December we had to call a halt to the Trager sessions, as we were both finding them quite exhausting because of the distance involved. Besides, we had to think about our first Christmas together since the stroke and all the challenges this might involve.

CHAPTER 16

OUR FIRST CHRISTMAS SINCE THE STROKE

On Thursday, 13 November 2011, Vivien had a follow-up appointment at the ophthalmology department at the Scottish General Hospital. Consultant Ophthalmologist Dr Anne Travers confirmed that she was blind in her divergent left eye, with her visual acuity being perception of light. Dr Travers examined her fundi (the backs of both eyes) and noted that her left retina was now a mass of fibrous scar tissue. Fortunately, her right eye was completely healthy. Dr Travers asked us if we wanted any further appointments, and I said I didn't think there was any point in her being seen again by the eye department as there was no treatment for her condition.

In early December I was contacted by Mr Graham McWhirter, our solicitor at Bannisters who had now looked through all the case notes and papers I had passed on to his firm. He said that it was not yet possible to determine whether there had been a breach of duty of care, since this would require a detailed review of the case notes by an independent medical expert, which in this case would have to be a consultant rheumatologist.

The cost of such a report would be at least several hundred pounds, so Mr McWhirter said that he would apply for what is known as an after-the-event insurance policy, which would cover the cost of litigation, including court action if necessary. If the case was a very strong one, it was also possible that the insurance company might fund the preliminary independent medical report. Mr McWhirter said that he would get back to me once the insurers had given him their response.

We now had to think about what we were going to do on Christmas Day. For the last few years we had alternated between spending Christmas at home in Dunblane – with David, Gillian, and Vivien's mother, her sister, Margaret, and her friend Alice as guests – and going to Vivien's mother's house in Bearsden, Glasgow.

In recent years my elderly mother had usually spent Christmas with my sister, Sally, and her husband Alastair at their house in Sway, Hampshire, but she hadn't done that for a few years because her increasing frailty made it difficult for her to travel long distances, and so she had started to spend Christmas with us in Dunblane. Unfortunately, Christmas 2009 had proved to be a very emotionally draining experience for the whole family as my mother was now affected by dementia and was behaving very oddly.

We gave her our spare bedroom, but she kept getting up during the night to use the toilet, and every time she came out of the bathroom, she couldn't remember which room to go back into and went into the wrong bedrooms. Then on Christmas night she got stuck in the bath, and I had to go into the bathroom to lift her out. I found this an extremely upsetting experience. It was the first time I'd seen my mother naked and also the first time I had glimpsed the scar from her Caesarean section dating from my birth.

By Christmas Day 2010 my mother had been resident at Altnacraig nursing home in Greenock for eight months, and as she was very confused and doubly incontinent, we didn't think it would be a good idea for her to leave the nursing home to spend Christmas with her family. Instead, I travelled to Greenock to visit her on Christmas Day and had lunch with her in her room at Altnacraig.

Vivien's stroke had changed everything, and now it was impossible for me to see my mother on Christmas Day. I did ask Vivien if she would be willing to come down to Greenock with me to visit my mum on Christmas Day, but she indicated that she couldn't do this as she didn't want my mother to see her in her current state. I was now Vivien's full-time carer and had to take the view that my fifty-five-year-old wife was more important than my ninety-one-year-old mother.

It was also impossible for us to have the rest of the family over to our house on Christmas Day. Apart from the problem of cooking the Christmas lunch, there wasn't really room for everyone. When we first moved into our house at the end of 2001, we had a large conservatory constructed round the back which we used as a dining room on special occasions such as Christmas. Unfortunately, the conservatory could no longer be used for this purpose. Before Vivien had come home from hospital, I cleared out our main lounge and got rid of the three-piece suite in order to create a large 'stroke recovery room' with plenty of space for Vivien to do exercises. This meant that much of the furniture, and other contents of the lounge, had to be transferred to the conservatory in order to give us room, turning it into just a storage area.

The main lounge now had only three main items of furniture, namely Vivien's special electrically adjustable armchair, which her family had kindly purchased for her; a small two-seater sofa; and a rocking chair, for any guests who might visit. We simply didn't have the facilities to have a large number of people round at Christmas anymore, so the only option was for the whole family to go to my mother-in-law's house on Christmas Day.

Christmas 2011 went very well, although it was clear that things were vastly different from before. Vivien couldn't help me put up the Christmas tree or decorate it. Nor could she buy presents or send Christmas cards. If I wanted a Christmas present from my wife, then I would have to buy it myself, wrap it up, put a little card on it saying 'Love from …,'and then get Vivien to scrawl the three letters Viv with her left hand.

Hogmanay 2011 proved to be a bit of a non-event for us. In previous years Vivien's brother, Andrew, and his family had spent the New Year period in a small cottage in the grounds of Crieff Hydro, and we had joined them on Hogmanay for a lavish dinner in the main hotel. Now that was not possible because Vivien went to bed every night at 7.30 and now disliked alcohol, so Hogmanay became like any other night of the year to us.

As 2011 came to an end, I realized that it really had been the worst year of both our lives. I just hoped that 2012 would turn out better and that Vivien's condition would start to improve. Unfortunately, this proved to be not the case, and in early 2012 some aspects of her condition took a turn for the worse.

When Vivien suffered her stroke back in May, her right arm and hand became completely paralyzed and lay motionless by her side. Over the next few months, with help from the NHS physiotherapists, she started to get some movement back in her right arm and regained a little function in her hand, to the point where she could just about hold a knife to butter a slice of toast.

By early 2012 though, it was obvious that something strange was happening to Vivien's right hand. I had noticed that her little and ring fingers were starting to curl up, and within a few weeks the other fingers became affected. In addition, her right arm floated up in the air when she sat down at the kitchen table, and when she walked it pointed straight ahead as though she were about to press a doorbell button. I pointed out these new developments to Tony, the jack-of-all-trades from the NHS rehab team, who was still visiting Vivien weekly, and we both agreed that she had developed spasticity (increased tone) in her right arm, which was impeding its function.

I made an appointment for Vivien to see her GP. He noted the problem and said that he would discuss this with Dr Brian Sutton, the stroke consultant. In the meantime he prescribed a drug called baclofen, a muscle relaxant used to treat spastic conditions.

Vivien started taking baclofen, and it soon became apparent that these tablets had a very serious side effect: they made her very drowsy, which meant that she spent much of the day sleeping. Out of interest I took one of her tablets just to experience the effect for myself and found that it was indeed very soporific.

We made another appointment to see the GP, and he agreed that – as the side effects were so severe and the drug didn't seem to be reducing the spasticity – he would refer Vivien to Dr James Courtney, a consultant in rehabilitation medicine who specialized in treating spasticity problems. The only snag was that we would have to wait a few months for her appointment, which was scheduled for June 21.

The problems with Vivien's right hand were a great blow because up to that point we were optimistic that she might get back some useful function in her right hand and arm. There had also been very little improvement in her speech and language, and Vivien became very depressed at her situation. I also felt a bit down about everything because for the past few months I had hoped that she might make an excellent recovery. A number of factors suggested this might be true. She was relatively young for a stroke survivor, she was very intelligent, and I believed that she was highly motivated to recover. She had always been a feisty individual, and I also thought that all the alternative therapies she was receiving would help her make a better-than-average recovery.

All our friends and family thought that Vivien would recover well. When I discussed her situation with them it seemed that almost everyone knew someone who had had a really terrible stroke and had then made a miraculous recovery to the point where you wouldn't really know there was ever anything wrong with them. For example, there was the well-known case of the actress Jean Marsh who suffered a stroke and then returned to acting within a fairly short period.

What our friends perhaps did not realize was that not all strokes were the same, and people who made quick and miraculous recoveries from them had usually suffered only a small amount of brain damage. I can illustrate this point by considering the group of people who normally attended the Going Forward stroke group every week in Bridge of Allan. On a typical week fifteen people might be attending. About four of these people had recovered so completely that you wouldn't really know they had ever had a stroke. Then there might be another three or four people who were still severely affected by their strokes – even many years afterwards – as evidenced by the fact that they were still in wheelchairs or severely aphasic. The rest of the people attending the stroke group were between these two extremes.

Vivien had suffered a total anterior circulation infarct (TACI), which was classified as a very severe stroke. She had lost much of the parietal and temporal lobes of the left hemisphere of her brain. In addition, the frontal lobe of her left hemisphere – although not destroyed by the stroke – was unable to communicate with the other parts of her brain. I believe it was the loss of her left frontal lobe which was responsible for the personality changes that we had all witnessed.

On average, 30 per cent of people who suffer a stroke die in the first twenty-four hours. In the case of a TACI stroke this percentage is higher (40 per cent), and within a year a staggering 60 per cent of people who have suffered this type of stroke are dead. Only 4 per cent of people with a TACI make a complete recovery, and even in such cases the recovery is not really complete, as there are often persisting personality changes and other problems.

Although we all hoped and prayed that Vivien would make a complete recovery from her stroke, by early 2012 I realized that this was now unlikely and that she would be left with permanent severe disabilities particularly affecting her speech and language function. It was a depressing scenario, and even with all her cognitive difficulties, I think Vivien knew deep down that this was going to be her future. In the first few months after coming home, she did her physiotherapy exercises religiously every morning, but now she was losing interest in them and wanted to spend all day watching television.

If 20 May 2011 had been the worst day of my life, then 26 January 2012 proved to be almost as bad. That was the day Vivien went missing. For the previous week or two she had been convinced that she had suffered another stroke. I had examined her a couple of times and reassured her that this had not happened. As I pointed out to her repeatedly, her atrial myxoma had been surgically removed, and her repeat echocardiogram just four months before had confirmed that the myxoma had not grown back following surgery, so it was impossible for her to have another stroke. However, nothing I could say seemed to satisfy her, so I made an appointment for her to see her GP, as I knew she would accept his opinion more readily than mine.

On the morning of Thursday, 26 January, I drove to Tesco to buy some groceries, leaving Vivien in the house. About thirty minutes later I returned home. 'Darling, I'm back,' I cried out as I opened the door. Even with her aphasia, Vivien would usually respond in some manner even if it was just a friendly 'Hi', but there was no reply. I checked the lounge. She wasn't there, so I looked in the bathroom. Nothing. A feeling of panic started to rise from deep within me. I then went through the entire house, checking every room. She was nowhere to be found. Then I looked in the key box on the kitchen wall. Her set of house keys had gone, although she had not taken her handbag with her.

I began to fear the worst. In the last couple of weeks she had been very down, feeling that she had suffered another stroke. Where had she gone, and what was she up to? I wondered if she had gone down to the main road to try and kill herself by walking in front of a lorry or bus or if she intended to stand on the railway line. But how could she do this, since she could only walk a few steps?

I picked up the phone and dialled Susie, one of our neighbours, and asked her if she had seen Vivien walking out the house or indeed if Vivien was with her, as they had spent a bit of time together recently. She said she hadn't seen her. The only thing to do now was to phone the police.

I rang the Dunblane police station and started to tell them what had happened. I was about two minutes into my call when the mobile phone in my trouser pocket started to vibrate. I pulled it out and discovered that it was someone else in the police station trying to contact me. To my relief I discovered that Vivien had somehow managed to make her way down to the police station – an incredible achievement, bearing in mind that she was half-blind and had great difficulty walking (I learned later that she had got a lift from a neighbour she saw leaving). She had told the police that she had suffered a stroke, and they had called an ambulance, which was on its way. I pointed out that she had not had a further cerebral infarct and that they should cancel the ambulance, but the policeman said that he could not do this, so I agreed that I would get down to the police station immediately.

Within five minutes I was reunited with Vivien in one of the rooms at the police station. I was delighted to see her alive but also angry at what she had done. She looked very distraught, and once again I explained to the police that she had not suffered a stroke and was suffering from a delusion, but they said that they were unwilling to cancel the ambulance callout. The ambulance arrived fifteen minutes later, and – despite my protestations that all this was unnecessary – the crew spent some time checking Vivien medically, recording her blood pressure and pulse and pupil reactions. Eventually they agreed with me that nothing new had happened to her medically, and I apologized for wasting their time.

It was clear though that Vivien had suffered a psychological crisis. When people suffer a life-changing injury such as a stroke or paralysis or severe burns or losing limbs, then they often go through a suicidal phase when they don't want to live. Fortunately, they usually pass through this stage and recover psychologically. Often all they need is a bit of support to get them through the worst part.

I phoned Tony from the NHS rehab team and told him what had happened and also made an emergency appointment for Vivien with her GP, who saw her later that same day. He increased her dose of citalopram (which she had been on for some weeks) to 40 mg per day and said he would keep an eye on the situation. It had been a grim day – truly the second worst day of my life – but at least it had not ended tragically as I feared it might.

CHAPTER 17

LONDON CALLING

By February 2012 Vivien's emotional crisis had passed. She had accepted that she had not had another stroke, and my fears that she wanted to take her own life also receded. The GPs believed this improvement was due to the increased dose of citalopram, although I was very sceptical. For decades I have doubted that antidepressant drugs actually have any real therapeutic benefit since it is known that about 70 per cent of the effect of these drugs is due to placebo. While I was at medical school in the 1970s I read an article in *Psychology Today*, written by a psychiatrist who shared these views. He believed that all antidepressant drugs did was make people slightly drowsy, which meant that they tended to be less aware of their problems. (In those days the standard antidepressant medication was the tricyclic group of drugs. Nowadays these have largely been replaced by the more modern SSRI drugs.)

When I was at Glasgow University, we had several months of lectures on materia medica (practical pharmacology), and I recall one of the lecturers saying that he considered that antidepressant drugs didn't really have a therapeutic effect, only side effects.

In more recent times psychiatrist Dr Joanna Moncrieff of the University College, London, has criticized the excessive prescribing of antidepressants and has even written a book about it, The Myth of the Chemical Cure.1 Dr Moncrieff has been practising psychiatry for more than twenty years and believes antidepressants 'don't do any good at all.' She has also gone on record as saying she wouldn't take these drugs herself under any circumstances, even if she was suicidal.

There is no doubt that many people who are given SSRI drugs by their GP could be treated much more effectively using other therapies like hypnosis, NLP, and TFT. Indeed in the last decade an Edinburgh GP, Dr Alistair

Dobbin, has been in charge of a project which has treated tens of thousands of people with minor psychological illness, such as stress, mild depression, and lack of confidence, using nothing more than a series of prerecorded self-hypnosis CDs. The results have been very impressive, and it is possible that this project may eventually be extended to other regions of Scotland.2

A lot of people who met Vivien said that she seemed depressed, particularly as she had been left with a permanently downturned mouth, giving her a very sad expression. In reality it was quite difficult to truly assess Vivien's mood because of her aphasia, and I felt that her changed personality was largely down to the fact that her left frontal lobe, though not damaged by the stroke, was unable to communicate with the other parts of her brain. The frontal lobes are known to be the most important part of the brain connected with personality, and I believed it was this organic change in her brain rather than true depression that was causing her change in affect.

However, the members of the Rehab team took the latest developments very seriously, and Tony arranged for Vivien to receive a few visits from Diana, a psychiatrically trained nurse (RMN) who was attached to the team.

As the winter of 2011/2012 came to an end, my thoughts turned to the possibility of us taking a spring break. If nothing else it would help me determine whether we could go on holidays again.

I'd always enjoyed going to London for short breaks, but one problem had always been finding suitable accommodation. Central London hotels tended to be very expensive. They were also very noisy at night, making sleep difficult.

In May 2008 I attended a TFT training course in the Victory Services Club (VSC) in Seymour Street, just off Edgware Road, quite close to Marble Arch. I was very impressed with this establishment, which was one of a number of military clubs scattered throughout the capital. Membership of the VSC was open to serving members of the British Armed Forces, but on checking their website, I was delighted to discover that I too would be eligible for membership, as my father had served in the British army from 1942 to 1945 and had been a reservist for another fourteen years. All I had to do was provide documentary evidence of his army service, which I was able to obtain quite easily from an army administrative unit based in Yorkhill, Glasgow.

In August 2008 my application for membership of the VSC was accepted, and I have since made use of their facilities many times when staying in London. The VSC offers very comfortable overnight accommodation at reasonable prices, with the most expensive rooms being equivalent to four-star hotels but at a much lower price. The club also has an excellent bar and restaurant; their buffet breakfasts were especially impressive. Although some bedrooms at the front of the building could be quite noisy at night, the rear-facing rooms were reasonably quiet, and I usually didn't have any problems sleeping overnight in the club.

I'd always wanted to take Vivien to the VSC. I used to tell her how great it was, but I had never had an opportunity prior to her stroke. Now I thought I could take her on a two-night weekend break to London, which would give me an opportunity to assess whether it would be possible for us to start going overseas on holidays again.

We travelled down to London on Friday, 25 May 2012, on the East Coast train service from Stirling station which left about 11.30 a.m. I decided to travel first class; this would give Vivien greater room and privacy and there was also the additional benefit of complimentary snacks during the journey.

The seats in first class were big and comfortable, but it was obvious that the train was very old and had clearly seen better days. There was quite a lot of vibration in the carriage, which made it difficult to read without feeling travel sick, and there seemed to be a problem with the air conditioning as, the train was too hot. The toilet was also very dirty.

Despite these problems we had a reasonably comfortable journey and arrived on time at King's Cross station about 5 p.m. After waiting about twenty minutes for a taxi in the baking hot sunshine, we took a cab to the VSC. The summer of 2012 was probably the worst in living memory, but the last week in May was dry, hot, and sunny and as our taxi sped down

Edgware Road with its windows open, I could smell all the various aromas of a London summer. One thing I've always liked about the Edgware Road area is that there are a large number of Lebanese and Arab restaurants – where I love to eat – and the various smells which emanate from these establishments, such as exotic spices and water pipes (hookahs), always seem to trick my brain into believing that I'm really in the Middle East rather than central London.

After checking into our room at the VSC, we relaxed for a while, and then at 6 p.m. we met one of Vivien's old friends, Anne Jamesston, who lived in Northwood and worked for a publishing company with offices in the city. We went to a little Lebanese restaurant a couple of doors down from the VSC, which I had visited many times before, and had a really excellent dinner.

The next morning my old friend Rosemary Wiseman (I first met her while doing a hypnotherapy course in 1998) and her husband, Lawrence, came to meet us at the club, and we had morning coffee together. After they had left, we went to nearby Hyde Park and relaxed in deck chairs, enjoying the early summer sun. In the afternoon we went to the Dominion Theatre, near Tottenham Court Road underground station, to see a performance of We Will Rock You, the musical based on the songs of Queen.

Although it was the hottest and sunniest day of the year so far, the theatre was packed and it was a memorable performance. We have always enjoyed Queen, and we had a great time. Despite her disabilities, Vivien did her best to dance in the aisles during the more rousing numbers!

Then it was back to the VSC for an early dinner and then bed. I hadn't slept a wink the first night at the club because of a combination of Vivien's snoring and traffic noise in the road outside, but on this Saturday night I went to bed at 7.50 p.m., feeling quite drowsy after two pints of draught beer, and fell asleep almost immediately. After sleeping for several hours, I woke feeling very refreshed.

The next day we went on a river cruise from Westminster Embankment to Greenwich Pier and back. It was another glorious sunny day, and the

River Thames had never looked more beautiful. The cruise boat arrived twenty minutes late, and the guide apologized profusely for this, saying that this was because of rehearsals for the Jubilee River Pageant, which was to be held in exactly one week's time. On the way down the river we saw many of the boats that were due to take part in that event. (Sadly, in a week's time the weather had taken a turn for the worse, and the pageant was held in cold, cloudy and rainy conditions).

After we had enjoyed our cruise, we went back to the VSC for a bar lunch, collected our baggage, and then travelled to King's Cross Station for our train home. That morning we had agreed that we would catch an earlier train than originally planned, as this would give us more time to catch a connection from Edinburgh Waverley Station to Dunblane. I had phoned up East Coast trains customer services and (as is the norm these days) was put through to a call centre in India. I explained that we wanted to travel on an earlier train but would like to have a seat reservation in the first class carriages as we did not want to turn up and find that there were no seats.

Unfortunately, when we boarded the train at King's Cross and went to the designated carriage, I discovered that we had been given seats in second class. Vivien became very upset because she realized she would not have as much room and no complimentary food. Fortunately, I was able to get this matter sorted out, and we moved to the first class compartment.

The rest of the journey went without incident, apart from a delay, but this error in the reallocation of seats, combined with all the problems with dirty toilets and faulty air conditioning two days earlier, put me off travelling with East Coast, and I decided that if we were going to London by rail again, we would definitely choose Virgin Trains. I should add that Virgin Trains have now taken over the East Coast service and plan to introduce new rolling stock on the route.

As I indicated earlier, one of the reasons I was keen for the two of us to go on a break to London was that it would give me an idea if it would be possible for us to go on a foreign holiday together. The indications were that this would now be feasible. Vivien couldn't carry luggage, so I would have to handle all the bags, but she seemed to cope with staying at the Victory Services Club. She had even managed to have a bath with my assistance, the first time she had ever done so since her stroke a year earlier.

As soon as we got back to Scotland, I started looking for a suitable holiday for the two of us. Since the beginning of our relationship in 1999 we had always booked vacations during school holiday periods, for obvious reasons. Now that was not a consideration, I decided that our next holiday would be in late September. It was often difficult to book holidays in Holiday Property Bond accommodation at such short notice, so I chose a break in a five star all-inclusive establishment in Crete called Aquis Vasia beach hotel. One advantage of this facility was that, for a little extra money, you could choose a VIP suite that featured its own patio and sunbeds and a small swimming pool. I felt this would give us the extra privacy that we craved, so I made a booking for seven nights' holiday starting on Thursday, 27 September.

While I was dreaming of our trip to Crete, we had to endure the terrible summer of 2012. We had one week of warm, sunny weather at the end of March and another glorious few days in late May but — apart from these two periods — there were no long spells of balmy, sunny weather during the whole summer. We did get the odd mild, sunny day here and there, and we tried to make the most of it when it did happen. I purchased a small portable barbecue and a camping gas stove, and when the weather permitted, I cooked dinner on our patio, and we enjoyed eating it outside.

On Sunday, 3 June, one of our neighbours held an afternoon tea in their garden to celebrate the Jubilee and raise funds for charity. It was a superbly organized event which was well attended, and the catering was excellent. But in stark contrast to the weather a week earlier, it was cool, cloudy, and overcast.

We also had a few day trips by rail that summer making full use of Vivien's disabled rail card. One day we took the train to Glasgow Queen Street and then transferred to another from Glasgow Central to Wemyss Bay where we caught the ferry to Rothesay on the Isle of Bute. I've always had a soft

spot for Bute as I have visited it many times during cycle runs. Rothesay –
although being very beautiful and picturesque – is a bit run-down, and
most of the shops and restaurants look much the same as they did during
the 1960s.

In Dunblane at present we have a single boarded-up former Chinese
restaurant which is a bit of an eyesore and greatly concerns the local
community council. But in Rothesay there are many such properties,
and the island clearly needs a massive injection of cash to get it back into
pristine condition. Rothesay used to be a popular holiday destination, and
every summer thousands of Glaswegians would travel there by steamer.
The advent of cheap package holidays to places like Spain put an end
to that. I recall going on a family holiday to Rothesay in July 1962 and
remember that it rained almost every day.

However, the place still has a great deal of charm, and the views of the
Firth of Clyde are breathtaking. For lunch we went to one of the two
Indian restaurants in the centre of Rothesay. The food was quite good,
but the decor reminded me of a typical Glasgow Indian restaurant in the
early 1970s with cheap plastic chairs, paper tablecloths, and vinyl flooring.
Halfway through our meal two of the waiters pushed a full supermarket
shopping trolley through the front doors into the centre of the restaurant
and started to unload it in full view of all the customers. Somehow I can't
imagine that happening in the Koh-I-Noor restaurant in Glasgow!

Another day we took the train to Largs on the Clyde Coast and then
took the ferry to the Isle of Cumbrae, where we caught a bus to the town
of Millport. I was quite impressed by how good Millport was looking.
Again this was somewhere that I'd visited many times during cycle runs
in the seventies, eighties, and nineties, but it looked much smarter than
I'd ever seen it. There was no litter, and all the buildings appear to have
been refurbished. We had a pub lunch in a local hostelry, and I was very
impressed with both the food and decor. Clearly Rothesay really needed to
follow Millport's lead and spruce itself up, and I am sure that one day this
goal will be achieved, as the island of Bute has a great deal to offer tourists.

CHAPTER 18

PROGRESS ON THE LEGAL CASE

While we were enjoying the summer of 2012 as best we could, things were progressing with our legal case. Back in early February our solicitor Graham McWhirter had received a response to his request for an 'after-the-event' insurance policy from DAS. They said that they would not issue a policy until they had seen an independent medical report on Vivien's case which confirmed that there had been a breach of duty of care.

Mr McWhirter contacted a few consultant rheumatologists in Scotland who did medico-legal work and could not find one who was willing to do a report for us because they all knew Dr Green personally. This is a common problem in medical negligence actions, so Mr McWhirter said he would look for someone suitable in England and would get back to us.

A few weeks later he sent me a letter stating that he had found a suitable medical expert – Dr Nick Packer, a consultant rheumatologist at an English general hospital, who did a lot of medico-legal work. He enclosed Dr Packer's CV. He also indicated that the likely cost of this report would be in the region of £1400-1500. I replied immediately, saying I was quite happy with his choice of medical expert and also the fee. Although the report was expensive, I knew that it would be worth every penny if it helped us win our legal case.

There was a bit of a delay in obtaining this report, largely because additional case notes had to be obtained from the NHS Medical Records Department, but in late June the first draft of Dr Packer's report arrived in the post.

My fingers were trembling when I opened the envelope and started to read its contents. My greatest fear was that Dr Packer would conclude that, because atrial myxoma was such a rare condition, Dr Green could not be reasonably expected to diagnose it. The first part of his report suggested this might be his conclusion because he spent a lot of time explaining how rare atrial myxoma was and how many consultant rheumatologists might not even see a single case during their entire professional career. He then pointed out that Vivien had never had any cardiac symptoms.

But in the latter part of his report Dr Packer stated that atrial myxoma was recognized as a less common cause of vasculitis (or pseudovasculitis, as in this case) and that this had never been considered in the differential diagnosis. He spent some time discussing Dr Green's interest in Vivien's cervical ribs and pointed out that the way such abnormalities caused problems with hand circulation was by causing damage to the blood vessels, resulting in small emboli which then travelled to the hands. He then said that it was unfortunate that Dr Green had not considered other causes of emboli in his differential diagnosis.

Dr Packer concluded by stating that he felt that Dr Green should have ordered an echocardiogram and that under the circumstances his failure to do so 'represents care that is below the level that I would expect to be provided by the majority of consultant rheumatologists and therefore, potentially a breach of duty'. He also agreed that if Dr Green had ordered an echocardiogram, then the atrial myxoma could have been excised before it had caused the stroke and central retinal artery occlusion.

Dr Packer's report was music to my ears. In his conclusion he had said everything I had wanted to hear for the last year. The insurers must have thought so as well because they granted an 'after–the-event' insurance policy as soon as they had read the report.

I was overjoyed because after thirteen months of uncertainty I now felt that we had a very good chance of winning a medical negligence action. Even if our legal action failed, I was still glad that we had an independent medical report because it confirmed my suspicions about the standard of Vivien's medical care. Clearly they were not paranoid fantasies.

In early July, Mr McWhirter made an initial claim to the NHS Central Legal Office (the solicitors for Scottish General Hospital), enclosing a copy of Dr Packer's report. His hope was that once the solicitors read it, they would realize that we had a very good chance of winning a medical negligence action and might agree to an out-of-court settlement.

There was no response from the Central Legal Office, and after three months had elapsed, Mr McWhirter made contact with a firm of advocates in order to bring an action at the Court of Session in Edinburgh, the highest civil court in Scotland. Now that we had an 'after-the-event' insurance policy, this course of action was possible without risking our own personal finances.

On Wednesday, 12 December 2012, we travelled to Edinburgh by train for a meeting with our designated advocate, Mr Frank Munro, which was held in the Faculty of Advocates at 142 High Street, near the rear of Waverley Station. Mr McWhirter was ill that day and was unable to attend the meeting, so one of his colleagues, June Grant, attended in his absence and took minutes. Mr Munro was a very personable man who looked about forty, with a slim build, dark hair, and black spectacles.

Mr Munro opened the meeting by giving us a quick summary of what was going to happen. He said that the action for damages was only concerned with obtaining financial compensation for what had happened and nothing else. I asked if it would be possible for me to make a complaint to the General Medical Council about Dr Green and if that would affect the outcome of the legal case. For example, I asked what might happen if I complained to the GMC and they replied saying that they were not going to do anything about Dr Green. Could this then be used against us in the legal action?

Mr Munro said that I was perfectly entitled to complain to the GMC, as this would not affect the outcome of the case. However, he pointed out that such a complaint might stir up a hornets' nest, resulting in the lawsuit being more vigorously defended than it might otherwise be, so I decided that I would leave such a course of action until after all legal proceedings had been concluded.

Mr Munro then said that there were two main issues in medical negligence actions, namely causation and liability. He said that he did not think there would be an issue with causation in this particular case as even Dr Green had admitted in print (in the NHS response to my complaint a year earlier) that if the myxoma had been detected a few months earlier, then it could have been removed and the stroke avoided.

So it seemed the only issue in this case was liability. He said it was very hard to find information about similar cases of stroke resulting from undetected atrial myxoma, and I suggested to him that this might be because many such cases were not reported. It was also possible that the victims of such tragic incidents didn't even know that possible medical negligence had occurred. He agreed that this was very likely to be so.

One possible defence that the NHS might use was that, as atrial myxoma was such a rare condition with only one new case per 2 million people per year, then it was not reasonable to expect a consultant rheumatologist to consider it in a differential diagnosis. However, Mr Munro said he had been in contact with Dr Nick Packer (our designated medical expert), who had pointed out that Dr Green had not just ignored the possibility of atrial myxoma but had also failed to consider much commoner causes of embolic phenomena (such as endocarditis) which would also have required an echocardiogram for accurate diagnosis.

Mr Munro also said that, as Dr Packer was a consultant in a teaching hospital (and not a district general hospital), then it might be necessary to obtain a second medical opinion from another consultant rheumatologist who worked in a district general hospital, since some teaching hospitals might investigate people more thoroughly.

He stated that the court case would not happen for least another eight months and that it would probably take two weeks, with each week consisting of four days in court. He said that it would be good if Vivien could testify as to the effects of the stroke. I pointed out that – as Vivien was aphasic – it would be very difficult for her to do this. However, I felt that if she got into the witness box, attempted to speak, and obviously failed in front of the judge, then this in itself would be very convincing evidence of the true effects of this dreadful medical error.

Mr Munro pointed out that it would be necessary to obtain independent medical reports on the effects of Vivien's stroke, and this would require examinations by a consultant in stroke medicine and a consultant ophthalmologist. He would also ask an actuary to visit us at home to carry out an in-depth assessment of the financial effects of Vivien's stroke and partial blindness.

Mr Munro concluded the meeting by saying that he felt there was a reasonable chance of success in this case and that he had won medical negligence cases which were much weaker than this one. I went away from this meeting feeling very buoyed up by what happened. I had a great sense of confidence in Mr Munro, as he seemed to be intimately acquainted with every detail of the case and was very thorough in his approach.

In early 2013 Bannisters informed us that Vivien would now need to be independently examined by doctors and others to confirm the true effects of her stroke and central retinal artery occlusion. On 4 February we received a visit from Liz Shaw, who worked for a firm called Doris Goldman and Co. Liz was what is known as an actuary, an expert at calculating the true effects and costs of injury and disease. Her background was in occupational therapy, but she now worked in this highly specialized field.

Liz spent a full three and a half hours with us and carried out a very detailed enquiry into the effects Vivien's tragic misdiagnosis had had on both our lives. She did a thorough clinical examination to assess the true effects of Vivien's stroke and also enquired about what it had cost us financially.

Until Liz's visit, even I had probably not fully realized just how much Vivien's stroke had cost us financially. As Liz explained, if we won our legal action, we would be entitled to claim reimbursement for all sorts of things which had probably never even occurred to us. For example, we would be allowed to claim for all the travelling expenses, rail fares, and mileage, etc., involved in visiting Vivien every day for three months. Also, the cost of all the special clothing and footwear we had to buy Vivien was a legitimate expense. Prior to her stroke, Vivien took great pride in her appearance, and she still had three wardrobes full of beautiful clothes, but since her cerebral infarct, her daily attire had consisted of a T-shirt, jogging bottoms, fleece jacket, and trainers with Velcro straps. She also had to ditch all her old bras and change over to using special one-piece ones which could be put on single-handed.

This was one of the most upsetting consequence of the stroke. When I was doing the housework, I would often open the wardrobes to put clothes away and gaze upon all these beautiful outfits, suits, dresses, skirts, and blouses which Vivien used to wear but which she would never put on again because it was too difficult for her to don them and take them off. She also had a large number of beautiful shoes, none of which she would ever wear again. And in her bathroom she had several trays full of cosmetics which were now gathering dust.

Vivien always used to like wearing some make-up when she went out to work or we went out for a meal, but now – apart from using some moisturising cream in the evenings – she shunned cosmetics completely because they were simply too difficult to put on because of her stroke and partial blindness. There were a couple of occasions after she came home from hospital when she applied a little lipstick, such as on Christmas Day 2011, but apart from that she never wore any cosmetics.

As Liz explained, we would be perfectly entitled to claim for all sorts of domestic expenses. For example, I had purchased a Sony widescreen television in late 2011, solely for Vivien's use. This was one of the latest models, which included Internet access and built-in Skype which I felt would increase the quality of her life. Liz said we would be perfectly entitled to claim for this. Also, Vivien's family had very generously bought her an electrically adjustable armchair costing about £1100, and again Liz said they would be perfectly entitled to receive reimbursement for this cost. We were also allowed to claim for all the alternative treatments which Vivien had received since her stroke, even though these treatments were not accepted as effective by the NHS.

Liz explained that the way compensation worked was that they would try as much as possible to put our lives back to the way they were before the stroke. Clearly it would be impossible to do this completely, but that was the aim.

Three weeks later we received the first draft of Liz's report, which was sixty-six pages long. Liz recommended that Vivien should really have full-time support workers and also the services of various professionals such as chiropodists, physiotherapists, speech therapists, psychotherapists, and others to try and make her life as comfortable as possible. The annual cost of providing all these personnel would run to tens of thousands of pounds. This would of course be in addition to any large lump sum payment the NHS would be required to pay us to compensate Vivien for her severe disabilities and loss of quality of life if we were successful in our legal action. When I read this report, I realized that the cost to the NHS of their diagnostic error could be millions of pounds over the remainder of Vivien's life.

I was also pleased to see that Liz had fully recognised the devastating effect of Vivien's stroke. I had felt that some of the NHS professionals who had assessed Vivien since her stroke had tended to understate the impact of her blindness and cerebral infarct. For example, on looking at the GP case notes, I came across an entry in the autumn of 2011 which stated that Vivien's speech was 'almost back to normal' and that she was walking 'with a slight limp'. However, Liz's report painted a much more depressing (and of course, realistic) picture of the true extent of Vivien's disabilities, and I was pleased that this had finally been recognized.

A couple of weeks later, on 19 February 2013, we travelled to Ashbridge Hospital for an appointment with Stroke Consultant Dr James Henderson.

I had heard a great deal about Ashbridge Hospital over the years but had never visited it. I remember that when it first opened in the late 1970s, people were impressed by the sheer size of the building, and I recall that Surgo (Glasgow University medical journal), which I then edited, reported that some junior doctors were using scooters to get about, such was the size of the building. Since then the hospital complex had been further increased in size.

It was a beautiful, cold, crisp, sunny day when we drove up to the hospital, and the sunshine was sparkling off the river to our right as we turned left and drove up a steep hill towards the hospital. The hospital clearly had a problem with car parking as hundreds of cars were jammed into every possible parking space in all the surrounding residential streets, so I was very glad that we had a 'blue badge' disabled parking permit which enabled us to park quite close to the hospital entrance.

We arrived at the stroke unit at 1 p.m., exactly half an hour before the appointment. This was typical 'Colin Barron', as I have a habit of arriving early; in mitigation, however, I wasn't sure exactly how long it would take me to drive there or whether I might get lost or have difficulty finding a parking space. As it happened, Dr Henderson was able to see us a little bit earlier than planned at 1.20 p.m. and he spent a full fifty minutes taking a careful history and examining Vivien.

Dr Henderson did a very thorough and careful assessment of the effects of Vivien's stroke. I was already familiar with all the different physical problems she had, but when he did an examination of her visual function and carried out a visual field test, he reported that he felt that she had some loss of visual field affecting the temporal (outer) side of her right field of vision.

I was quite surprised to learn this because Vivien had had a visual field examination carried out by ophthalmologists at the Scottish General Hospital about fifteen months earlier, and at that time it was thought that she had a normal visual field in her right eye. It was known that she had a right-sided homonymous hemianopia immediately after her stroke, but it was believed that this had now resolved. However, Dr Henderson's examination cast doubts on this claim.

Dr Henderson had carried out his visual field examination using the very simple clinical 'confrontation' method, in which the tester stands in front of the patient, who is asked to cover one eye with a hand and then stare at the doctor's nose. The patient is then instructed to keep their gaze fixed on the doctor's nose while he slowly brings his fingers in from the periphery, and the subject is instructed to speak whenever the fingertips become visible. In view of his findings, Dr Henderson said that he would recommend that Vivien be checked out by a consultant ophthalmologist and a report prepared.

On 27 March 2013 I took Vivien to a private hospital in Glasgow to see Dr Naismith, an NHS consultant ophthalmologist who also saw some patients privately. Dr Naismith spent a whole hour examining Vivien and took a very detailed history. He checked her visual fields using the same confrontation method that Dr Henderson had employed and then did them a second time using an automated visual field testing machine. Dr Naismith confirmed what Dr Henderson had previously found: in addition to her being completely blind in her left eye, she had a significant amount of visual field loss in the right eye which was effectively a partially recovered right-sided homonymous hemianopia. Dr Naismith explained that automated visual field testing machines can often give inaccurate results in stroke patients because of problems such as diminished reaction time, difficulty pressing the button, etc. He said he was absolutely certain that there was visual field loss affecting Vivien's right eye. This had very serious implications, as there was now the possibility that she could be registered as partially sighted. It would also affect the legal case and the amount of damages claimed.

On the downside it also meant that she would never drive a car again. People who have only one functioning eye are allowed to hold a driving licence providing they have normal vision and a complete visual field in the other healthy eye. But if there is any kind of visual field loss in the good eye then it is clearly impossible to hold a driving licence as it is too dangerous to drive.

I was pleased that that we now had these three independent reports. As well as helping us win our case and hopefully receive a huge damages payment, it was good that Vivien's disabilities had been much more comprehensively assessed than they ever had been by the NHS. In particular, the Health Service had not recognized that she had visual field loss in her right eye, and they might not have even realised she was blind in her left eye if I hadn't pointed it out to them in July 2011!

CHAPTER 19

SUMMER HOLIDAY

While things were proceeding slowly with our legal case, Vivien was receiving further treatment, both alternative and orthodox. On 22 June 2012 she finally saw rehabilitation consultant Dr Robert Courtney who examined her right arm and hand and concluded that she was suffering from a dystonia (abnormal muscle spasm due to brain injury) rather than simple spasticity (the main difference between dystonia and spasticity is that the first can be controlled by a lot of mental effort whereas the second cannot). Accordingly, he considered that she would not benefit from either muscle relaxant drugs (like baclofen or clonazepam) or from Botox injections. He felt the best treatment would be a tight Lycra glove which, by applying pressure to the hand and fingers, gave the brain a better indication of where they were in space.

He was so confident that this would work that he arranged for a video to be made showing her right hand and arm 'before' and 'after' the Lycra glove, which he intended to show at clinical meetings. We both gave our consent for this, as we realized that it might help other people. Six days later Vivien was seen at the orthotic clinic where she was measured up for her Lycra glove, which would be manufactured by an Irish firm called Jobskin and would probably be ready in a few weeks.

Unfortunately, months passed, and there was no sign of the Lycra glove. In early October we were asked to come back to the clinic on the tenth, as the factory reportedly didn't have all the measurements required to make the glove. Senior technician Mr James Brown was very apologetic at the length of time it had taken to make up the item and said the new measurements would be faxed through to the factory in Ireland that day. A couple of weeks later we were informed that the glove had finally arrived, and on 29 October I took Vivien back to the orthotic clinic to be fitted with it.

I had expected that Vivien would get a glove with a long sleeve which extended all the way up to the elbow but the one she got was very short and only went as far as the wrist. It had to be put on every morning and taken off last thing at night and required to be washed occasionally. It was quite difficult to put it on correctly without tearing it, but with practice I got quite good at it and could eventually do the job in about three minutes.

Unfortunately, it soon became obvious that the glove was not helping. I wondered if the reason for this was that it was too short and that there would be a much greater effect if it went all the way up to the elbow. I remembered that when we had seen Dr Courtney on 22 June, he had demonstrated the likely effect of a Lycra glove by gripping Vivien's right forearm just below the elbow, and as soon as he did this her fingers relaxed.

I wrote a letter to Dr Courtney pointing out that the glove didn't seem to be having the desired effect and also asking if perhaps the wrong type of glove had been provided. I also wrote to Elaine, the physiotherapist, to explain what had happened. On 30 November Elaine visited us at home and had a quick look at Vivien's right hand. She said that she had discussed my concerns with Dr Courtney, who had pointed out that he had always intended Vivien to have a short glove and not a long one. Apparently Lycra gloves were not made in a size that only went as far as the elbow; the next size up was a full-length sleeve which went all the way to the shoulder joint and was extremely difficult to put on every day. Elaine concluded her visit by saying that Vivien would be reviewed at the orthotic clinic in the New Year.

On Thursday, 24 January 2013, Vivien saw Mr James Brown at the orthotic clinic for the fourth time. He said that he had now discussed her case with Dr Courtney who felt that, if the short Lycra glove had done nothing, then a long glove would also be ineffective. However, he did agree to see Vivien once more for a further opinion the following month.

On 22 February Dr Courtney saw Vivien for the second time. Once again he examined her right arm and hand and said that – since the Lycra glove had no effect – the only other option worth considering would be a Botox injection, and an appointment for this treatment was arranged for 4 April. He said it would also be possible to treat this problem using clonazepam, which was a benzodiazepine drug similar to Valium, which had serious side effects namely dependency and sedation.

He also said that the Botox injections would have to be followed up with the prescription of a splint which would have to be worn three times a day for an hour at a time. The aim of this splint was to hold all the fingers in a more natural physiological position. This, combined with some physiotherapy sessions, might help Vivien regain some function in her right hand. Unfortunately, nothing could be done to stop Vivien's right arm from floating up in the air when she sat down, or pointing straight ahead when she was walking. The reason this was happening was because her brain simply didn't know where her right arm was in space.

I was very impressed by the courtesy and professionalism of Dr Courtney and all the other members of the rehab team but was rather dismayed at the length of time it had taken for Vivien to receive effective treatment for this problem. It is an issue that has dogged the NHS since its inception in 1948. As I knew from experience, the NHS could move very fast when attending to an emergency, such as Vivien's stroke on 20 May 2011. But at other times, when dealing with non-emergencies, it seemed to move with all the speed of an arthritic tortoise.

If the NHS was working properly, then Vivien should have received treatment for her dystonia within weeks. She shouldn't have had to wait several months for each appointment. I am sure the length of time she had to wait for treatment must have led to her condition worsening, as contractures would have developed over time in her hand, making treatment much more difficult.

I have the greatest respect for people who work in the NHS. They do a very difficult job in the face of chronic underfunding, but it is clear that they cannot always provide the service that they really should be providing, because of lack of money and the bureaucracy of the system. I remember that when I worked as a junior ophthalmologist in the early 1980s, there was another eye department in Glasgow (which has now been closed down) which had a two-year waiting list for cataract operations. I also recall that when I had dental problems in 1991 – which required me to have surgical extractions of all four wisdom teeth – I was told I would have to wait two years to have this operation on the NHS. Fortunately, at that time I had private medical insurance and had the procedure done at the Nuffield Hospital in Glasgow just two weeks later.

I was also aware that stroke rehabilitation services in Scotland were resources-led rather than needs-led. In other words, stroke survivors only got a fairly minimal amount of physiotherapy, speech therapy, and occupational therapy, probably less than they really needed. If Vivien lived in the United States and was receiving privately funded stroke rehabilitation services, then she would probably have had the services of a physiotherapist, speech therapist, and occupational therapist at least five days a week, for a period of about five years.

Vivien's NHS speech and physiotherapy sessions had stopped some months before, not because there was nothing more that could be done but because it simply was not possible to continue rehabilitation services for life, for financial reasons. What usually happened in the NHS was that stroke rehabilitation was provided at home for a few weeks or even a few months, and then it was stopped as the NHS didn't have the money or personnel to keep providing the service indefinitely. This is not the fault of the people delivering the service. It is really something that the politicians need to get sorted out, and I hoped that once the dust had settled on Vivien's case, I might be able to add my voice to the debate on this issue.

Meanwhile I was continuing to investigate possible alternative therapies which might help her. For about a year after her stroke she had received psionic medicine treatment, a form of homoeopathy in which the diagnosis and appropriate remedy were both determined by dowsing a hair sample. Now that this course of treatment had concluded, I wondered if she might benefit from classical homoeopathy.

While perusing the Glasgow Yellow Pages I came across an advert for a medically qualified homeopathic doctor called Dr Mary McTavish. I already knew Mary because she had been my predecessor as editor of Surgo (the Glasgow University medical journal) in 1976–77, and she was also a fellow member of the British Society of Medical and Dental Hypnosis (Scotland).

On 4 July 2012 we travelled into Glasgow to meet Mary. This was more stressful than I anticipated because my Jaguar was being repaired and I had to use a hire car fitted with satellite navigation. Rather than making the journey easier, I found the satnav to be an annoyance as it took us on a 'Magical Mystery Tour' round parts of Glasgow I'd never been to before. Eventually though, it did take us to Mary's doorstep.

Mary saw her patients in a small consulting room in her house, just as I did, and I was allowed to sit in while she carried out her first consultation with Vivien. I'd never witnessed a classical homoeopathic session before and found the whole thing fascinating. The average GP appointment lasts just eight minutes, but Mary spent a full two hours with Vivien, asking her all sorts of questions about her life to date, her mood, her habits, her dietary preferences, and even her sleep pattern and dreams. Vivien had difficulty answering these questions because of her aphasia, so I had to help out as best I could.

At the end of the consultation Mary gave her a homeopathic remedy, which had to be dissolved slowly on her tongue, and arranged a follow-up appointment for the following month. One other treatment she suggested interested me greatly. She said it would be a good idea if I could buy some natural progesterone cream from Amazon and rub it on Vivien's body for three weeks out of every four.

This was a new treatment for strokes and other brain injuries, which had resulted from experience gained from treating soldiers returning from Iraq and Afghanistan. It had been noted that female soldiers seemed to recover better from brain injuries than men, and it was suggested that this was because they produced the hormone progesterone, which is one of the two hormones involved in the menstrual cycle. As a result of this observation, brain-injured servicemen were now receiving intravenous progesterone infusions as part of their treatment. Stroke survivors like Vivien could benefit from this discovery simply by applying natural progesterone cream to their bodies. It seemed to work by stimulating the formation of new neural connections.

I was very intrigued to learn this. As far as I could see, there was a chance that progesterone cream could help Vivien make a better recovery – and even if did not help, she had nothing to lose by trying as it had no side effects. So I bought a tub of progesterone cream and started applying it as suggested to four different sites in rotation, namely the front of the neck, upper chest, the breasts and the inner upper arms.

As with all the other unorthodox treatments that Vivien had received, I took the view that it was worth trying. Since it appeared to me that the NHS had given up on my wife, I was keen to try anything that might help her, even if the chance of improvement was small.

By early September 2012 we were looking forward to our first proper holiday together since the stroke, and I'd chosen a five-star all-inclusive hotel in Crete with a flight departure date of Thursday, 27 September. I had picked this date very carefully because it was just before the mid-term October school holidays, so the resorts were likely to be quieter, but it was still close enough to summer to ensure good weather.

We had previously gone to Crete in July 2007 and had flown out from Glasgow airport just two days after the terrorist car bomb attack which led to the emergence of 'local hero' James Smeaton. At that time, we had stayed in a small apartment complex called New Kydonia, only a few miles from the town of Chania, which we visited many times.

This time I had chosen a full-service hotel because I thought it would make things much easier for Vivien. Unfortunately, in early September she developed a new health problem which put our holiday under threat. She had started her menopause a few years earlier and had had a lot of unpleasant symptoms like hot flushes and so had seen a gynaecologist a few times. One morning in early September I heard Vivien crying for help. I went into her bedroom and discovered a bloodbath. There was blood all over the toilet seat, inside the pan, on the bathroom floor, all over the sheets, and on the mattress protector, which (being waterproof) had saved the mattress from staining. I made an emergency appointment with the GP and got to work cleaning up the bedroom. I also bought in a supply of extra-strong sanitary towels.

Our GP very kindly saw Vivien the same day and told us that she was suffering from postmenopausal bleeding which would require emergency investigation. He explained that this was a very common problem and that a special postmenopausal bleeding clinic at Scottish General Hospital usually saw new cases within two weeks. In the meantime he gave Vivien a prescription for norethisterone (a synthetic progesterone drug), which should stop the bleeding within a couple of days.

I was pleased that the NHS had taken this matter so seriously and had given Vivien such an early appointment, but I was rather worried about what the cause of the bleeding might be. I read up on this and discovered that the majority of such cases were caused by temporary hormonal imbalances. More worryingly, a small percentage were due to tumours of the reproductive system, and this was the reason that people were seen so quickly. Vivien received an appointment within ten days, but unfortunately it was for Thursday, 27 September, the day we were due to fly out to Crete. I phoned the gynaecology department to explain the situation, and they gave her another appointment for Monday, 17 September, ten days before we were due to fly on holiday.

Vivien was seen exactly on time at 9.10 a.m. that day. Dr Humphrey took a brief history and then carried out a gynaecological examination, including an ultrasound scan of the uterus. Much to my relief, he pronounced that there was no evidence whatsoever that she had any malignancy in her reproductive system. He believed the bleeding was just due to the ovaries briefly starting up again after a period of inactivity due to the menopause. I asked him what we should do if the bleeding returned. He said that it was unlikely it would come back but agreed that she could continue on the norethisterone until she returned from Crete, as this would prevent any further bleeding while we were on holiday.

I was greatly relieved that there was no evidence of a tumour because up to now Vivien had been incredibly unlucky as far as her health was concerned. She was extremely unlucky to have developed an atrial myxoma in the first place (since this was extremely rare), and she was also very unlucky that it was not picked up before it could cause a stroke and a central retinal artery occlusion.

On Thursday, 27 September, we woke at 2.30 a.m. and, after a quick breakfast of coffee and toast, drove to Glasgow Airport. I had booked the car into the Flying Scot long-stay car park in Paisley. Check-in was even more stressful than usual, as I had to manhandle both suitcases plus our combined hand luggage. I was annoyed to discover that our flight had been delayed a couple of hours.

I had booked Vivien in as a special assistance passenger on the understanding that this would mean that she would be allowed to board first and get seating with extra legroom. In the event, this didn't happen, and when the call to board was made, there was just a mad scramble as everyone tried to board at the same time. However, she did at least get a seat that was very close to the toilet.

Heraklion Airport Terminal compares very unfavourably with most other European airports. It is really too small for the number of passengers it handles and has very ineffective air conditioning, and the public address system is almost impossible to hear. In addition, we had to wait a long time at baggage reclaim.

The coach which collected us from the airport was comfortable enough but was rather old and appeared to have faulty air conditioning as it was very hot inside. Vivien asked me for water, but I told her not to drink too much as we would have a very long journey ahead of us, and there was no toilet on the coach.

As luck would have it, the Aquis Vasia Hotel was the last one on the driver's run, and we were feeling very hot and tired by the time we pulled into the village of Sissi. We had only a few hundred yards left to go when the traffic came to a complete stop because the road was blocked by a large tarmac-laying machine which was resurfacing the main road through the village. After we had been stationary for about twenty minutes, the driver got out and had some angry words with the construction workers. Then he returned to the coach and reversed it back up the road about a mile to a point where he could do a three-point turn and return the way he came. His plan was to get to the hotel by a different road, bypassing the obstruction. Unfortunately, by the time we had made this lengthy detour, the tarmac-spreading machine had itself moved on and was now blocking the route that the driver had chosen. This time the driver got out and screamed at the construction workers for ten minutes. Eventually they relented, the machine was moved out the way, and we finally got to our hotel.

The Aquis Vasia Hotel was a very large complex with several swimming pools, a huge main buffet restaurant, and two other à la carte restaurants situated on the seafront. Our VIP minisuite had a large bedroom and a separate sitting area, though curiously the flooring was laminate – rather than the more usual tiled floor that I was used to in Mediterranean countries – and was already starting to show signs of wear. At least it did have effective air conditioning.

The holiday was quite enjoyable, though it was probably our least active one ever. We both used to love going long walks on holiday, but that was now a thing of the past. Unfortunately, on the first full day of our holiday, Vivien developed blisters on her feet caused by new shoes, and I had to spend much of the week walking to the local chemist to buy stocks of special blister dressings.

An additional problem was that the shower cabinet did not have a non-slip mat in the bottom tray, and there were no grab rails in the bathroom. I made some enquiries but found it was impossible to buy such items in Crete, so I made a note that in future I should bring our own non-slip shower mat and suction cup–fitted grab rail with us. Another problem was that every time Vivien had a shower, the floor got very wet, and I had to spend a lot of time on my hands and knees with a little microfibre cloth drying it out, so I also decided that it would be a good idea to take a small collapsible microfibre mop or a large microfibre towel on holiday with us in future.

We had a similar routine every day. We would have breakfast about 8 a.m. in the main buffet restaurant and then spend most of the day relaxing on our private patio. This featured a pair of sunbeds which were fitted with a large canopy, giving the appearance of a four-poster bed. This proved ideal as we could lie together on the sunbeds, shaded from the fierce Cretan sun. I could read my Kindle, and Vivien could relax and doze.

There was also a very small, shallow swimming pool which I used every day. On the first day I managed to get Vivien into the pool, but it was soon obvious that she could not swim because of her right-sided paralysis. This was unfortunate because swimming together had always been a very enjoyable part of our holidays.

The food at the hotel was very good, but I soon found that an all-inclusive package was not really ideal for Vivien. Because she only had one useful hand, it was very difficult for her to serve herself at the buffet and carry her plate, so she simply chose what she wanted, and I served it up for her and then carried it back to our table. I realized that in future we should really go somewhere with waiter service.

It was a very inactive holiday compared with what we were used to, but at least I was getting a break from food shopping, cooking, cleaning, and laundry (although I was dreading having to do a massive washing and ironing when I got back to Scotland!).

Vivien had become a recluse as a result of her stroke, and so had I. One evening the hotel held a large barbecue party. Previously we had loved attending such events and had been to just such an occasion on our last big holiday together, to Majorca in 2010. Now Vivien felt very anxious at the thought of going to a barbecue party, having to eat in front of other people, and trying (and failing) to have a conversation. Also, with the event starting at 7 p.m. and her usual bedtime being 7.30, she would have found it very tiring. I fully agreed with her reasoning and we opted out of this event.

On Wednesday, 3 October, we went on a short trip round the local area on a road train (rather like the trams at Universal Studios) which ran on the local roads. I think Vivien enjoyed seeing a little of the local countryside, and for that brief hour it seemed just like all our previous holidays.

The following day we flew back to Glasgow. The holiday was very enjoyable, although very different from what we had experienced before, since Vivien didn't show much interest in going on trips or attending social events. But at the very least, it did prove that it was still possible for us to have some kind of summer holiday together in spite of her disabilities.

CHAPTER 20

ANOTHER PROBLEM DEVELOPS

In early 2013 we learned that the court case was to be postponed until June 2015. This was because it had now been decided that a full three weeks (twelve days) of court time would be required, and this was the earliest date that such a slot was available. I was disappointed at this development but not surprised. I knew that the average time for settlement of a medical negligence case in Scotland was three and a half years (from the time of the claim being made, not the date of the original incident which led to the claim). Many claims took much longer; the record in Scotland was twenty-one years. However, these lengthier cases tended to involve birth injuries and cerebral palsy, which often took many years to settle.

There was a good side to this news, though. I could now go ahead and book another holiday. Our previous vacation in Crete had been a success, although I realized that an all-inclusive hotel package was not really suitable for us. My thoughts therefore turned to the possibility of a holiday in Cyprus. It had a special place in our hearts because we had got married there in 2002 and had visited the island on two other occasions. In the summer of 2001 we had rented a property at Argaki Villas near Polis. As well as being an enjoyable holiday in its own right, this also gave us an opportunity to check out our wedding venue and fill out all the appropriate paperwork in the council offices in the village of Pegia. Vivien also chose the restaurant for our wedding breakfast – the Coral King in Coral Bay – after sampling its cuisine.

In October 2009 we had visited Cyprus for a third time, staying at the Avanti Hotel on the outskirts of Paphos. We loved everything about the island – the hot, sunny weather, the beautiful beaches, the views, the friendliness of the local population, and, most of all, the cuisine.

I knew that Holiday Property Bond accommodation wouldn't be available at such short notice, so I hired a villa in the centre of Coral Bay, the same resort we had stayed in when we got married in 2002. About two weeks before our holiday we were informed that the villa we had chosen was no longer available as a consequence of the financial crisis affecting the island. A number of Russian investors had pulled out of Cyprus, and these included the owners of the villa who had cancelled all future bookings. Fortunately, the villa hire company was able to find us another one at short notice.

When we arrived at Paphos airport on 8 May 2013, we discovered that our villa had been changed once more as there was a problem with the swimming pool. Instead of a villa within Coral Bay we were allocated a property in the hills overlooking the resort. However, I didn't consider this to be a problem as we had a hire car and Vivien couldn't walk much anyway.

The replacement villa proved ideal as it was a bungalow with three large bedrooms, all with en suite bathrooms, which were disabled-friendly. It was also well-equipped with air conditioning, Wi-Fi, a dishwasher, and a washing machine.

As was the case with our previous holiday abroad, Vivien's disabilities meant that we couldn't do all the things we used to do on foreign vacations, and most days were spent lying by the small pool at the rear of our villa. Even though it was the second week of May, and the weather should have been very hot and dry, there was a lot of rain and half the time we were in Cyprus we had to stay indoors because of wet weather.

One day we drove to Pegia, the small village where we had got married eleven years earlier. It was a grey overcast day, and the secluded courtyard where we had tied the knot looked damp and depressing. As I gazed at the spot where we had signed the marriage register, I detected a strong smell of urine emanating from a nearby public toilet. Then it started to rain. It was as if Mother Nature was shedding tears over what had happened to Vivien and our life together, a fairy-tale romance that had turned into a tragedy. The visit to Pegia proved a sad reminder of how our lives had been destroyed by a medical error. Still, despite this one depressing episode, the holiday was a success.

That July I had a weekend break in London on my own for the first time since the stroke. Gillian very kindly offered to look after her mother while I was away. As usual I stayed at the Victory Services Club (VSC) in Seymour Street. On the Friday night (12 July) I met my old friends Gary Leigh and Sheldon Collins for a drink and a meal. Gary was the former editor and publisher of DWB (Doctor Who Bulletin), a magazine that I had contributed to in the mid-eighties, and Sheldon was a London taxi driver who I knew through attending a few Doctor Who conventions in those days.

On Saturday, 13 July, I took a train from London's Liverpool Street Station to Whittlesford, from where I walked to Duxford airfield, near Cambridge, where the annual Flying Legends air display was being held. This was the first time I'd visited Duxford since 2008 and the first air display I'd been to there since 2001. There was a heatwave that weekend so it was baking hot on the exposed airfield. Although it was good to be doing one of the normal things I used to do, I found it didn't really take my mind off my problems. There were many times during the day when I was standing in a long queue or sitting on a stationary train, and during these moments my mind tended to focus on all the horrible things that had happened in the last couple of years. As John Milton said in Paradise Lost: 'The mind is its own place, and in itself can make a heaven out of hell, a hell out of heaven.' At these times I was indeed experiencing my own personal hell. Since Vivien's stroke I have always found the best remedy for my constant mental anguish to be keeping my mind occupied by doing things, and sitting by myself on a sun-baked bench on an airfield didn't help at all.

That night I slept poorly at the VSC, as there was a noisy police helicopter hovering overhead for hours. The next day I discovered this was because of the Rolling Stones concert in nearby Hyde Park. After breakfast I went on an open-top bus trip round the sights of London before heading back to the VSC to have dinner and then pack before flying back to Scotland the next day.

Unfortunately, when I got home I had to deal with another problem. Back in 2004 Vivien had bought a one-bedroom flat in the centre of Dunblane for her son David so that he could enjoy an independent life. This proved to be a good decision as he liked staying on his own.

One snag about the building was that it was very old (built at the end of the nineteenth century) and required constant maintenance, particularly frequent roof repairs. There was an even more serious problem looming, though. In 2006 a local contractor had carried out repairs to the ceiling of one of the two shop properties on the ground floor of the block. This involved the removal and replacement of some timber joists which were affected by dry rot. Unfortunately, the contractor had failed to support the building properly while these vital structural members were being replaced, and as a result a large hairline crack had appeared on the front facade. At the time the contractor had inspected the damage and concluded that no remedial work was required. But in the spring of 2013 some of the owners noticed that the crack on the front of the building had now widened to the point where you could put a hand in it, and the front facade appeared to be bulging forward slightly. A structural engineer surveyed the property and confirmed that there was now a serious defect affecting the front of the building which could result in the whole facade collapsing if nothing was done.

Obviously we had to contact the contractor who did the original work and request that the building be repaired at their expense. Unfortunately, things moved extremely slowly, and it took repeated phone calls, letters, and emails before things started to happen. Eventually the contractor informed us that their own insurers would be investigating the matter, and in mid-June a loss adjuster inspected the property and agreed that there was a serious structural defect.

Weeks passed without anything happening. Then in late July, after I had returned from my London break, I took a late-night phone call from one of the owners. She had a friend who was a civil engineer and who had just viewed the property. He felt that the building was in danger of imminent collapse and that urgent action was required to support the facade, followed by an extensive repair.

On 8 August a surveyor commissioned by the insurance company viewed the building and agreed that there was a serious structural defect but declined to comment on whether the original contractor was responsible for the current damage. He did say though that he would recommend that the insurers fund the fitting of a building support – without prejudice to liability – to prevent a collapse until liability could be ascertained.

More phone calls and emails to the insurance company followed, but no progress was made while engineers pondered over what kind of building support might be needed. At this point I was sick with worry. If nothing was done, the front of the building might collapse, and people could be killed. The owners could simply have clubbed together and arranged for the building to be repaired as a communal repair but the cost could be astronomical. One builder told us it would cost a six-figure sum to fix. Obviously the cost would be shared between all eight of the owners, but even so that was a lot of money. Some of the owners were in low-paid jobs and didn't have that kind of cash to hand. There was also the problem that if we got the building fixed at our expense it might be difficult to claim the money back from the insurers. I realized it was obviously better if the insurance company could agree to fix the building and pay their own contractors directly.

Another problem was what might happen if Stirling Council became involved. They might slap a 'dangerous building' notice on us, ask for the entire block to be evacuated, have it repaired by their own contractors, and then present us with a huge bill, far greater than the estimates we had received. Local councils are not concerned about keeping costs down in such a scenario.

I was already under considerable strain because of the effects of Vivien's stroke and the ongoing legal case with all the problems this was causing. Vivien had lost her job and was now receiving only a small pension and some benefits. My own business had also collapsed as I was only averaging one or two hypnotherapy clients a week and was no longer able to hold training courses.

I was having great difficulty sleeping because of constant worry about what might happen. As if things couldn't get any worse, another problem arose. I started to develop severe pains and tingling in my arms and hands. I knew from my medical training that this was caused by degenerative changes in my cervical spine causing nerve root irritation, a condition known as cervical radiculopathy.

Unfortunately, this is a very difficult condition to treat. Painkillers such as paracetamol, aspirin, codeine, and ibuprofen don't alleviate this kind of nerve root pain. My GP had offered me amitriptyline, an old tricyclic antidepressant which was no longer used to treat low mood but was found to be helpful in treating some kinds of pain. I declined to take this medication because of the severe side effects, which included drowsiness and a dry mouth. Another drug that was offered to me was gabapentin; again I refused this because it had side effects similar to those of amitryptiline.

The early autumn of 2013 was therefore one of the worst times of my life. As well as all the problems caused by Vivien's stroke and resulting lack of income, I couldn't sleep because of a combination of stress and severe pain in my arms and hands.

After consulting all the other owners in the block, I decided to do two things. First of all, I made an appointment to see a commercial solicitor at the Glasgow branch of Bannisters to discuss what we could do to get the building fixed by the insurers. Second, all the owners agreed that it would be a good idea to get another engineer's report on the building, as the original engineer's report had not commented on the issue of liability. After discussing the matter with Rod Simmons of Bannisters, a second engineer's report was commissioned which did conclude that the original contractors were at fault.

There were a few anxious weeks while the insurance company studied the second engineer's report, and then in early December 2013, much to my relief, they finally accepted liability and agreed that the building should be repaired as soon as possible. In early February 2014 a metal building support was fitted to the front of the block to prevent further movement of the masonry, and three months later repair work started on the building, directly funded by the insurance company. The insurance company even agreed to pay all the legal expenses and engineers' fees that we had incurred.

There was also some good news about my neck problem. Conventional physiotherapy and painkillers were completely ineffective, so I tried a few sessions of acupuncture, which also didn't help. Then in December 2013 I saw Dr James McGee, a chiropractor in Bridge of Allan. Even after the first session of this treatment, there was an immediate improvement in my symptoms, so I started seeing him regularly, and within a few months my pain and tingling had almost completely resolved.

By early 2014 I was feeling a bit more relaxed because the crack in the block of flats was going to be fixed soon at the insurance company's expense. In addition, my cervical radiculopathy symptoms were starting to improve, thanks to the chiropractic treatment. Unfortunately, there was another problem looming on the horizon.

My elderly mother Nancy had suffered from dementia for several years, and in April 2010, as documented earlier, she had been admitted to Altnacraig nursing home in Greenock. At the time she was admitted, we expected her to live for only a few months, but almost four years later she was still alive, although her condition was continually deteriorating. For the last few years I had jumped every time my mobile phone went off and the display said 'Altnacraig', as I thought I was going to hear some tragic news. And every night when I went to bed, I wondered if I was going to be awakened by news of my mother's demise. Since her admission to Altnacraig she had suffered frequent health crises, usually caused by a chest or urinary infection, and every time we had wondered if this was going to be the end. But on all previous occasions she had pulled through. By early 2014 it was clear that she didn't have much longer to live, as she was becoming increasingly frail, and her dementia had worsened to the point where she didn't even know who I was.

On Sunday, 25 April, I took a phone call from Altnacraig at about 7.45 a.m. The nurses informed me that my mother looked rather blue and was having difficulty breathing and had been taken by ambulance to the Accident and Emergency Department at Inverclyde Royal Hospital. A couple of hours later I got a phone call from one of the A & E doctors who told me that my mother was not expected to live much longer. Just after 11 a.m. I got another phone call to inform me that she had died.

Her death was obviously a shock, but my overwhelming feeling was of great relief that her years of suffering were finally over. The real tragedy wasn't that she had died of dementia a few days short of her ninety-fourth birthday but that she had endured such a poor quality of life in the last few years because of her illness.

Three weeks later on 17 May I paid tribute to her at her funeral service in Greenock Crematorium. Although my mother had been a churchgoer up to the early 1970s, she had no formal religious beliefs in her later years, so I agreed with my brother and sister that there would be no religious trappings at the funeral. In my eulogy I mentioned all my mother's great achievements. She had been a hospital physician, an eye surgeon, a Justice of the Peace, and also a very talented artist, public speaker, and piano player. I also inserted a considerable amount of humour into my presentation, and the anecdote which seemed to get the most laughs was a tale I related about my mother's strange attitude to ansaphones. I explained how she believed that because they were machines, she had to speak to them like a Dalek, or else they wouldn't work.

I also told a funny tale about how my mother suddenly became interested in disco dancing in May 1973 and how every time the record Roll over Beethoven by the Electric Light Orchestra came on the radio, she started bouncing round the room.

I was touched by the number of cards and messages of support I got from friends and family after my mother's death, but what was curious was how little emotion I felt about her passing. I think this was partly explained by the phenomenon of anticipatory grief. Because she had suffered from dementia for six years before her death and the person I knew had more or less disappeared a long time ago, I had really done my grieving some years earlier. Another reason why I was unable to mourn for my mother was because I was grieving for my wife. Although Vivien was not dead, I had now been mourning for three years for the loss of the person I loved and knew and the life we once had.

Vivien had declined to attend the funeral because she didn't want people to see her in her current condition. It would also have been difficult for her to put on the smart clothes and shoes that people normally wear when attending funerals, because of her disabilities.

At the wake, in Greenock's Beacon Arts Centre, a lot of people asked me how she was doing. Many people believed that she would continue recovering over time to the point where she would eventually be much the same as she was before the stroke. Some people do make this kind of recovery, for example the actress Sharon Stone, who made a remarkable recovery from a brain haemorrhage. However, it was clear that this wasn't going to happen in Vivien's case as many of her problems were actually worse than they had been two years before.

As related earlier, Vivien had some Botox treatment for the spasticity and dystonia affecting her right hand in the spring of 2013. Unfortunately, this had only a slight effect which wore off after a couple of weeks and by late 2014 the right hand was worse than ever, as all her fingers were curled up. Gillian was so concerned that in the autumn of 2014 she went to Vivien's GP to ask if anything more could be done. Her GP agreed to refer Vivien to the rehabilitation department at Scottish General Hospital, and so between late November 2014 and mid-January 2015 Vivien attended for seven consecutive Mondays to receive physiotherapy treatment.

I could not praise the dedication and commitment of the staff enough, but despite some excellent treatment there was no improvement in Vivien's right hand and arm. In particular, nothing could be done to stop Vivien's right arm pointing horizontally straight ahead when she walked or rising vertically into the air when she sat down.

There had been a little improvement in Vivien's speech over the past two years, but all the same she was tending to use the same small number of phrases repeatedly, e.g. 'Love you', 'Going to bathroom', 'Bog roll', 'Tea,' 'What are we doing today?,' and 'Going to bed.' This is because aphasic people find it easier to use a few stock phrases to communicate rather than coming up with sentences made to order.

There was also evidence of a shrinking of her comfort zone in other areas of her life. Earlier in this book I mentioned how Vivien had developed a dislike of many common foods following her stroke. This had now worsened over time to the point where she would eat very few foods. She now disliked pasta, corned beef, potatoes in any form, almost all vegetables, and most fruits, which meant cooking for her was very difficult. We seemed to be having chicken and rice dishes a lot because that was one of the few things she still enjoyed. One thing she did relish though was curries, and she particularly liked Indian restaurants, so that was always our choice for a special meal out.

There had also been changes to her daily routine. For the first couple of years after her stroke she had gone to bed about 7.30 p.m. and then risen earlier and earlier until eventually she was getting up at 5.30 a.m. By 2014 she was now going to bed at 6.30 p.m. and not getting up till 9 a.m. This meant I had to change my own schedule, and eventually I started going to bed at 8 p.m. and then rising between 5 and 6 a.m. so that I could get a lot of the day's housework done before Vivien got up.

It was clear that Vivien's 'comfort zone' was shrinking in many areas of her life, and she became reluctant to leave the house at all, sometimes even feigning illness to get out of going to things like the stroke club. It was the same sort of behaviour I had indulged in at primary school, as I had sometimes pretended to be ill in order to avoid going to my classes.

One very positive thing did happen in 2014, though: we got a Crossroads carer for a few hours a week. Ever since I had become Vivien's carer, I had thought of getting in some help even if it was only one day a week. In January 2014 I went to the Stirling Carers Centre to see if this could be arranged. Because of all the paperwork and assessments that were involved this took several months to arrange, but in mid-September our Crossroads carer, Caroline, started her first shift. She worked every Tuesday from 11 a.m. to 4 p.m., and we agreed that she would do things with Vivien. Caroline had been a fully trained cook before she became a carer and suggested that she do some cooking or baking with Vivien every week. She was also keen on arts and crafts, and Vivien did some card making with her.

I benefitted too, as I could get out of the house for a few hours a week. On good days in the spring and summer I could go cycling. In the winter I could go swimming and shopping or simply spend some hours in the library, something which I've always enjoyed. As Vivien was under sixty-five, we had to pay a monthly fee to the Social Work department for the service, but I still thought it was well worth the money.

The years 2013 and 2014 had been very challenging for us, but in early 2015 things started to happen with the legal case.

CHAPTER 21

THE END GAME APPROACHES

Someone once wrote that war consists of 'long periods of great boredom interspersed with short periods of great excitement'. This could equally well be a description of a medical negligence action because nothing happens for months or years on end. In late 2012 our case had gone to first proof – the first stage in bringing about a civil court case for damages. The NHS had responded with what is known as a 'skeletal defence' in which they had denied there was a breach of duty of care and backed it up with a lot of legal gobbledygook. Since then we had heard nothing from the defenders (the NHS), and I was beginning to wonder whether they were taking us seriously.

But in the autumn of 2014 things started to happen. In October, Bannisters informed us that the defenders wanted to have Vivien examined by two experts who would prepare their own reports. The first of those was Susan Cairns, a care expert who worked for an organisation called the Fry Partnership. She had the same role as Liz Shaw (who had visited us in February 2013). On 26 November Susan saw us in Dunblane. The other expert was Dr Alan Henley, an NHS stroke consultant, and he examined Vivien at our home on 17 October. I saw these visits as a positive step because it indicated that the Central Legal Office was finally taking our case seriously.

Then on 5 January 2015 there was a significant development. Janet Stranks of Bannisters emailed me to inform me that the Central Legal Office had just sent them an independent medical report on Vivien's case, based on a review of the case notes. This report came with an offer of a fifty-thousand-pound out-of-court settlement. In addition to this sum, the Central Legal Office was willing to pay all our legal costs.

I was pleased that something was happening at last but was disappointed at the rather derisory offer. That amount wouldn't even cover Vivien's loss of earnings, let alone the costs that we had incurred so far as a result of the stroke. Neither would it be sufficient to provide ongoing care such as the employment of care support workers. In addition, this relatively small one-off payment wouldn't cover the cost of Vivien being admitted to a nursing home in the future, if that proved necessary. Nor would it compensate her for the devastating brain and eye injuries she had suffered. But it was still a step in the right direction and clearly better than nothing. When I had first started the legal action in 2011 I took the view that even if it took twenty years and we only got a hundred pounds' compensation, it would still have been worth it.

The independent medical report was written by Dr James Parsons, a consultant physician and rheumatologist. I already knew James because I had met him when I was a medical student although we were hardly bosom pals, as I shall explain.

Back in the autumn of 1977 I had recently taken over as editor of Surgo (the Glasgow University medical journal) and was keen to find new contributors. James attended a committee meeting in the Surgo office in the basement of George Service House in University Gardens, and the first question I asked him was 'What did you think of the latest issue?" (It happened to be my first as editor and featured a lot of material I had written.)

'Not much,' replied James. 'I thought all the articles were of a very poor standard, and I didn't like the jokes. There was only one decent joke in the whole issue.' James was particularly scathing about the motoring page, written by 'Fanny Belt' (actually my brother, Alistair, using a nom de plume). Alistair had a similar writing style and sense of humour to my own, something which seemed to irritate James. 'People think you wrote it', he said.

Despite being a non-fan of my comic writing, James eventually submitted a humorous article which was published in Surgo. It was a Bond spoof, and James couldn't think of a title, saying that he would leave that up to me. I came up with a title, and the article was illustrated with some Bond-style graphics by my friend and fellow artist David Carlile. I later heard that James didn't like my title.

I met James again a few years later when I was an ophthalmology registrar in Glasgow. At that time James was a medical registrar, and one day he asked for an ophthalmology opinion on one of his patients. I was given this task, and when I arrived in the medical ward, James greeted me with a dismayed expression. 'I was hoping for an ophthalmologist,' he muttered, 'but I suppose you will have to do.'

However, leaving our rather difficult past relationship to one side, I was aware that James was a very intelligent, highly skilled rheumatologist and physician with a lot of qualifications. He was also a superb writer and had penned many articles, papers, and short stories and some non-fiction books. He was also adept at marshalling facts in support of an argument, as evidenced by an article he had published in a Scottish newspaper in which he very ably defended the hospital he worked in against allegations of poor standards. He was clearly someone who saw himself as a defender of the NHS.

It was undoubtedly these highly developed skills which had led to the Central Legal Office asking him to be their 'independent' medical expert. There would never have been any possibility of Dr Parsons preparing a report for our side because at the start of the legal action our first solicitor, Graham McWhirter, had contacted a number of Scottish rheumatologists who did medico-legal work, and all had declined to do a report for us as they were personally acquainted with Dr Green.

I also understood that most of the doctors who do independent medical reports for the Central Legal Office never work for pursuers and only write reports for the defenders, i.e. the NHS. At the beginning of his report Dr Parsons mentioned that he was acquainted with one of the hospital practitioners mentioned in the text, though he didn't specify which one.

Dr Parsons' report was lengthy, detailed, and extremely well written. He had clearly covered every angle, as every possible complaint about the investigation and treatment of Vivien's symptoms had been carefully considered and then rebutted. Despite our tense past relationship, I found, on reading the report, that I admired and respected him in the same way that General Bernard Law Montgomery thought highly of his worthy adversary, Field Marshall Erwin Rommel.

All the same I felt that his sympathies lay with all the doctors involved in this case, as he appeared to be bending over backwards to exonerate them of any blame for what had happened. Almost every clinical decision made by various doctors seemed to be given a positive spin by Dr Parsons, even Dr Green's rather questionable prescribing of azathioprine when there was a doubt about the exact diagnosis.

He did say that he sympathized with the 'disappointment' felt by the patient (Vivien) and others at the outcome. It was kind of Dr Parsons to consider the emotional impact of this 'late diagnosis', but I think he was understating things a bit. 'Disappointment' is the emotion I feel when I order poppadoms in an Indian restaurant, and they don't come with spiced onions. Anger and anguish, completely off the Richter scale, are what I experience when my wife ends up blinded and brain-damaged due to an NHS cock-up.

Dr Parsons also said that Vivien had made a 'good but not complete' recovery. That claim again astounded me. I can only assume that he drew this conclusion from the rather odd comments made by one of the GPs in the case notes in late 2011: 'Walks with slight limp, speech almost back to normal.' A truer assessment of Vivien's severe disabilities could be found in the reports by Liz Shaw and Dr Henderson, which Dr Parsons had probably not seen.

It all made me wonder just how neutral some of these 'independent' medical reports really were. It looked to me as though a prominent member of the Scottish rheumatology establishment had been brought in to get one of his colleagues (who may even have been a friend) off the hook. I remembered George Orwell's words in Animal Farm: 'All animals are equal, but some animals are more equal than others.' Perhaps in the same way all independent medical reports are neutral, but some are more neutral than others!

The punchline of Dr Parsons' report was that he did not consider that Dr Green had been negligent. While he agreed that the stroke could have been prevented if an echocardiogram had been carried out sooner, he affirmed that this had happened purely because Dr Green had not thought of the diagnosis. Although he said it was 'disappointing' that Dr Green had not thought of the possibility of a myxoma, he did not consider him negligent for not doing so.

Dr Parsons' conclusion was based on his interpretation of the Hunter v Hanley test, which stated that for a case of negligence to be proven, it had to be shown that the doctor in question had done something that no other doctor would have done. He said that it was thus difficult to see how failing to think of a particular diagnosis could be considered negligent.

This is something that might surprise members of the general public and even some doctors. Over the previous three years I had discussed Vivien's case with a large number of acquaintances. Some of them were lay members of the public, while others were doctors in various fields, including a consultant cardiologist, a consultant haematologist, and a few GPs. All of them were of the opinion that what had happened constituted negligence. These were some of the comments I received:

'Wow! That sounds really incompetent. I hope you are putting a claim in!'

'Why on earth did that man not ask for a second opinion?'

'It's a cut and dried case. Any fool can see he should have ordered an echocardiogram!'

'If you can't get him on negligence, you should be able to get him for incompetence!'

'You will definitely win your case. I can't see you losing a case like this!'

'The investigation was very poor right from the start. You'll walk it!'

Of course it must be realized that none of these people were experts in medico-legal matters, even though some may have been highly qualified in medicine, and the responses I have shown above were really emotional reactions rather than a serious legal opinion. For example, when claiming damages, you can't 'get people for incompetence'; you have to prove negligence.

Dr Parsons also made another very interesting point about the Hunter v Hanley test. As I've mentioned previously, this states that the doctor in question must have done something that no other doctor would have done in order for negligence to be proved. However, Dr Parsons pointed out that several doctors had examined Vivien, and none of them had considered the diagnosis of atrial myxoma. According to his interpretation of the Hunter v Hanley test, this proved that Dr Green could not be negligent, as all the other doctors were in the same position and had all failed to think of the correct diagnosis.

I would argue though, that all these other doctors were not in a position to make a final diagnosis. For example, the vascular surgeon who was asked to see Vivien was given the job of determining whether her cervical ribs were causing her hand lesions. She wasn't asked to find out what was wrong with her. The GPs' role was really just to refer Vivien to a specialist for further investigation rather than being unduly concerned with what was actually causing the vasculitis. In the case of dermatologist Dr Brown, he had referred her to Dr Green for further investigation rather than doing such investigations himself. In my personal opinion (as someone who has a medical qualification but is not a legal or medico-legal expert), therefore, responsibility for investigating the lesions had been passed on to Dr Green in a medico-legal version of 'pass the parcel', and full responsibility for the non-diagnosis of the myxoma should therefore fall on his shoulders.

This is what I personally believed on a common-sense basis, and I'm sure the majority of the general public would agree with this opinion. Unfortunately, though, there are many occasions when the peculiarities of law seem to fly in the face of common sense, and this may be one of them.

Dr Parsons claimed that the main issue in this case was that Dr Green had not thought of the diagnosis of atrial myxoma and had therefore not ordered an echocardiogram. I saw things slightly differently: I believed the problem was not that he had failed to think of the possibility of a myxoma but rather that he had not ordered a sufficient number of investigations which would have revealed the presence of the myxoma, whether he had actually thought of it or not.

By this time our side had two independent reports from consultant rheumatologists, one from Dr Nick Packer dating back to 2012 and a second recent report by Dr Roy Carrington, a consultant rheumatologist in England. Both of these rheumatologists considered that an echocardiogram should have been carried out in this case and that the failure to do so constituted a possible breach of duty of care.

Dr Carrington went even further, saying that, as the vasculitis had gone on for a second year without any improvement or even a definite diagnosis, a further round of investigations, including an echocardiogram, whole-body scan, creatinine clearance test, and pulmonary function tests should have been carried out. He also suggested that a second opinion from another rheumatologist and dermatologist would have been valuable.

Dr Parsons had implied that the only reason for ordering an echocardiogram would have been to rule out a myxoma. But there are other reasons why an echocardiogram should have been ordered in this case. First of all, there are other embolic disorders which would require an echocardiogram for diagnosis. For example, endocarditis (inflammation of the inner lining of the heart) is a rare condition that also requires to be considered in the differential diagnosis of vasculitis. Like atrial myxoma, it results in the discharge of small emboli from the heart into the bloodstream. Another laboratory test that may be required to rule out some cases of endocarditis in which there is a bacterial cause is blood cultures (a blood sample taken to detect the presence of bacteria in the bloodstream), and that was another test that was not carried out in Vivien's case. An echocardiogram is also advisable in vasculitis cases because it can show how the disease is affecting the heart.

Dr Carrington's report cited the British Society for Rheumatology guidelines on the management of vasculitis, which mentioned emboli originating from an atrial myxoma as being a condition which should be considered in the differential diagnosis of this condition. The guidelines also mentioned that an echocardiogram should be carried out in cases of vasculitis. The only problem with these guidelines from our point of view was that they were written for cases of ANCA positive vasculitis, and in Vivien's case the ANCA test was negative (ANCA stands for anti-neutrophil cytoplasmic antibody, which is a marker in the blood of an underlying autoimmune process). I would suggest though that the same investigations should have been carried out regardless of whether the ANCA test was positive or negative. In addition, the guidelines were advisory, not mandatory.

Nevertheless, I personally considered that the root cause of this tragedy was a failure to carry out a sufficient number of investigations which would have revealed the presence of the myxoma whether any of the doctors had thought of it or not. After all this is how the myxoma was eventually discovered. Dr Brian Sutton had ordered an echocardiogram, not because he thought Vivien had a myxoma but because it was part of the routine investigation of a stroke in a relatively young person. He would have been looking for things like a blood clot in the left atrium (a heart chamber) or an abnormality of the heart valves and was probably quite surprised to discover an atrial myxoma. However, the outcome of our case wouldn't depend on anything I said or wrote, it would hinge on an appraisal of the expert medical evidence provided by both the defenders and the claimant.

Despite Dr Parsons' report, I still felt we had a good chance of winning our case. We had independent reports from two separate consultant rheumatologists, which suggested that there may have been a breach of duty of care. On the other hand, the defenders had produced an extremely well-written report by Dr James Parsons which clearly stated that – in his opinion – Dr Green was not negligent.

We also knew from our research that the majority of consultant rheumatologists in the UK would have carried out an echocardiogram in a case such as Vivien's. In addition, the rheumatology department at Scottish General Hospital now carried out an echocardiogram in all cases of vasculitis and suspected vasculitis as a direct result of Vivien's case.

However, our legal team was not entirely confident of success, and at a meeting in Edinburgh on 26 January 2015 with Janet Stranks, James Munro (our advocate), and our designated QC Edward Conroy, it was agreed that the best option might be to accept an out-of-court settlement. The problem was that in order to win the case, we would have to show that there was some kind of agreed national standard for the investigation of vasculitis and that Dr Green had fallen below that standard, something which could be difficult to prove. The fact that the rheumatology department at Scottish General Hospital was now carrying out an echocardiogram in every case of vasculitis and suspected vasculitis as a direct result of this case could not be used as an argument to support our case, as doctors are allowed to change their practice as a result of clinical experience without any implications for liability. Also the fact that the majority of rheumatologists would have carried out an echocardiogram in this case didn't mean that the minority who wouldn't have done so were negligent.

Obviously this meant that we wouldn't get the millions of pounds damages I had hoped for. On the other hand, we would be spared the ordeal of a three-week court case in the summer which could end with us losing the case and receiving nothing. If Vivien's case had been an episode of the BBC-TV series Judge James Deed, then I'm sure it would have gone to court and we would have won. Judge Deed, on seeing Vivien's disabilities, would have ruled in our favour and savagely criticized the NHS for their incompetence. After awarding Vivien a multimillion-pound settlement, he would have stomped off to eat an Indian takeaway and bonk one of the jurors while the NHS legal team drowned their sorrows in the nearest pub!

Unfortunately, real life isn't like TV, and the movies and legal cases don't always go the way you would expect. It all reminded me of a classic scene from the 1971 film Dirty Harry. Clint Eastwood's maverick cop, Inspector Harry Callahan, is called to the district attorney's office to discuss his recent capture of the psychotic serial killer Scorpio. The DA berates

Callahan for not following correct legal procedure and rules that the suspect's sniper rifle is inadmissible as evidence, as it was obtained during an illegal search which had not been validated with a search warrant. He then says that he couldn't convict Scorpio of spitting on the sidewalk and that he is going to walk free. Callahan is so outraged that he storms out of the office declaring, 'The law is crazy!'

George Chapman expressed the same sentiments in 1654 when he asserted that 'the law is an ass!' However, we had to face reality, which was that we would probably lose a court case and would have to accept whatever we could get from an out-of-court settlement. It was yet another blow and one we would have to come to terms with.

CHAPTER 22

A SETTLEMENT IS AGREED

In late March 2015 we decided to accept the offer of an out-of-court settlement of £50,000 plus legal expenses since I thought our chances of winning the case were poor.

The settlement was nowhere near the level we had hoped for. I had read of some cases in the USA involving people who had undergone investigation for transient ischaemic attacks (TIAs) and had subsequently suffered strokes as a result of an atrial myxoma that had not been picked up because an echocardiogram had not been carried out. The damages awarded through resulting lawsuits were about £5 million. In Britain compensation payments tended to be lower than in the USA, but a sum of between £1m and £2m would probably have been awarded to Vivien if we had gone to court and won our case. I also read of a recent case in Scotland involving a man who was struck in one eye with a golf ball, resulting in the loss of the eye. He put in a claim for £800,000 and was subsequently awarded £400,000 at the Court of Session. Vivien was completely blind in her left eye, had some visual field loss on the right side, and also had severe brain damage and yet was only getting an eighth of what had been awarded in that case.

But no amount of money could really compensate Vivien for her destroyed life. If someone were to suggest that I take part in a medical experiment in which I was surgically operated on to give me a total anterior circulation stroke and blindness in one eye in return for a large cash payment, then I would decline the offer. Even if someone offered me a hundred million, a thousand million, or even a thousand billion, I would always say no, because no amount of money can ever compensate for such disabilities.

Nevertheless, although we didn't have the satisfaction of a clear win in a court case, I thought we could claim a moral victory, as we had forced the NHS to give us some money as compensation for what happened. We never got an admission of liability. We never proved negligence in a court of law. The NHS never admitted that it had done anything wrong or made any mistakes. We never even got what I would consider to be a proper apology. But we had done the best we could and won some kind of victory.

In summary then, what had really gone wrong with Vivien's investigations? It had all started with some painful fingertips in August 2009, thought to be caused by allergy to a plant. Within a few days a rash developed in her hand which was diagnosed as 'vasculitis'. Apart from an ECG, no investigations for vasculitis (or referral to a dermatologist or rheumatologist) took place at that point. The case notes suggest this was because the GPs thought that the vasculitis was a local reaction caused by the plant allergy and that further investigation was therefore not required (This may have been a reasonable diagnosis at the time, but with the benefit of hindsight I think it is likely that the red fingertips, and the subsequent rash, were both part of the same embolic episode, probably the very first one originating from the then-undiagnosed atrial myxoma, and the idea that it was all caused by touching a plant was just a red herring.) So the GPs simply put Vivien on a short course of corticosteroids, and the lesions subsequently resolved.

In March 2010 Vivien developed another rash on her left hand. Again the GPs diagnosed vasculitis – and in doing so would of course been influenced by the previous diagnosis in August 2009. After some blood tests, Vivien was again put on high-dose oral corticosteroids. On 6 May she was seen by Consultant Dermatologist Dr Brown. Unfortunately, the rash had faded by the time he saw her, so he decided not to carry out a skin biopsy. This was unfortunate because, had he done so, it is possible that particles of myxoma would have been identified in the tissue sample, as they would likely have been present for some time after the rash had settled. It is also possible that the high-dose corticosteroids prescribed by the GPs accelerated the resolution of the rash as they would have reduced the inflammation associated with the embolic episode. Had they not been prescribed, then it is possible that the rash would still have been present when Dr Brown saw Vivien, prompting him to do a biopsy. An opportunity to correctly diagnose the problem was therefore missed.

Vivien was seen on two occasions by Dr Brown and was then referred to Dr Green, who also saw her twice. Unfortunately, neither of the consultants saw Vivien when the lesions were present, leading to difficulties in diagnosis. Had they actually seen the lesions, then they could have done a skin biopsy, which would probably have revealed the true nature of the lesions and prompted a decision to order an echocardiogram. It is indeed unfortunate that neither of them considered the possibility of asking Vivien to come back to the hospital the moment the lesions returned, enabling them to actually see these lesions for themselves and do a biopsy.

This is not some flight of fancy on my part but a serious observation. During my research for this book, I came across a case in France very similar to Vivien's.1 A thirty-five-year-old woman presented at the dermatology department of Fournier Hospital with a small erythematous macule (a red area) on the sole of one foot. A previous biopsy of the lesion had shown an intravascular thrombus (blood clot inside a blood vessel) but was otherwise inconclusive, as were her blood tests. As her lesion had faded by the time she was seen, she was asked to return immediately to the department the next time her condition flared up. Two months later she returned with some fresh skin lesions on her foot. These were immediately biopsied, myxomatous material was spotted in the lesions, an echocardiogram was carried out to confirm the diagnosis, and emergency cardiac surgery then done to remove the myxoma. The woman made a complete recovery.

This happy outcome occurred because the French doctors did all the right things, i.e. they asked the patient to come back to the hospital for another biopsy the moment the lesions returned and also withheld any treatment such as corticosteroids or azathioprine which might have masked the diagnosis.

A number of doctors who studied Vivien's case were critical of the decision to give high-dose corticosteroids every time the lesions appeared. They said there was really no clinical reason to do so since this was a non–life threatening, localized, and unexplained rash which could simply have been left untreated pending a definite diagnosis. In my personal opinion the only clinical situation in which a vasculitis should be treated urgently with high-dose steroids before a definite diagnosis is made would be suspected temporal arteritis (aka giant cell arteritis), in which failure to treat promptly can result in permanent blindness. This is a condition I have some personal experience with, as I was involved in the treatment of a number of cases when I worked in ophthalmology. Thorough investigation is very important in the management of temporal arteritis, and in cases where there is any doubt about the diagnosis, a biopsy of the temporal artery is carried out.

High-dose corticosteroid therapy would also have reduced the constitutional symptoms of the myxoma, since the corticosteroids would counteract the effect of inflammatory cytokines produced by the tumour. This contributed to a masking of the symptoms. Also, to repeat, they would possibly have accelerated the healing of the pseudovasculitic lesions, giving the false impression that the skin lesions were vanishing because of the corticosteroid 'treatment' when what was actually happening was that the lesions were resolving spontaneously. I would suggest that a far better clinical decision would have been to withhold all medication until a definite diagnosis had been established. Thus the fact that these lesions were appearing and disappearing spontaneously would have become apparent, and this might have raised suspicions that they were caused by emboli.

Giving high-dose corticosteroids to a patient with suspected vasculitis before any investigations have been carried out can sometimes be dangerous as well, as some cases are caused by infections which can be worsened by steroids. Furthermore a number of conditions which can mimic vasculitis should be ruled out at an early stage in the investigation. I fully understand that there are occasions in clinical medicine when empirical treatment with steroids is justified, but I would suggest that this is not one of them.

Even more puzzling was Dr Green's decision to change Vivien's medication from corticosteroids to azathioprine. Azathioprine is a dangerous, toxic drug which is very similar to chemotherapy agents used to treat cancer. In the treatment of vasculitis, it works as an immunosuppressive drug; i.e. it suppresses the activity of the immune system. Azathioprine should therefore be used in cases of vasculitis only when it is caused by autoimmune processes (i.e. conditions in which the body's immune system attacks its own healthy tissues).

I understand that it is recognized by the rheumatology establishment as an evidence-based treatment for certain types of vasculitis. It is often described as a steroid-sparing therapy, since it allows steroids to be prescribed at lower dosages or indeed to be stopped completely. However, I would question its use in this case since the diagnosis was unclear. It would be like putting someone on insulin if you weren't sure whether they were diabetic or giving them chemotherapy agents when they didn't actually have cancer (something that has happened in the NHS, by the way, and has led to lawsuits). The latter is a more valid analogy because azathioprine can be used as a chemotherapy drug.

The azathioprine made Vivien ill and contributed to her diminished quality of life in the months leading up to her stroke. Also, some of the symptoms of her myxoma were then attributed to the azathioprine. For example, the facial swelling and rash in March 2011 was thought to be a side effect of azathioprine but were almost certainly due to another embolic episode. Thus the azathioprine side-effects masked the symptoms of the myxoma just as the corticosteroids had. So the decision to prescribe corticosteroids and then azathioprine made diagnosis more difficult.

There was also the issue of Vivien's cervical ribs. There was never any possibility that they could have been connected with her symptoms because she had rashes in her feet as well as her hands, and cervical ribs can only cause problems in the upper limbs. Dr Green's flagging up of the cervical ribs may also have influenced the decisions of the GPs when Vivien presented with a 'funny feeling' in her right hand in early May 2011.

With the benefit of hindsight, it is likely that this was either a transient ischaemic attack (TIA) or even a small stroke which would have been caused by a small embolus originating from the atrial myxoma. By definition the symptoms of a TIA last no more than twenty-four hours, so on this basis it is likely that the correct diagnosis was a small stroke.

I can understand the GPs' predicament when Vivien presented with these symptoms in early May 2011. I myself gave her a brief clinical examination and could not find any evidence of weakness or loss of sensation in her right hand. One of her symptoms was that she complained of difficulty with handwriting. I asked her to write a short sentence on a piece of paper, and her handwriting looked much as it always did. The GPs thought her symptoms might have been caused by her cervical ribs, which can cause problems by pressing on blood vessels and nerves. They might not have come to this decision if Dr Green had not emphasized their possible role in a letter to the GP practice.

A number of doctors who have examined Vivien's case notes have commented on this episode and have suggested that, as the symptoms suggested an upper motor neuron lesion (i.e. a stroke or a TIA), then Vivien should have been referred urgently to the stroke unit or a neurology department for investigation.

This may have been the correct thing to do, but I have my doubts about whether there would have been enough time to save Vivien. Even urgent NHS appointments are sometimes not that urgent at all, and I rather doubt that the wheels of the NHS would have moved fast enough to diagnose the myxoma and then have it surgically removed before she had her stroke. Her myxoma was eventually diagnosed on 25 May, but she didn't have cardiac surgery till 13 June, eighteen days later. Bearing in mind this timescale, even if the GPs had acted promptly to have her symptoms investigated, I think it is likely that Vivien would have had her stroke before surgery could be carried out.

So I feel that by the time she presented to the GPs in early May with her hand symptoms, she had already run out of time. The window of opportunity to correctly diagnose the myxoma probably closed several months before. On the other hand, it is always possible that things could have moved very quickly and her stroke could have been prevented by an urgent referral to the appropriate experts. We will never know. It is one of the many what-ifs in this case.

On reviewing the case several years later, it is clear that not one but several opportunities to correctly diagnose the myxoma were missed. For example, with the benefit of hindsight, I believe the attack of 'viral labyrinthitis' on 30 May 2010 was almost certainly a transient ischaemic attack caused by an embolus from the myxoma. A number of factors lead me to that conclusion. First of all, Vivien's symptoms came on as quickly as turning on a light switch. I know because I was only standing a few yards from her at the time. Almost instantaneously she became very dizzy and started crying out, 'I'm dying, I'm dying.' Symptoms which come on instantaneously usually indicate a vascular origin. That is something I remember from my medical training.

As far as I can recall, she did not have a fever (which you would expect with acute viral labyrinthitis). Also her symptoms cleared up within a few hours. Viral labyrinthitis is supposed to last between one and six weeks, so suspicions should have been aroused that she had suffered a transient ischaemic attack. In addition, dizzy turns (presumably due to TIAs) are recognized in the scientific literature as occurring in atrial myxoma sufferers. The investigation of transient ischaemic attacks in the NHS does not always include an echocardiogram, but nonetheless if it had been recorded in her medical notes that she had had investigation for a possible TIA in the summer of 2010, then that might have prompted Dr Green or Dr Brown to consider that her lesions could have been embolic in origin.

There is also the question of her 'acute gout' on 4 September 2009. Vivien had presented with pain and redness affecting the M/P joint (the big joint) of her left big toe. The GP diagnosed gout purely on clinical grounds and did not order any appropriate investigations such as a blood test, which would have shown a raised uric acid level if she really did have gout. Vivien did not have a previous history of gout. There have been no attacks of 'gout' since, and all the many blood tests she has had both before and since this episode have shown a normal uric acid level. Almost certainly this was an embolus affecting the toe, and had a blood test been carried out then, the GPs might have realized that they were dealing with something other than acute gout. Another opportunity to correctly diagnose the problem was missed.

So it should be clear that the tragic outcome in Vivien's case wasn't just caused by the failure to order an echocardiogram. Multiple mistakes were made in the investigation. It was a tragedy of errors. In Appendix 2 at the end of this book, I have listed all the miscalculations that I believe led to the tragic outcome, and in Appendix 3 I have listed the lessons that I feel need to be learned from this case.

In summary then, each doctor who saw Vivien chose to go down the path of previous diagnosis and accepted a diagnosis of 'vasculitis' made by another doctor, even though there was never any real evidence (in the form of biopsy samples or conclusive blood tests) that vasculitis was her problem. As Dr James Parsons said in his report for the NHS Central Legal Office, 'If there is one lesson to be learned from this case, it is the dangers of presuming that other doctors' assumptions are correct.' Most rheumatologists would agree that a diagnosis of vasculitis should be made using a combination of clinical features and laboratory results, something that did not happen in this case, as the diagnosis was made purely on the clinical appearance of the lesions. There was far too much emphasis on hasty treatment rather than thorough investigation. In my opinion the mantra of a doctor investigating a vasculitis case should be 'Investigation, investigation, investigation', whereas the mantra of all the doctors involved in Vivien's case seems to have been 'Treatment, treatment, treatment'.

So although it was the end of the legal case, we still had to live the rest of our lives, every day of which had become a challenge. It wasn't the end of Vivien's story. As Churchill once said, it was 'not even the beginning of the end. But it [was], perhaps, the end of the beginning'.

I believe that many positive things will come out of this book and the discussion it causes. First of all, I hope that the echocardiogram becomes recognized as an investigation that must be carried out in all cases of vasculitis and suspected vasculitis. I do not believe such a policy would be that expensive to implement. If we take the Scottish General Hospital as an example, the policy since late 2011 has been to order an echocardiogram in every case of vasculitis. As the hospital has a catchment area of 600,000 people and the incidence of vasculitis is one in 50,000, then we can assume that six people will develop vasculitis every year in this part of Scotland. As the cost of an echocardiogram is £180, then the total cost to the local NHS of this new policy with be £2160 per year. Even with twice that many suspected cases whose tests are negative, the cost is only £6480, a trivial sum compared to their total budget. Most such echocardiograms will be normal, but I would argue that it is far better for a hundred people to have an echocardiogram they don't need than for just one person to have a massive stroke and a central retinal artery occlusion.

By contrast, the cost to the taxpayer of Vivien's stroke will have been colossal. She has gone from being a £32,000 a year wage earner paying tax and national insurance to becoming a highly dependent individual receiving benefits. When you add up the cost of the out-of-court settlement, legal costs, loss of tax revenue, costs of benefits, the cost of three months in hospital, and all the subsequent rehabilitation costs, then it is likely that the total cost of her stroke to the taxpayer over the rest of her life could exceed £1 million. Compared with this the £180 cost of an echocardiogram seems like small change.

(By the way, the quoted £180 average cost for an echocardiogram was given to me by a consultant radiologist friend in 2013. I have since learned that the true cost is probably much less, as that quoted figure includes capital costs. Echocardiograms may in fact cost as little as £50 per person.)

The case has also illustrated some of the problems with the current system for claiming compensation for medical accidents. These cases linger far too long, and the requirement that claimants prove negligence according to the Hunter v Hanley test (Bolam test in England and Wales) means that many people who are the victims of medical mistakes don't receive the compensation they should get. The current system – which is very adversarial – seems to reflect the need to protect the reputation of the doctors involved and hide errors rather than meet the care needs of people whose lives have been destroyed by medical accidents.

Vast amounts of taxpayers' money are used to defend these cases. If only 1 per cent of the effort that had gone into defending Vivien's case had been spent on investigating her vasculitis more thoroughly, then the tragic outcome would never have happened.

For years the Scottish government has been investigating the possibility of a no-fault compensation system for medical accidents, similar to that which operates in Scandinavian countries. I would hope the controversy stirred up by Vivien's case will lead to a rapid introduction of a similar system here in Scotland and perhaps the rest of the UK.

One feature of the current system is that doctors rarely seem to make a proper apology for their errors, and this is partly explained by a fear that such an admission could be construed as an admission of liability. But it is the lack of an apology – and the anger this causes – that drives many people to seek redress through the courts. As one victim of a medical mistake once said, 'If only the NHS would put up its hands and say, "We made a mistake and we're terribly sorry", then I wouldn't have taken legal action.' So I believe a proper apology from the doctor concerned should be a part of any new system for dealing with compensation for medical accidents.

Also the government needs to ensure that the lessons learned from a medical mistake in one area of the UK are then passed on to medical professionals in the rest of Britain. I am not convinced that this happens to any great extent at present, since health authorities are probably too embarrassed to admit that one of their doctors made a dreadful mistake. Similarly, the practice of making victims of medical accidents sign non-disclosure agreements (NDAs or gagging orders, as they are more commonly known) as part of any out-of-court settlement should be discontinued, since they prevent a free discussion of the issues involved.

The only reason for having an NDA as part of the deal, in my personal opinion, is to protect the reputation of the doctor involved. In my view though, ensuring that similar mistakes do not happen again is more important than an individual doctor's reputation. I think it is highly likely that what happened to Vivien has probably befallen others elsewhere in the UK but has never become public information because it was not reported. It is also possible that many such cases have never come to light because the relatives of the victim didn't realize a mistake had been made, lacking the necessary medical knowledge to understand that a stroke due to a myxoma is sometimes preventable if people are correctly investigated.

Finally, I hope this case leads to a review of NHS stroke rehabilitation services. I think it is fair to say that the acute treatment of strokes in the NHS is excellent, but the long-term follow-up is perhaps not as good as it could be. Politicians need to realize that people with severe strokes, such as Vivien, have long-term care needs that are not currently being met by the system and that this needs to be looked at.

Vivien's story does not have a happy ending; it only has a resolution. But I do hope that by publicizing what has happened, in the long term there will be many positive benefits. As Dr John Larkin once said in an article in The Glasgow Herald in 1998: 'Somebody somewhere has to write all this down. It might as well be me.'

CHAPTER 23

WHY DID THE MISTAKES HAPPEN?

In this book I have described the unfortunate mistakes which led to Vivien suffering a stroke and central retinal artery occlusion. But how could this disaster have happened? In the twenty-one months leading up to her stroke, Vivien was seen by about ten different doctors, including two hospital consultants. All of them were highly qualified and experienced, yet the correct diagnosis was repeatedly missed. How could this have come about?

Some medical mistakes happen because the doctors involved are lazy, tired, poorly trained, or under the influence of alcohol or drugs. Other errors occur because staff are overworked, and the service they provide is chronically underfunded, resulting in a poor standard of care. However, I don't believe any of these possible causes were a factor in Vivien's case. Instead, I feel that what transpired can be explained in terms of the failings of the human conscious mind.

To be precise I think the tragic sequence of events – which I have already explained in detail – can be explained by the inadequacies of the human conscious mind in the left brain which, under certain circumstances, can be easily fooled. Looking through Vivien's case notes – with the benefit of hindsight – it is now blindingly obvious that she was suffering from the effects of microemboli, and the likeliest source of this would be the heart. Yet none of the doctors involved realized this at the time. As far as they were concerned, Vivien was suffering from vasculitis, the treatment for which was corticosteroids or azathioprine, and if no cause for the vasculitis could be found, then so what?

I think weaknesses of the mind were to blame for this tragedy of errors. The mind can be considered to have two parts – the conscious mind, which resides in the left hemisphere of the brain, and the subconscious (or unconscious) mind, which occupies the right hemisphere. The left hemisphere is involved with mathematical and analytical functions, symbols and speech, while the right hemisphere is concerned with feelings, intuitions, creative processes, and musical ability.

Left-brain thinking is endemic in modern medicine. 150 years ago, doctors had no laboratory tests to rely on, and so they had to depend on intuition and careful observation to make a diagnosis. By comparison, modern doctors are almost exclusively left-brained thinkers who deal exclusively in facts and figures. Intuition and right-brain thinking don't have much of a role in modern medicine.

One handicap of the left brain is that it has a tendency to get 'stuck in the groove', unable to consider alternatives. This also means that people have a tendency to 'follow the herd' and not think for themselves.

A fascinating psychological experiment that was carried out many years ago illustrates this. Experimenters put six people in a room. One of them was a genuine subject who did not know full details of the experiment. The other five people were 'stooges' who had been briefed to respond in a certain way to a given question.

The experimenter asked each of these people the same question, 'What is the capital of the USA?', ensuring that the five 'stooges' were asked the question first. The first five people had been briefed to respond to the question incorrectly by saying that the answer was 'New York' (I'm sure you know that the capital of the USA is Washington). But then, when they asked the sixth person the same question what do you think he said? That's right, he also said that the capital of the USA was 'New York'. Deep down he knew that this was the wrong answer, but because everyone else had said 'New York', he felt he had to do the same.

Something similar happened several hours after the Japanese attack on Pearl Harbor on 7 December 1941. After enduring two waves of Japanese air attacks earlier in the day, US Army and Navy anti-aircraft gunners were understandably nervous and trigger-happy. Knowing this, the commanders at Pearl Harbor told all the gunners that eighteen US

Navy planes – Douglas SBD Dauntless dive bombers and Grumman F4F Wildcat fighters – from the carrier U.S.S. Enterprise were going to be landing at airfields near the harbour and that they were not to open fire on these 'friendly' aircraft. Unfortunately, a single jumpy anti-aircraft gunner on one warship panicked at the sight of planes approaching and opened fire. Almost immediately other guns started firing and soon every anti-aircraft gun in the area was blazing away at the US Navy planes. Several were shot down. At an inquiry held later, the gunners said that they started shooting because everyone else was firing, so they thought it was the right thing to do even though they had been told that the planes in question were friendly. This unfortunate 'friendly fire' incident happened because human beings have a tendency to agree with the majority view under certain circumstances and not challenge other people's decisions.

This, I think, is one of the factors that led to the tragic missed diagnosis in my wife's case. As soon as one GP diagnosed vasculitis, all further signs and symptoms were attributed to this cause, despite the absence of any real evidence. In my personal opinion, the doctors should not have allowed themselves to become fixated on one particular diagnosis (vasculitis). Instead, they should have considered all the possible causes of episodes of painful red fingertips and toes and associated rashes, and investigated Vivien accordingly. Had they done so, they would likely have considered the possibility of her lesions being caused by emboli, with the heart being the likeliest source.

Dr Green had his doubts about whether Vivien really was suffering from vasculitis but seemed unable to think of what else might be causing her symptoms. When Vivien asked him what was wrong with her (on 8 December 2010), he said, 'I don't know.'

Another failing of the human mind is that we all have a tendency, under certain conditions, to see things that are not there and not see things that are there. Almost everyone knows what the word hallucination means: it describes the phenomenon when we see something that is not there. It can happen during a hypnosis session but can also occur during everyday life.

Hallucinations are not just visual; they can be olfactory as well because it is very easy to trick the human mind into believing that a smell is present when it is not. Here is a little 'hypno-trick' I picked up some years ago which I have demonstrated at lectures. Prior to the lecture I would fill a small bottle with brightly coloured liquid, created with water and food colouring. Then, at one point in my lecture, I would produce this bottle and explain that it contained a highly concentrated form of perfume and that I was going to open it to demonstrate how keen the human sense of smell was.

I would then open the bottle, sniff it, and flinch as if I'd been confronted with a powerful odour. I would then hold the bottle in front of me with the cap removed and explain that very soon this powerful scent would start to fill the room. Then I asked members of the audience to put up their hands as soon as they started to smell the perfume. Within a couple of minutes a few hands went up, and soon a forest of hands would be held high in front of me. Then I would take the bottle of 'perfume', drink from it, and announce that there was in reality no smell.

I experienced this phenomenon myself at home recently. My home office is next to the utility room where we keep the litter tray for the cats. One day as I was working on the computer, I heard the sound of one of the cats rummaging about in the litter box, which usually indicates that they are burying their faeces in the litter. I knew I would have to clean out the litter box shortly but didn't want to do it immediately as I was so engrossed in what I was doing.

After a couple of minutes, I was aware of a smell of faeces pervading the room. I tried to ignore it, but soon the odour was so strong that I realized I would have to stop what I was doing to attend to the litter tray. When I went through to the utility room and checked the tray, I discovered that it was completely clean and there was no waste in it whatsoever. The bad smell had been created entirely by my imagination: part of my mind heard the sound of the cat rummaging about and expected this to be followed by a nasty smell. So belief and expectation created a smell in my mind that did not exist in reality.

The great American actor and director Orson Welles first came to prominence in 1938 when he produced a version of H. G. Wells's classic novel The War of the Worlds for American radio. Welles modernized the drama, setting it in contemporary times, and included fake news broadcasts describing Martian war machines landing and rampaging across the United States. Many people who heard portions of the dramatization believed that what was happening was real, and mass panic ensued. Some people even claimed to have seen the Martian war machines, even though they obviously did not exist. What was happening here was that people were experiencing hallucinations. They expected to see the Martian war machines, so their minds came up with the goods for them.

It is also possible to experience what is known as a negative hallucination, when we fail to see something that is there. This is also an everyday occurrence. I'm sure we've all had the experience of going frantic looking for our lost car keys and then, after a long search, suddenly finding them on the kitchen table. We had looked there earlier but failed to see them. What happened was that the image of the car keys clearly registered on our retinas but somehow didn't reach conscious awareness.

Some recent research has confirmed that this phenomenon may be a factor in some cases of medical mistakes. An experiment was carried out recently, published in the American Psychological Science journal,1 in which twenty-four radiologists were shown a series of MRI scans. However, these scans had been doctored, as a small image of a gorilla had been placed on them. Rather curiously, twenty of the radiologists taking part correctly identified pathological lesions in these MRI scans (as one would expect), but most of them failed to see the image of the gorilla. The experimenters concluded that this was because their brains were only trained to see certain images and simply ignored the gorilla. (Once the images of the gorilla had been pointed out to them, they were able to see them.)

This investigation followed an earlier one known as 'The Invisible Gorilla' experiment2 conducted by American psychologists Christopher Chabris and Daniel Simons, in which experimental subjects were shown a video showing six people passing a basketball from one to the other. Half of the people wore white, and half wore grey. The subjects were asked to view this video, concentrate on it, and count the number of times that a person wearing white made a pass with a basketball. As the video played, a man in a gorilla suit walked across the scene and then back again.

When the subjects were quizzed afterwards, they were able to recount exactly how many times the people in white passed a basketball, but most of them failed to see the man in the gorilla suit. As with the other experiment with MRI scans, once the subjects had been told about the presence of the man in the gorilla suit and were shown the video a second time, they could see him.

Experimenters concluded that human beings sometimes suffer from a phenomenon they called inattention deficit, which means that when they are looking for one particular thing, they fail to spot something else that should be blindingly obvious. I think this was a factor in Vivien's case. All the doctors concerned became so fixated on her 'vasculitis' and on treating this with steroids and then azathioprine that they totally failed to consider the possibility that she might be suffering from pseudovasculitis caused by emboli, even though she had many other symptoms suggesting this was the true cause.

When I was a medical student, one thing that I was taught early in my clinical years was the maxim that 'common things commonly occur'. I can remember one instance when I was being taught by a consultant during a ward round. I was shown a patient with certain symptoms and signs and was then asked what I thought the likely diagnosis was. I started off by mentioning something that wasn't very common. The consultant immediately interrupted me and reminded me that I should always begin by considering the most common diagnosis.

The only problem with this maxim – which is usually a reasonable rule to observe – is that common things do indeed commonly occur, but uncommon things also occur as well, although less commonly, and one of these uncommon things is an atrial myxoma.

Yet another factor that could explain some cases of medical mistakes is the limited storage capacity of the conscious mind. Whereas the unconscious mind in the right hemisphere of the brain has almost unlimited storage capacity, the conscious mind in the left hemisphere can only hold a maximum of nine pieces of information at the same time (to be precise, the conscious mind is considered to have a storage capacity of 'seven plus or minus two' pieces of information).

This means that when presented with a difficult case doctors may be unable to think of all the possible causes because the conscious mind simply doesn't have enough storage capacity to consider them all at one time. I am sure we have all had the experience of trying to remember someone's name or the title of a film we have seen. We simply can't remember, and the harder we try to remember, the more difficult it becomes (this in itself is a rule of psychology used in hypnosis called the 'law of reversed effort' [aka the 'law of reversed effect'], which means that the harder we try to do something the more difficult it becomes).

The remedy in such situations is simply to stop 'trying'. Relax, and do something else, and in a little while the required information will simply appear in our conscious mind. What actually happens is that when we stop 'trying' to remember and do something else, the information 'downloads' from the unconscious mind.

I can remember an experience I had which illustrates this very well. When I was a final year medical student, I sat a clinical exam in paediatrics, a subject which I found very difficult. I was presented with a young baby and told to listen to her heart with my stethoscope and then palpate the baby's abdomen. I heard a heart murmur with my stethoscope, but when I felt the baby's tummy, I couldn't find anything wrong (probably due to lack of experience). When I looked at my examiners' faces and saw their expressions of dismay, I realized that I must have missed something important, though I didn't know what it was. About a half hour later, as I was driving home, I suddenly realized what it was that I was expected to find. The baby must have been suffering from heart failure caused by congenital heart disease, which would have been the cause of the murmur, and what I was expected to find in the abdomen must have been an enlarged liver, which in young babies is a sign of heart failure as it becomes congested with blood. The information 'downloaded' from my unconscious mind while I was driving home, although sadly it hadn't happened a bit earlier when I was sitting the exam!

This problem of limited storage capacity of the left hemisphere of the brain (the conscious mind) may also have been a factor in the repeated failure of various doctors to come up with the correct diagnosis in Vivien's case, since their conscious minds could only hold a small number of possible diagnoses at one time. A doctor possessing intuition might have come up with the correct diagnosis through a flash of insight, a Eureka moment, but right-brain doctors are today in danger of becoming an extinct species as the medical selection and training process favours left-brain people.

All this has implications in the causation of medical errors. Such cases don't just involve a doctor going into the operating theatre under the influence of alcohol and cutting off the wrong leg, as most people imagine. It can involve a consultant developing a mental block about the possible causes of certain symptoms, as happened in Vivien's case.

Another weakness of the human conscious mind is something which is known as post hoc, ergo propter hoc, which means 'after this, therefore because of this'. Put simply, it means to conclude that because Event B follows Event A, therefore Event B must be caused by Event A. It is a logical fallacy but is also an everyday occurrence. For example, an old man has sore arthritic joints and takes a new supplement. Within a day or two the pain lessens, and he assumes it must be due to the supplement, when in fact it might have happened anyway, since arthritic symptoms tend to wax and wane.

Post hoc, ergo propter hoc is such a powerful 'Rule of the Mind' that it even appears in Simon Lancaster's excellent book Speech Writing – the Expert Guide as a rhetorical trick often used by politicians. For example a left-wing politician might make a statement such as this: 'In May 1979 Margaret Thatcher was elected to power. Six months later the last washing machine factory in the UK closed down.' Because the two statements are presented in sequence, the listeners assume they are connected and that the closure of the washing machine factories must be due to Tory policies, when in reality it had nothing to do with them.

Even though this logical fallacy is well known, even doctors can fall prey to it. In Vivien's case the GPs put her on corticosteroids for her 'vasculitis', and when it improved due to this 'treatment', it reinforced in their minds (plus those of the dermatologist and rheumatologist who took over the case) the idea that this was a steroid-responsive autoimmune vasculitis when in reality it was a pseudovasculitis caused by microemboli that would have resolved without any treatment.

So the human conscious mind has its weaknesses and long before Vivien fell ill I had some personal experience of these failings. Back in August 1980 I was working as a senior house officer (SHO) in an accident and emergency unit. One day an unconscious patient was wheeled into the recovery room. The sister in charge of the department told me not to do anything as the receiving physician was already on his way to see the patient and would arrive any moment. Out of interest, though, I looked at the handwritten letter which accompanied the patient. It was written by his GP and stated that he had found the man unconscious in his home and thought he had suffered a massive brain haemorrhage. Then I looked at the man's face and realized immediately what the problem was. Without further hesitation I asked the nurses to give me a large syringe full of dextrose solution (a form of sugar) and injected it into one of the man's veins. Within a minute he had regained consciousness and started moving his arms and legs.

How was I able to perform this miracle? Dead easy. You see, I recognized the man. He had been a patient in the medical wards when I was working there a few weeks before, and I remembered he was an unstable diabetic who had a tendency to have hypoglycaemic attacks (periods of unconsciousness due to low blood sugar).

When a person collapses unconscious, then a brain haemorrhage is indeed a possibility. However, if the person is a known diabetic, then is quite likely that the unconsciousness is due to a diabetic coma, either a hypoglycaemic episode (as in this case) or a hyperglycaemic episode known as diabetic ketoacidosis, caused by insufficient insulin (resulting in high blood sugar). In an emergency situation where you don't know which sort of diabetic coma you are dealing with, it is quite permissible to give some intravenous dextrose, because if the coma is hypoglycaemic, then the dextrose will immediately cure the patient, and if it is a hyperglycaemic coma, it won't help but also won't make things any worse.

What was extraordinary about this case was that the patient's own GP somehow forgot he was a diabetic, something which might have had tragic consequences if he had not been treated promptly.

I have also personally experienced a misdiagnosis which had some similarities with Vivien's case. Back in 1994 I started to get episodes of pain in my scrotum. At that time, I had private medical insurance, so I arranged to be seen by a urologist at a private hospital. The urologist took a very detailed history, carried out a very thorough examination of my testes, and did some further investigation, including blood tests and an ultrasound scan of my testes. All were normal, so he eventually concluded that no cause could be found to explain the pain which eventually vanished after a few weeks.

Fourteen years later in 2008 I suffered an episode of severe lower back pain which was thought to be due to a slipped disc. As most people know this is often accompanied by sciatica – nerve root pain which runs down the back of the leg. In my particular case the nerve root pain I experienced was felt in the scrotum. The location, character, and intensity of the pain I felt was exactly the same as that I experienced in 1994, which led me to believe that that earlier pain was due to nerve root irritation rather than any disease in the testes.

What had happened was the urologist had mentally flipped through a list of conditions in the testes which might cause pain but had not thought of the possibility of nerve root pain originating from the spine. No harm at all resulted from the urologist's mistake, but it does illustrate the kind of diagnostic mental block that led to Vivien's tragic misdiagnosis many years later.

So in summary the doctors who treated Vivien fell into a series of 'thinking traps' which prevented them from coming up with the correct diagnosis. What is the solution to these problems? Unfortunately, human minds will always suffer from these weaknesses. But one way of getting around this problem would be to ask organizations such as the British Medical Association, the Department of Health, or the medical defence unions to produce printed checklists or protocols that doctors could follow when investigating particular conditions.

We all know that when we put our car in for a service, the mechanics usually consult a printed sheet that has details of all the different checks that have to be made for that particular model of car of that age and mileage. Nothing like this happens in medicine at present, but I think if there was a set of guidelines in the form of a checklist which could be used when investigating vasculitis, then it could be drafted in such a way that it would be impossible to miss any cases of atrial myxoma, particularly as it could specify that an echocardiogram needs to be carried out in every single case or at least in cases where all the blood tests are normal and the vasculitis is 'unexplained'. I believe this will happen one day and that this will be one positive legacy of Vivien's tragic illness.

PART 2

COLIN'S STORY

'You only live twice:
Once when you're born,
And once when you look death in the face.'

—Tiger Tanaka (Ian Fleming in the James Bond novel
You Only Live Twice*)*

CHAPTER 1

THE BEGINNING OF THE END?

By the summer of 2015 I had been Vivien's carer for four years. We had had three holidays, to Crete, Cyprus, and Portugal, plus a weekend trip to London and numerous day trips. Although our quality of life was certainly less than it had been prior to 20 May 2011, we had at least adapted to our new existence and had a daily routine which made life easier. For a few weeks either side of the 2015 summer solstice I had often got up at 5 a.m. to go a ninety-minute cycle run to Causewayhead and back while Vivien was still asleep. Though 2015 was not a particularly good summer, I still had the thrill of riding my bike down empty streets and seeing the sun rise above the horizon as I rode along the cycle path next to the railway track on the way back through Bridge of Allan.

I also had a new car (or at least a newer second-hand car), which gave me great pleasure. In October 2003 (as described in the first part of this book) I had purchased an ex-demonstrator Jaguar X-Type saloon. By early 2014 it was clear that it required replacement.

I was still keen on the X-Type but felt the estate version (which wasn't available in 2003) would meet our needs better. One thing I liked about the X-Type was that it had four-wheel drive, which I considered essential, bearing in mind the amount of snow and ice we got in Dunblane. I also felt that I should go for the top-of-the-range Sovereign model with every conceivable extra and the more powerful 3.0 litre V6 engine.

Very few of these Sovereign X-Type estates had ever been manufactured (and X-Type production had ceased in 2009), but a quick search on the Internet showed that a single example was currently available at Arnold Clark, Wishaw, very close to the site of the former Law Hospital where I had worked in 1979–80. A few other examples were available in England, but they were too distant for me to consider them because of my caring responsibilities.

In mid-February 2014 I viewed the car I was interested in. It had recently been delivered to Arnold Clark and so had not yet been valeted. All four alloys were badly scuffed, there were a few small scratches, scrapes, and dents on the bodywork, and cheap Arnold Clark car mats had been fitted. The car also had three previous owners and had a towing hook fitted, a feature which I did not want. But it was relatively cheap at just £8900, and the following month I drove the car from Arnold Clark to Dunblane. My previous X-Type had a 194 bhp, 2.5 litre motor, but this model had 231 bhp under the bonnet, giving it rocket-like performance. In addition, it had a true Jaguar engine rather than the Ford power plant in my previous car.

It also had every conceivable extra – automatic transmission, satnav, electrically adjustable heated seats (with two heat settings), front electric screen, climate control, front and rear parking sensors, a single-slot CD player plus a second multidisc autochanger in the boot, and leather upholstery with contrasting piping. It was quite simply the best car I had ever owned, and over the next few months I had all the little scratches, scrapes, and dents professionally repaired. I had the alloys refurbished, got new Jaguar carpet mats from eBay, and shone the paintwork till it gleamed like glass, using an electric polisher and a bottle of carnauba wax. Though I had a tough life looking after Vivien, my car gave me a great deal of pleasure.

Over the past four years we had taken more than a few knocks – Vivien's stroke, the discovery she had an atrial myxoma and then a central retinal artery occlusion, her visual field loss in her 'good' eye, her incomplete recovery, the death of my mother from dementia, the stress caused by the huge crack in the block of flats that David lived in, the collapse of my hypnotherapy business, and the disappointing outcome of our legal case against the NHS. By July 2015 I held the view that things couldn't possibly get any worse and that the only way was up. How wrong I was, because things did get worse. I faced a health crisis which was potentially even more serious than Vivien's stroke and myxoma, as I very nearly died not once, but three times.

For years I had assumed that serious health problems were many years away. I had expected that by my sixties I would have issues like prostate enlargement and cataracts. I feared that by my mid-seventies I might develop dementia (as had happened to my father). I also worried that I might develop some form of cancer eventually since this is such a common health problem.

I never thought for a moment that at age fifty-eight I would have a heart attack, particularly as I had none of the risk factors connected with coronary artery disease. I exercised daily, ate a heathy diet, and had never smoked. I was not diabetic and did not suffer from high blood pressure (hypertension). In addition, no one on either side of my family had ever had a heart attack or angina. The only risk factors were that I was a bit overweight and was probably under stress caused by caring for my wife. However, in July 2015 – against all the odds – I suffered a coronary thrombosis.

The first inkling that something was wrong came on Wednesday, 29 July. I had picked up my friend Tom Christie from his house in Plean, and we went to the Bo'ness and Kinneil Railway and Museum, where our mutual friend Raymond MacFadyen worked. The first thing we did after arriving at the museum was to have some lunch in a nearby pub. Mine consisted of spicy noodles in barbecue sauce (which were delicious). However, a few hours after eating the noodles, I started to get stomach pains and heartburn.

By the next day (Thursday) the stomach discomfort was worse, so I bought a bottle of Gaviscon, which I thought would alleviate the pain. I did not sleep Wednesday or Thursday nights and at 3.45 a.m. on Friday, 31 July, I was awake and pacing around the living room. Suddenly I felt a sensation like a tight band around my chest which radiated down my left arm. From my medical training I knew that this was typical of the pain of a myocardial infarction (heart attack) or perhaps angina pectoris. (The difference between angina and a heart attack is that angina involves a temporary reduction in the blood supplying the heart muscle, resulting in ischaemic pain, whereas a true myocardial infarction involves the permanent cutting off of the blood supply to a section of the heart muscle, resulting in an area of necrosis, i.e. tissue death.)

The chest tightness only lasted 45 minutes and was not very severe. This suggested that I had not suffered a heart attack. In addition, the level of pain was not that usually described by heart attack patients, which usually requires the administration of opiate painkillers such as morphine or diamorphine. In addition, I had always believed I would never have a heart attack in middle age because I had none of the risk factors associated with the condition.

With the benefit of hindsight, the episode of chest tightness must have been a myocardial infarction. What was muddying the waters was that I had indigestion symptoms, which initially may have been caused by food but later may have been a result of the heart attack. Though the level of pain was not great, this is also recorded in the medical literature, as there is a so-called 'silent' myocardial infarction in which pain is slight or even absent. In any case I had no intention of leaving my disabled wife on her own in the middle of the night to seek medical attention.

The next day my indigestion symptoms were gone, but I still felt unwell and could not eat or sleep. My stepdaughter Gillian was so concerned that she made an appointment for me to see one of the GPs at 4 p.m. on Tuesday, 4 August.

On the day I was due to see my GP, I started to get breathless walking up stairs. I knew from my medical training that this was a sign of congestive cardiac failure (CCF) but still had not twigged that I had had a heart attack. Just before 4 p.m. I drove to the surgery, parked the car, and was promptly seen by my GP. She was horrified to see how ill I looked, and when she put the oxygen saturation sensor on my finger, she found it was only 45 per cent (it should be 95 per cent or more). She then listened to my heart and heard a murmur. My blood pressure was also very low.

My GP said she was certain I had suffered a heart attack, and she would call for an ambulance that would arrive within five minutes. As I was waiting for the ambulance, I rang home to tell Vivien what had happened. I also left a message on Gillian's mobile voicemail telling her to drop everything and get up to Dunblane as soon as possible to look after her mother. Five minutes later I was in an ambulance on my way to the Scottish Heart Hospital. An ECG carried out on board confirmed I had suffered a massive heart attack. I had only hours to live.

CHAPTER 2

AT DEATH'S DOOR

4 August 2015, 5.45 p.m.

The ambulance screeched to a halt outside the entrance to the Scottish Heart Hospital. The rear doors were flung open and I was taken inside the hospital on my trolley. I have only a hazy recollection of what happened in the next few hours, as I was slipping in and out of consciousness.

The next thing I remember is waking up in the high dependency unit (HDU) the following morning and discovering that I was unable to move. A type of life support machine called a balloon pump had been attached to my body to take over the pumping action of my heart. Sitting at the foot of my bed it was basically an electric pump which exerted its effects through a long thick cannula inserted into my right femoral vein (at the groin) which went all the way up my main veins until it was sitting close to my heart.

Unfortunately, this meant I could not move my right leg at all, and I also had to lie flat on my back. If I wanted a pee, I had to call the nurses and ask for a urine bottle. If I needed a shit, I had to request a bedpan. All meals were served via a tray which sat horizontally on my chest, so much of the food spilled everywhere.

It was sheer torture. How long could I stand this? I soon discovered that much worse was to follow. Eventually a cardiac surgeon visited me and explained the dilemma. An operation had to be carried out to seal the hole in my ventricular septum using a patch made from cow heart. The problem was that a procedure too soon was likely to fail as the tissue surrounding the hole was too soggy to hold stitches. On the other hand, if several weeks were allowed to elapse, then there was an ever increasing risk of death from the consequences of a large hole in the heart, such as heart failure, an embolus, or a stroke.

207

Eventually the operation was carried out on 18 August, about three weeks after my heart attack. To this day I have complete amnesia for what happened from about a week before the operation until the time I woke up in the intensive care unit in late August. What I learned some months later was that this initial operation had not been successful. It had proved impossible to seal the hole completely, partly due to the sogginess of the surrounding tissues and also because the hole went right up to the mitral heart valve.

In addition, my body developed a massive inflammatory reaction the day after the operation, and I had to be kept in a medically induced coma while I hovered between life and death. At this point my family were called in and were told that nothing more could be done for me. The operation had failed, and I was almost certain to die. But as was to happen so many times over the next few months, I proved the doctors wrong.

CHAPTER 3

TO SLEEP, PERCHANCE TO DREAM

Intensive Care Unit
Scottish Heart Hospital, late August 2015

Slowly I opened my eyes. I was alive but only just. I had a tracheotomy tube inserted into my windpipe and a collar round my neck so I couldn't speak. An intravenous infusion was in my arm. I could move my hands and arms a little but could only wiggle my toes. I did not have a true paralysis (which would have been caused by severe brain damage or spinal cord injury) but had what might be termed a pseudoparalysis caused by extreme muscle wasting. I had lain on my back for two weeks awaiting surgery and had then been in a coma for a week or two, so it was no wonder my muscles had atrophied. Muscles start to waste within eight hours of not being used.

My mouth felt dry, but I was not allowed to drink any water. Nor could I eat. I was being fed via a nasogastric tube as the doctors thought the risk of choking from normal eating and drinking was too great.

I was also doubly incontinent. If I wanted a pee, I was supposed to use the buzzer to call for a urine bottle. In practice I would flood the bed with urine almost immediately. Later I was fitted with a long-term urinary catheter to alleviate this problem, but the issue with my bowels remained. I would feel the urge to defecate, and before I even had time to buzz for the nurse, I was lying in a puddle of my own warm, stinking faeces.

I was hallucinating wildly for much of the time. At one point I thought I was in ancient Rome, then in Nazi-occupied France. My dream world and the real world dovetailed into one another, so looking back, it is hard to remember what actually happened. A common occurrence was that I would hear the exact words that were being spoken by people next to me, but my deluded brain would come up with totally different pictures. Some evenings I imagined I was attending a concert, with all the other ICU patients being audience members. On another occasion I hallucinated that the Intensive Care Unit was a gigantic model railway shop.

My raging thirst bothered me, and I would fantasize about drinking large glasses of ice-cold freshly squeezed orange juice. I imagined that in front of me was a machine that prepared fresh orange juice from real oranges. At other times I visualized myself quaffing pints of ice cold Moretti lager. One hallucination sticks in my mind. I was lying on the floor of a futuristic concrete bunker, and the senior physiotherapist was observing me through a thick window made of armour-plated glass. My packed suitcase was beside me, and Gillian was standing in front of me.

'I don't want to be here,' I screamed. 'I want home. Take me home so I can have a drink of cold lemonade. I don't care if I choke to death.'

'You are too ill to leave,' said Gillian. 'It is too dangerous for you to come home.'

I was soiling myself regularly, and every time, the nurses had to clean me up and change my incontinence pad and my bedding. I felt totally ashamed and humiliated that I was now as helpless as a baby, totally dependent on others for care.

Eventually it was agreed that I could be moved to the Intensive Care Unit at the Scottish General Hospital. There was a delay in getting the ambulance, and I hallucinated that I was back in the Second World War as part of the cast of the BBC series Secret Army. I was being hidden by the Belgian resistance while Albert and Monique stole a German ambulance to smuggle me out.

When I was finally transferred to the Scottish General Hospital, I hallucinated that I was dressed in a suit, shirt, and tie complete with highly polished lace-up shoes and lying on the floor of the ambulance. I imagined that two Italian eye surgeons were in the vehicle with me carrying all the specialist equipment required for cataract operations.

Staying in the intensive care unit of any hospital is not a pleasant experience. Often you are kept on a ventilator much of the time, which itself feels horrific and claustrophobic. Subjectively it feels as though you have an anchor chain round your neck and a metal pipe stuck in the front of your neck. Everyone who goes on a ventilator becomes very 'chesty' and has to have their bronchial secretions sucked out several times a day. This is because air enters your lungs through a hole in your neck and doesn't go through the 'filtering' system inside your nose.

You don't have a room to yourself, just a 'bay'. In theory a highly trained specialist ICU nurse is assigned especially to you, but staff shortages often mean this ideal target of a 1:1 staffing ratio is not achieved in most hospitals.

The noise level at night is horrendous, as there is the constant sound of monitors bleeping, buzzers sounding, and alarms going off. It is like trying to sleep in a bed situated in the middle of Piccadilly Circus. This is no exaggeration. An article in the Daily Mail on 30 May 2016 mentioned that the noise level in ICUs could be up to 101 decibels, louder than a revving motorbike or a heavy lorry.

Occasionally I got visitors, but in these early days I found the experience draining and exhausting. There weren't even any meals to break up the monotony of existence, as I was nil by mouth. There was no TV, and I lacked the concentration to read, so I spent most of the time staring at the ceiling, something I was to do a lot of over the next few months.

Back in the late eighties there was a bad joke which went as follows:

Q: 'What would be Terry Waite's specialist subject on Mastermind?'

A: 'Lebanese radiators, 1986–88.'

My specialist subject on Mastermind would be 'NHS hospital ceiling tiles'.

On the credit side the physiotherapists had started to work on me. Their first task was to try to get me from a horizontal to a vertical position using a device called a stand aid, a machine designed to help paralyzed patients attain a vertical position.

Initially I found it impossible to use this machine, and on one occasion the physios had to use a power-operated hoist to transfer me from one bed to another. This was very uncomfortable, and the position adopted by my body during transfer, which was similar to the well-known 'squatting' position, cause my bowels to open spontaneously. The physios had to race for cover as a brown rain descended from the ceiling. Eventually I was able to use the stand aid. The next step was to transfer from the stand aid to the Zimmer frame, though I never achieved this goal while I was in ICU. There was some good news though, as it was eventually agreed that I could eat and drink normally, though my nasogastric tube remained in place so parenteral nutrition could continue.

I could not speak in the normal way, as I had a tracheotomy tube in place, but I was eventually able to talk using a mechanical device called a speaking valve. When the valve was on, I simply had to 'mouth' the words, and a kind of mechanical voice resulted. I sounded a bit like the Mark 2 Cybermen who appeared in two 1967 Doctor Who stories, 'The Moonbase' and 'The Tomb of the Cybermen'.

This was no surprise, as the Cyberman voices in these two stories were created electromechanically (rather than electronically) using an artificial palate attached to an electric buzzer which was worn by voice artist Peter Hawkins. A similar method was used to create the voice of Robert the Robot in the 1962 Gerry Anderson series Fireball XL5. Curiously, the voice artist for Robert's voice was none other than Gerry Anderson himself, who wore a buzzer-equipped false palate which was originally created by the Department of Artificial Intelligence at Edinburgh University to help people speak after laryngectomy operations.

Up to now I had coped quite well with everything that had happened to me. This was largely because I was so ill, so pumped full of drugs, and so prone to hallucinations that I found it impossible to feel any negative emotion such as depression or anxiety.

Then in late September I had what might be termed a nervous breakdown. I was feeling mentally OK that day until about 7.15 p.m., when I imagined a large trapdoor had opened in the ceiling and a tornado of negative emotions emerged, crushing me down. Subjectively I imagined that I was buried a foot below floor level, and a vast weight of negative emotions was pressing down on my chest.

I felt crushed by a combination of depression, anger, anxiety, and trauma caused not just by my recent heart attack and current condition but by all the things that had happened to me and Vivien in the last few years. I was at the lowest point I had ever been in my entire life. I was certainly suicidal, but there was no way I could kill myself due to my severe disabilities.

After discussing this with my designated nurse, I was given some Valium which I was written up for, but it did not help at all. At 4 a.m. I saw a junior doctor, who eventually agreed that she would call out the on-call psychiatrist, whom I saw at about 5.30 a.m. Looking back, I make no apologies for asking to see a psychiatrist at this unsocial hour, and I found the support I was given by her to be a great help.

The psychiatrist felt that one reason for my sudden descent into depression was that I had not slept for two nights. In fact, I was trying to sleep without using any kind of sedative, as I didn't want to become addicted to sleeping pills. While I was in ICU at Scottish General Hospital, I was prescribed 7.5 mg of zopiclone to be taken at 10 p.m. Some months later I learned that back in August 2015 the anaesthetists at the Scottish Heart Hospital had found this caused me to have hallucinations, so it should perhaps have not been administered to me while I was in ICU at the Scottish General Hospital. I have since learned that all the Z-class hypnotic drugs (including Zimovane) are associated with an increased risk of heart attack. Eventually I got myself off sleeping tablets by simply refusing to take them. I was determined to learn to sleep without medication in a hospital ward despite the noise and the discomfort. The psychiatrist prescribed some antidepressants and arranged for me to be followed up over the next few months. Calling out the on-call psychiatrist was undoubtedly the correct decision, as it was a key factor in my psychological recovery.

A few days later, after the doctors agreed that I no longer needed to be on a ventilator, my tracheotomy tube was removed. Immediately I experienced tinnitus, which subjectively was like a jet engine roaring in each ear to the point where I could barely hear. I also felt my sinuses were full of fluid.

My cardiologist could not explain these odd symptoms, so I was referred to an ENT surgeon, who was also puzzled by them. Fortunately, my tinnitus resolved in a couple of weeks. Personally, I think the symptoms were due a hole still being present in my trachea, as the wound left after tracheotomy tube removal is not sutured but left to heal naturally. On the credit side though, the removal of the tracheotomy tube and the end of my time on the ventilator meant I could now be transferred to the cardiology ward next door to ICU.

CHAPTER 4

THE WALKING DEAD

By early October 2015 I was breathing without mechanical assistance. The main reason I had stayed a few weeks in the ICU at the Scottish General Hospital was to wean me off the ventilator. My tracheotomy tube had also been removed and the hole covered with a dressing.

The improvement in my condition meant I could now be transferred to the cardiology ward which was next door to the ICU; this was done simply by wheeling my bed (with me in it) from one ward to another. In the ICU I only had a 'bay'; now I had my own single room in the cardiology ward, complete with WC, washbasin, and shower. Although I could not use the en suite facilities for the time being, I knew it would only be a matter of time before I could do so.

Though the cardiology ward had its fair share of noise from nurse call buzzers going off and monitors bleeping, it was still a lot quieter than the ICU. There was also greater privacy for any visitors who might call, though at this early stage in my recovery I still found such visits to be an exhausting experience. Even though my tracheotomy tube had been removed, I still had difficulty speaking, and I tended to talk using phrases rather than proper sentences. I had also noticed that I could not read anything. When I tried to read a magazine, it was as though it was written in Chinese. I also could not tell the time from the analogue clock in my room. All these observations lead me to conclude that I had a degree of aphasia (inability to read and speak), probably caused by slight brain damage as a result of my heart attack or the subsequent cardiac surgery.

I was still bedridden. Although my urinary incontinence had been dealt with by means of a long-term catheter (which at times could be very uncomfortable), this was eventually removed, causing a return of my bed-wetting problems. In addition, I alternated between spells of constipation and faecal incontinence.

Soon after I had arrived in the ward, two physiotherapists thought it was time that I learned how to use a Zimmer frame. The first step was to sit on the edge of the bed, put both hands palm down on either side of my legs, push myself up to a standing position, and then grab the handles on either side of the Zimmer frame. The first time I tried this, nothing happened. My arm and leg muscles were too wasted, and I simply didn't have the strength to do it. 'If you can't get up on the Zimmer, then you will never leave this ward,' said one of the nurses. This spurred me on, and suddenly I found myself standing upright, my hands gripping the handles.

Slowly I shuffled forward as instructed. Unfortunately, my rapid horizontal-to-vertical transition caused my bowels to open spontaneously, and suddenly I was like a horse, dropping faeces all over the ward floor. The two physios and a couple of nurses who were observing were horrified at what had happened. They told me that when I felt the bowel motion coming on, I should have made for a nearby commode, sat on it, and done my business there. But I felt so tired, weak, ill, and dizzy that I didn't really understand what I had done wrong and clearly didn't have any control over my bowels back then. Looking back on this incident now, I can laugh – it was a bit like the 'Lulu the Elephant' incident on Blue Peter which can be viewed on YouTube – but it wasn't very funny at the time.

This problem of spontaneous and uncontrollable opening of the bowels was – I later learned – a common problem with bedridden patients, particularly those who had spent some weeks in ICU as I had, and the first few times I used the Zimmer frame, I had to ensure the physio or nurse had a bedpan and a pack of wet wipes to hand.

I felt like shit all the time, and this was largely because most of the muscles in my body had wasted during my weeks waiting for – and then recovering from – my operation. It was like that horrible feeling you get when you have a bad flu, only a hundred times worse. When I walked using the Zimmer, I could not even feel my own legs; it was as though someone had amputated my lower limbs and sewed on a pair from a corpse. I was like one of The Walking Dead.

I had constant nausea, which worsened every time food was put in front of me, and I hated the food at the Scottish General Hospital. Breakfast was the best meal of the day, particularly as my friends and family had brought me supplies of Crunchy Nut cornflakes and some single-use coffee filters to give me real coffee. But lunch and dinner were usually awful. As soon as the meal tray was plonked down in front of me, I felt sick. Quite often I would only have a mouthful of what was offered, feel intense nausea, and then leave the rest. I later learned that the meals at the hospital were prepared elsewhere and trucked in, which meant that everything was reheated. This especially affected dishes like pasta, which really needed to be served fresh from the pan. Anything with egg in it was also a disaster, as powdered eggs were used, something which I thought had gone out with WW2. To quote a line of dialogue from the 1990 film Memphis Belle: 'These powdered eggs would gag a buzzard.'

Normally one of my favourite foods is curry, but what was served at the Scottish General Hospital was dreadful, consisting of a large lump of cauliflower floating in a disgusting, poor quality curry sauce. These curries didn't come with rice, just a tiny nan bread wrapped in aluminium foil, which was so hard it could have been used for body armour. As someone with appetite problems, I was entitled to dishes from an additional menu, but these were just as bad. For example, a 'hot dog' was nothing more than a poor-quality sausage served with a dry, stale finger roll.1 There was no butter, margarine, mustard, or onions.

The underlying problem was that NHS Trusts throughout Scotland had slashed their budgets for patient meals, in some cases spending just 89p per person per day on them. A Daily Mail campaign had highlighted this problem of disgusting food in NHS hospitals.

I worried that I was going to starve to death in hospital, and my weight plummeted. The poor quality of the food on offer was a factor, but it was also clear that my taste buds were not working properly. This interference with taste sensation could have been due to the lingering effects of general anaesthetic or some of the drugs I was on (such as powerful antibiotics), which can impair taste sensation.

One solution might have been for my friends and family to bring in good quality sandwiches from the M&S shop on the ground floor of the hospital, but this was only rarely possible. Because Vivien had had a severe stroke and was partially sighted, she could not drive in to see me every day as would have been the case if her stroke and central retinal artery occlusion had not happened. Instead, she could only visit me on Friday nights and Saturday afternoons, when Gillian could drive her in. Gillian had a full-time job in Bonnyrigg and could not get any more time off.

This lack of visitors was one factor which made my four-month incarceration in hospital so unbearable. Some of my friends visited me whenever they could, but they often had long distances to travel and had other commitments. Tom and Julie Christie (who lived in nearby Plean) visited me as often as they could and were also very helpful in buying things I needed, such as shaving cream and Crunchy Nut cornflakes. All the same, I could sometimes go for days without a single visitor. On one occasion I went a whole week without a single person coming to see me.

The operative policy at the hospital on personal laundry was that patients' relatives were expected to pick up dirty laundry, wash and dry it, and return with it the next time they were visiting. When Vivien was in hospital for three months in 2011, I had done this for her every day. But although I had a loving wife – who I also loved dearly – she could do nothing to help me. Nor could I do anything to assist her.

Furthermore, at times I came very close to running out of clean clothes and sometimes had to wear the same ones two or three days running. On one occasion the ward sister very cleverly made me a T-shirt out of two NHS hospital gowns to keep me going.

Although I was eternally grateful to the NHS for saving my life by acting so promptly, I still felt anger at the failure of the hospital's rheumatology department to investigate my wife's vasculitis thoroughly enough in 2010.

Had the consultant rheumatologist in charge of my wife's care ordered an echocardiogram (as I believe he should have done), then her atrial myxoma would have been diagnosed and excised in late 2010 or early 2011, preventing both her stroke and her central retinal artery occlusion.

In a letter to me in early September 2011, Abigail Bamber, director of nursing at the Scottish General Hospital, confirmed that every patient with vasculitis or suspected vasculitis seen by the rheumatology department from then on would be referred for echocardiography. The consultant rheumatologist (who had failed to diagnose the myxoma or order an echocardiogram) said this was 'as a way of learning from clinical experience'. A wise decision, but as far as my wife was concerned, it was a case of bolting the stable door after the horse had fled.

Had Vivien's stroke and partial blindness been prevented (as I feel they should have been), then she would have been able to support me more effectively. She would have visited me at least once a day, every day, and provided me with the psychological support I needed, as well as dealing with my dirty laundry and bringing me good-quality food.

For the first two months I was in hospital I had received bed baths, as I was too ill to be showered. I was also wet shaved by the nurses most days using cheap Bic razors, which tended to cut my face. Eventually I tried to shave myself using better quality razors, but my face still ended up as a bloody mess because I had a tremor in my hands. The problem was solved by changing to a cordless electric razor which Tom Christie bought for me. Although it didn't give as good a shave as a wet razor, I could at least use it without assistance. Eventually as my condition improved, I was showered by the auxiliary nurses using a special shower chair. They also gave my fingernails a good scrub, as I still had dried blood under them from my time in ICU.

A couple of weeks after my transfer to the cardiology ward I received a visit from Consultant Psychiatrist Dr Graham Sheard. I really liked him and discovered that he knew my old pal from university days, Dallas Brodie, who was also a consultant psychiatrist. Dr Sheard didn't prescribe any additional medication, as I had been on antidepressants since late September. Nor did he think psychotherapy was necessary. Instead he suggested that I keep myself as busy as possible by going on the Internet, watching DVDs, and even building Airfix models in my room.

I took his suggestions to heart and soon obtained two Airfix starter sets (a Curtiss P-40B Tomahawk and a Hawker Typhoon 1B). Unfortunately, I was unable to complete these models while I was in hospital because at that time I had a tremor which made the painting of models impossible. However, from then on I made sure I had plenty of DVDs which I watched on a small portable player, and this helped pass the time.

Once my aphasia had cleared up I was also able to read my Kindle and some aviation magazines I had subscribed to. I was making progress. But in mid-October I took a big step backwards.

CHAPTER 5

RUMOURS OF DEATH

By early October 2015 I had settled into my new existence in the cardiology ward. I still couldn't walk unaided, but I was gradually learning to get up from my bed to the Zimmer frame. By the middle of the month I could even use the Zimmer to get to my own en suite WC, which made my double incontinence a thing of the past. Then in mid-October there was a major setback which was to have implications for years to come.

One of the occupational therapists had visited me in the ward to assess my ability to cope at home. One task she gave me was to try to get up from the WC using just a single handrail. As I was attempting this, I collapsed unconscious. The next thing I remember was being lifted bodily onto my bed by several people. A sphygmomanometer (blood pressure) cuff was attached to my left upper arm while various doctors checked me out. It appeared that I had suffered some kind of epileptic seizure. Over the next few hours I had many such attacks of unconsciousness which were associated with total body paralysis and aphasia: when I tried to speak, the words would come out as 'Ga ga ga'.

On other occasions I had 'absence attacks' when I would stare into space, unresponsive and unaware of my surroundings. Dr Alan Thomas, my consultant cardiologist, ensured I was investigated very thoroughly. To start off, he carried out an echocardiogram himself with the assistance of one of the specialist nurses. 'There's no sign of any obvious clot or thrombus,' he said as he looked at the colour image on the screen.

One fear was that I might have suffered a thrombus (blood clot) in the 'hole in my heart' that had then fired off an embolus, causing a transient ischaemic attack or even a stroke. However, this did not appear to be the case. Over the next twenty-four hours I had numerous investigations including an MRI scan, a CT scan, and an EEG. The only pathology that could be found was a minor area of small vessel disease next to my speech centre. I was put on a drip of intravenous diazepam (Valium) to stop my seizures and was seen by a neurologist. The thoroughness of the management of my case contrasted sharply with the paucity of investigations that had been carried out on my wife by the rheumatology department five years before.

Within a day I was started on regular anticonvulsant therapy (levetiracetam, also known as Keppra) which eventually stopped my seizures. However, I was bedridden for a few days and even required to be fed by the nurses. As well as my seizures, it was clear that the patch inside my heart was gradually peeling off. This was evidenced by a worsening of my congestive cardiac failure symptoms such as breathlessness and ankle swelling. At times my legs and my hands swelled up as my damaged heart couldn't pump the blood around my body properly.

The doctors were worried that I was going to die, and for the second time my family was called in. They were told quite bluntly that the hole in my heart was increasing in size as the patch was coming adrift. As a result, I had severe congestive cardiac failure which was not responding to treatment. Around this time one of the ICU consultants had also told me that he had been in touch with the cardiac surgeons at the Scottish Heart Hospital, who had told him that there were no further surgical options in my case.

One evening as I was lying semiconscious in my bed, I heard some doctors discussing my case. 'Don't bother resuscitating this one,' said one of them. 'He's got a damaged left ventricle.' It reminded me of the scene in the film Reach for the Sky where a semiconscious Douglas Bader overhears a nurse telling a visitor to be quiet because 'There's a boy dying in there'.

I knew I was likely to die fairly soon, so I started to make tentative arrangements for my own funeral. I didn't want a religious funeral, so I asked my good friend Tom Christie (who is a brilliant writer and public speaker) to conduct the service and give the eulogy. I also chose the music to be played at the ceremony, which I recall was The Dambusters, 633

Squadron, the James Bond theme, and the Doctor Who theme. I had also planned for a number of my larger aircraft models to be placed round my coffin.

However, within a week my condition improved. My enormously swollen ankles gradually returned to normal, thanks to large doses of diuretics, and I was able to start getting out of bed again using my Zimmer. By late October I could manage to the WC without assistance, and by early November I could shower myself using the special shower chair. I could also shave myself again using my electric razor.

On 22 October I celebrated my fifty-ninth birthday in my room in the cardiology ward. Gillian brought in a coffee cake and some single-use coffee filters so I could have real coffee. We had our coffee and cake at about 3 p.m. Then at 4.30 Gillian went to the local Indian restaurant to collect a takeaway that I had ordered. It consisted of my favourite ethnic dishes: vegetable pakora, poppadoms, lamb Rogan Josh, and pilau rice. Unfortunately, I didn't have much of an appetite and only ate about three mouthfuls. The rest went in the bin.

Soon after my birthday I developed a new symptom though, which was extreme breathlessness. Although my ankle swelling had responded to large doses of diuretics, my breathlessness increased to the point where I could only sleep with the backrest of my bed raised bolt upright so that my chest was at ninety degrees to my legs. In addition to changing the angle of my bed, I was given a nebulizer mask to use as required, and this gave me a little symptomatic relief.

This dramatic development indicated that my congestive cardiac failure was worsening and that the drug treatment I was receiving was proving ineffective. However, in early November I received some news which was to give me a whole new future.

CHAPTER 6

A SECOND OPERATION?

In early November 2015 I received some dramatic news. Dr Thomas had been in touch with the cardiology and cardiac surgery departments at the Scottish Heart Hospital to see if anything more could be done for me. Their response was that I should be transferred to their hospital for a few days so that I could be properly assessed and investigated.

I was nervous at the prospect of a second cardiac operation since my perception was that the first one had nearly killed me. But Dr Thomas said that another option might be to do a procedure via an intravenous cannula in which a 'parachute' was opened inside my heart, partially sealing the hole between the ventricles.

As I had nothing to lose and everything to gain, I agreed to this proposal and in early November I was transferred by ambulance to the Scottish Heart Hospital. For the next three days I had a bed in the high dependency unit (HDU) while I underwent numerous investigations including a chest X-ray, MRI scans, and echocardiograms. The HDU was similar to the cardiology ward at the Scottish General Hospital. I had my own single room with an en suite shower and WC, although I was connected to a cardiac monitor during my entire stay, which meant I had to use urine bottles and commodes and could not have a shower.

One thing I did like about the Scottish Heart Hospital was that they supplied patients with large bottom wipes (called BedBath wipes) which were warmed using a special machine. During the entire three days I was at the Scottish Heart Hospital, absolutely no one managed to take a blood sample from me as I have very small veins, and my forearm and hands were much bruised from the hundred or so venepunctures I had had since I was first admitted to hospital at the beginning of August.

During the last day of my brief stay at the Scottish Heart Hospital, I was visited by Dr Petra Houghton (consultant cardiologist) and Mr Jack Vaughan (consultant cardiac surgeon). They had concluded that the parachute treatment by cannula would not be helpful in my case. However, I was told that a second attempt to patch the hole in my interventricular septum by cardiac surgery was likely to be successful. The problem with the original operation was that the tissues surrounding the hole were still soggy following the myocardial infarction, meaning there was really nothing to stitch onto. 'It would have been like suturing onto mushy peas,' as Dr Houghton put it. By this time, more than three months following my heart attack, the surrounding tissues would have scarred up, leaving firm tissue to suture onto.

As one of the cardiac surgery registrars put it very succinctly, 'You've gone from being a patient most cardiac surgeons wouldn't touch to one that most cardiac surgeons would be quite happy to have as a patient.'

One concern I had was that my body might react with a massive inflammatory response, as had happened the first time. But Mr Vaughan said this problem was not likely to happen this time round, as many months had elapsed since my myocardial infarction.

Mr Vaughan exuded great confidence that the operation would be a success, so I agreed that this was the way forward, and a provisional date of Wednesday, 18 November, was set for the operation. Soon after this I was transferred back to the Scottish General Hospital by ambulance.

A few days later I received further good news: the operation had been brought forward by two days to Monday, 16 November, and I was to be transferred back to the Scottish Heart Hospital on Friday, 13 November, so that I could be put on a balloon pump for at least forty-eight hours prior to surgery, to rest my heart. Going on a balloon pump wasn't a pleasant experience, as I already knew, but it was a necessary evil.

Mr Vaughan had requested that another CT scan of my chest be carried out prior to transfer back to the Scottish Heart Hospital, and on this occasion an intravenous cannula had to be inserted into one of my veins to enable a contrast medium to be injected. Unfortunately, this proved to be a difficult task. By then I must have had at least a hundred venepunctures since 4 August, so both arms and hands were a mass of bruises, and all the superficial veins had been damaged to the point where they could no longer be used. The cardiology registrar and one of the house officers spent a full fifty minutes making multiple attempts to put a cannula into one of my veins, without success.

Eventually, with only minutes left before I was due at the CT scanning room, I make the bold suggestion that perhaps they should try inserting a cannula into one of the superficial veins in my feet. The registrar warned me that this would be much more painful than a cannula into my arm and that I would have to prepare myself for great pain. He was right. As the needle went in I cried out in agony, and apparently my screams could be heard at the other end of the ward. However, after the cannula was in place and the needle pulled out I felt quite comfortable. Five minutes later I was in the scanning room and everything went to plan.

The following day I was transferred by ambulance to the Scottish Heart Hospital, arriving at the HDU unit about 6.30 p.m. Almost immediately I was taken to a small operating theatre where a consultant cardiologist, Dr Linstead, assisted by some specialist nurses, was preparing to attach me to a balloon pump. As had been the case on 4 August, this required the insertion of a large bore cannula into my right femoral vein, and exactly the same spot was chosen to push the sharp end in. Dr Linstead injected a little local anaesthetic into the surrounding area to numb it, but despite this, the pain when the cannula was inserted was the worst I had experienced in my entire life. For a full two minutes I was in agony, screaming, 'No, no, no!' Eventually the pain stopped and was replaced by the odd (though not painful) sensation of a cannula passing up my main veins until it was lying close to my heart. Exactly why this experience was so painful remains a mystery. Perhaps it was because the sharp end of the cannula was passing through scar tissue, or maybe it was because a nerve had been stimulated.

To my great relief the balloon pump had been attached to my body. Although there was a little bit of discomfort where the cannula was inserted into my groin, this diminished within a few hours. At least this time I would only have to put up with it until a few days after the operation.

Then it was back to the HDU and the familiar routine of lying motionless on my back, peeing into papier-mâché urine bottles and using a bedpan for bowel movements. I have always found using bedpans to be very difficult. They are extremely uncomfortable, and even the act of shoving a bedpan under my arse seemed to turn 'off' the act of defecation. In addition, it is very hard to shit in the horizontal position.

I didn't move my bowels on the Saturday and started to feel very uncomfortable. On the Sunday afternoon I did manage a bowel movement and felt much better. Despite being bedridden, I received numerous visits from the physiotherapists, who gave me several leg exercises to do in bed frequently to prevent my muscles from wasting. I took their suggestions very seriously. Before I was transferred to the Scottish Heart Hospital, I had learned to walk without a Zimmer or a stick, and I didn't want my recovery to go into reverse.

Then on the Sunday evening something happened that devastated me emotionally. Up to that point I had been fairly confident that the operation was going to be a success, and there would be no problems. However, at about 6 p.m. one of the cardiothoracic surgery registrars came to get my consent form signed. He didn't exactly exude optimism as he pointed out that a second operation was actually riskier than the first. There was a risk of a minor or major stroke, kidney damage, brain damage, other organ damage, and haemorrhage. I might not recover consciousness. I might get a wound infection. I might go blind. In fact, the consent form (which I did sign) listed about twenty different complications from the operation.

Five minutes later my anaesthetist visited me and gave me a similar gloomy prognosis. He had attended to me during my first operation and was well aware of what had happened. He pointed out that there was a risk that I might not wake up from the anaesthetic and need to be put on a ventilator. I might require to have my endotracheal tube kept in for weeks, which was apparently even more uncomfortable than a tracheotomy tube. He continued to reel out a list of possible complications from the operation.

When he left, I was devastated. Instead of being quietly confident about my forthcoming operation I was absolutely terrified. I started to cry. I was bubbling like a baby for about twenty minutes. As far as I was concerned, I was fucked. All the negative prognostications I had just been told had punched through my emotional armour plate like a hot knife through butter. Almost certainly they had gone straight into my unconscious mind, affecting my mood instantly.

I wasn't afraid to die. I had already accepted the possibility of death. But I was terrified at the prospect of becoming a vegetable, kept alive by machines, against my will, in a state of constant misery. This now seemed a likely possibility.

Eventually two of the nurses heard me crying and came in to see what was wrong. They reassured me that everything would be all right. Then one of them said some words which were to transform the situation. Just as things seemed hopeless, when there was no way forward, when I was at my lowest ebb, I suddenly realized what I had to do to change my fortunes.

CHAPTER 7

MY FATHER'S GHOST

I was a broken man. Then a staff nurse said a few words to me that completely changed my perception of what was going to happen:

'Why don't you use hypnosis on yourself? You teach this stuff. For goodness' sake, why don't you help yourself with your skills?'

After the nurses had left and I had calmed down, I thought over what she had said. I had been in hospital for three and a half months. Yet during this time I had never used my hypnosis skills on myself, largely because for much of the time I was unconscious, semiconscious, ill, dizzy, or fatigued.

The nurse was right. What did I have to lose by doing what I could with the skills I possessed? Quickly I put myself into a deep hypnotic trance. The first thing I did was delete all the negative suggestions that had just (inadvertently) been given to me by the two doctors. Then I used a technique called 'future pacing': I imagined the operation going really well. The hole in my ventricular septum was sealed completely. Mr Vaughan smiled with satisfaction as he sewed up my chest at the end of the operation. Then I imagined myself waking up after the procedure and my endotracheal tube being taken out after exactly one hour.

I saw myself recovering from the operation in record time. I visualized myself getting out of hospital in time for Christmas. Within a few weeks I was walking around Dunblane. By the summer I was cycling. Then I saw myself driving my car and going on a foreign holiday with Vivien.

Finally I talked to my unconscious and told it that it was to pretend that the operation was as routine as an appendectomy and that there was no need for the immune system to react in the way it had the first time.

Soon after this, the nurses gave me 20 mg of Temazepam (as instructed by the anaesthetist), and I fell into a deep sleep. At 6 a.m. I woke up and was given another 20 mg of Temazepam (as my pre-med). An hour later I was wheeled into the operating theatre area and felt the slight discomfort of a butterfly cannula being inserted into the back of my left hand. Some anaesthetic agent was injected into the cannula, and within seconds I was asleep.

The next thing I remember was waking up in the intensive care unit (ICU). It was 3 p.m. Right away I had the feeling that the operation had been a great success. The first thing I asked the nurses to do was to remove my endotracheal tube. They said it was too soon to take it out. An hour later I asked a second time for the tube to be removed and this time they were able to comply with my request. By that evening I was able to have a little water by mouth. The next morning, I ate a full breakfast.

The swiftness of my recovery amazed both the nursing staff and the doctors. Every tube and cannula was removed in record time, every milestone achieved with lightning speed. The only problem was my bowels. They hadn't moved on the day of the operation, for obvious reasons. Nor did they move for four days afterwards. I think the main problem was that I was compelled to lie flat on my back because of the balloon pump, and I already knew that my bowels rarely opened when I lay horizontal.

A few days after the operation the balloon pump was disconnected, and I was allowed to sit up. Even before I attempted this, I asked for a commode to be brought to my bedside. Within a minute I was sitting on it, and within thirty seconds my bowels opened, to my great relief.

Soon after this I was transferred to the HDU, as my condition had improved, and within a day I was in a post–cardiac surgery recovery ward. Unlike my first cardiac operation, everything had gone extremely well. The hole had been sealed completely, and the patch was holding. I had no chest or urinary infections (as I had the first time), and the wound was healing beautifully.

The only problem was pain from my broken breastbone and ribs. This had not been an issue after the first operation in August, but with my breastbone being cracked open for the second time in just three months, the tissue damage was greater, resulting in severe pain. For the first four days after the operation I was allowed to have an opiate analgesic called oxycodone (famous as Oxycontin). A small orange capsule, it had the most marvellous effect. Within minutes of taking it, all pain was gone, and I would fall asleep for about ninety minutes and then wake up with a feeling of euphoria. Even after waking, I found that when I closed my eyes I had pleasant dreams instantly, and this effect lasted for hours.

Unfortunately, I was only allowed to take this drug for four days because of the risk of addiction, and after this I was restricted to codeine-based drugs such as Co-codamol, which gave me constipation and nausea.

After a few days in the ICU, my condition had improved to the point where I could be transferred to the high dependency unit. I only spent a few hours there before being moved to an ordinary ward to continue my recovery. As I was lying in my bed, an apparition of my late father came into the room. He appeared as a translucent being, sepia in colour and only visible from the waist up. He didn't say a word but just looked at me with a benevolent smile. I felt his presence and the intense love he had for me. After thirty seconds he disappeared, but from that moment on I knew I was going to be all right, as if some kind of telepathic message had been transmitted to me. Did this event really happen, or was it some kind of hallucination? I don't know, but it certainly had a positive effect on me.

A week after the operation (Monday, 23 November) I had improved so much that a request was made for me to be transferred back to the Scottish General Hospital to complete my recovery there. Unfortunately, a day later I was still in the Scottish Heart Hospital, as there were problems getting an ambulance to take me to the Scottish General Hospital. This is a common issue in the Scottish Ambulance Service, as ambulances allocated to inter-hospital transfers are also on call for emergencies, which obviously must take priority.

The consultant who looked after the patients in the ward visited me that afternoon and suggested that I could be discharged home direct from the Scottish Heart Hospital, as I had already passed all the recovery milestones. I readily agreed to this, although I guessed that Dr Thomas would probably want me to stay in the Scottish General Hospital for a few days to allow another round of investigations to be carried out before I was allowed home.

A few hours later an ambulance crew arrived to take me back to the Scottish General Hospital. Soon after arriving back in the cardiology ward, I spoke to Gillian on the phone. She told me that there was some bad news, as one of our two beloved pet cats (Oscar) had died just before my second heart operation. She had decided to hold the news back until I was well on the way to recovery. This was undoubtedly the right decision. Gillian had put our two cats, Kiki and Oscar, into the local cattery for a few weeks and had then found a 'foster mummy' in Killin to look after them until I returned home.

Initially I took the news without any kind of emotional reaction, but then I found I could not sleep that night. The next morning, I was very upset, and I asked one of the junior doctors to prescribe me Temazepam 20 mg for the next two or three nights to help me sleep. For more than thirteen years Oscar had been my constant companion. Loving and loyal, he liked nothing more than lying on my lap or between my legs. When I was rushed to hospital on 4 August, I had no idea I would never see him again, and the heart attack had robbed me of three and a half months of his company and had meant that I never got the chance to say goodbye to him and thank him for all the love and companionship he had given me.

The next morning, Wednesday, 25 November, Dr Thomas visited me during his ward round and was delighted to see how much I had improved. For the first time in several weeks I could lie flat without getting breathless. I still felt winded when walking, but I knew this was largely because my leg muscles had wasted while in hospital; with enough time (and regular exercise) they would recover.

I suggested that Dr Thomas set a provisional date of Saturday, 28 November, for my discharge, as this would allow three days for further investigations and fine-tuning of my drug regime. The following day I had the most important investigation, a repeat echocardiogram, and to my great relief this showed that the patch was holding and my heart was working fine. However, that same afternoon something happened which was to delay my return home and have implications for the rest of my life.

At about 4 p.m. one of the occupational therapists visited me in the ward. I showed off how well I was walking and then stood next to the nurses' station as we discussed the possibility of my visiting their department the following day to see how well I would cope in the kitchen. He asked me whether I could walk there or would need a porter's chair. As I attempted to answer his question, I found that I had lost the power of speech. Everything started to go grey, and I felt dizzy. I walked the few yards to my room and collapsed on the bed. Within a couple of minutes I was unconscious and paralyzed from the neck down. Was I going to die?

CHAPTER 8

THE UNDISCOVERED COUNTRY

I was dead. As my spiritual body floated just below the ceiling, I looked to one side and saw a brilliant white light. Images of my mother and father appeared, beckoning me towards the light. 'Move towards the light,' they said. 'We want to see you again. Oscar and Jasper are here as well.'

I chose instead to look down. The lifeless husk of my body lay on the bed. The nurses were crying, and the doctors looked anxious. 'No pulse, no blood pressure, no heartbeat, fixed dilated pupils,' said one. 'He's dead. We'll have to call Gillian and tell her. Where's her phone number?'

'I am dead,' I said. Suddenly I opened my eyes and found I was really lying on the bed. Some nurses and doctors were in the room.

'No, you're not dead,' said one of the nurses. 'You have just had a funny turn.' Instantly I realized I had not had a genuine out-of-body experience, just a bad dream during a seizure.

This episode was witnessed by three junior doctors who happened to be in the ward at the time. Over the next few hours I had several further attacks, each following the same pattern: I felt dizzy and light-headed, and everything went grey. Then I would lapse into unconsciousness and have a terrifying nightmare in which I died. Then I would awaken to find myself aphasic (i.e. unable to speak) and paralyzed. Over the next few minutes my speech would gradually return to normal, and power would return to my limbs.

Several junior doctors who saw these attacks first-hand wrote in the case notes that I did not appear to have had classical epileptic fits. One of them must have used the term pseudoseizures to describe these episodes, since this eventually appeared in the immediate discharge letter. But this was not correct. Pseudoseizures is a condition in which people fake convulsions for psychological gain. However, it is not characterized by aphasia and paralysis and does not respond to anticonvulsant medication.

Some of the nurses thought I had suffered nothing more than a panic attack. As one said to me, 'You've been in hospital so long that you've got used to it, and you feel anxious at the thought of going home.' Nothing could be further from the truth, as I was desperate to get back to Dunblane to see Vivien.

That evening I had a few more of these attacks but had none overnight which I would attribute to the 20 mg of Temazepam (taken at 10 p.m.) which had been prescribed for three nights to help me sleep after the trauma of Oscar's death. Being a benzodiazepine drug similar to Valium, it tended to suppress fits, lending credence to the idea that these were genuine seizures and not psychological in origin. Much later I learned that what I was suffering from was what are known as non-convulsive seizures, i.e. fits which are not associated with a shaking of the body, and it was probably this which confused the junior doctors and led them to misdiagnose my problem as pseudoseizures.

Dr Thomas saw me at 9 the next morning. He asked me to describe what I experienced during one of these episodes, in exact chronological order. After hearing my report, he was in no doubt that I had had a return of the seizures I had first experienced in October and that the remedy would probably be an increase in the dose of my anticonvulsant. He said he would arrange for a consultant neurologist to see me, and just four hours later I received a visit from Professor Robert McKellar, one of the UK's leading neurologists. Professor McKellar only took minutes to realize that the fits had returned because I was on a relatively low dose of Keppra. 'I am not surprised that you are getting breakthrough fits on that dosage of Keppra,' he said. Then he confirmed that he would increase the dosage.

'When can I go home?' I asked.

'Immediately,' he answered.

'Do I need another brain scan?'

'No.'

Eventually I suggested that I should stay in hospital for another forty-eight hours to make sure the fits were being controlled by the higher dose of Keppra, and Professor McKellar readily agreed. That evening, after the higher dose of Keppra had started to work, the fits stopped. The next day I felt drowsy and nauseated, as my body had not yet adapted to the higher dose of anticonvulsant, but by Sunday I felt more like my former self.

The only problem was that, with the return of my fits, my discharge date had to be put back two days to Monday, 30 November. Gillian wouldn't be able to collect me on this date, as she was working, but Tom and Julie Christie said they could help. As it turned out, I had to change the time of my discharge to 2 p.m. on Monday, 30 November, as it would take a few hours for my bag of drugs to be made up by the pharmacy department.

On the Monday morning of 30 November 2015, I felt fine and was eagerly anticipating getting home. At 9.30 a.m. Dr Thomas saw me and agreed I could now be discharged from hospital. At about noon my lunch arrived – soup and sandwich – but I couldn't eat any of it, as I was so excited at the prospect of getting home, plus it seemed tasteless and nauseating.

At 12.15 p.m. I was taken in a porter's chair to the discharge lounge on the ground floor by the entrance. As my discharge had been put back to the afternoon, Tom wasn't able to meet me as he had to stay at home to let in a Sky engineer. I wasn't even sure if Julie could help either, as she had to go to a meeting. I was all set to order a taxi, but then about 1.20 p.m. I spoke on the phone to Tom, who told me that Julie had finished her meeting and was on her way to pick me up. At 1.40 p.m. she arrived, and within a few minutes I was on my way home. The day I had been l looking forward to for four months had finally arrived.

It was a cold, crisp, sunny winter's day, and I was glad to get inside the house as quickly as possible. The first thing I did after entering the house was kiss Vivien. Then I tried the main staircase. As expected, this was tough, as I felt I was walking upstairs while wearing lead diving boots. I was so breathless after doing this that I had to lie down on the bed for twenty minutes to let my pulse and respiration return to normal.

However, it was bloody marvellous to be home. I could go to bed when I wanted, sleep in a comfortable bed, and then arise at whatever time I chose. I could watch DVDs or satellite TV and surf the Internet. I could have bacon and eggs, fresh orange juice, and real coffee for breakfast. I also had a craving for a number of foods I couldn't get in hospital like hummus, taramasalata, oatcakes, and Greek salad.

For the first week after I came home I was aware that my taste buds were still not functioning correctly, but then on Tuesday, 8 December, I awoke to find that I was tasting everything normally again. This led me to believe that the impairment of my taste sensation was due to the lingering effects of the general anaesthetic, which had finally worn off.

I couldn't believe how tasty real coffee was or what a powerful caffeine kick it gave you. I had been used to poor quality instant coffee most of the time for the previous four months, as I only had a small supply of 'one shot' real coffee filters. I also tried a bottle of Cobra beer and was amazed at the strength of the taste and the soporific effect of the alcohol.

A couple of weeks after coming home I went for a meal at the Café Continental in Dunblane along with Vivien, Gillian, her boyfriend, Richard, and her brother, David. I had a pint of draught Moretti lager with my meal, and when I got home, I lay on the bed and slept for two hours, as I had lost my tolerance for alcohol while I was in hospital.

I voluntarily surrendered my driving licence to the DVLA in early December because of my fits. I couldn't drive my Jaguar, which in any case now had four flat tyres and a dead battery. I expected that I would get my licence back once I had gone a whole year without any further fits, which meant I would probably start driving again at the end of November 2016.

In the meantime I was heavily dependent on taxis to get anywhere, but I knew I had to organize my life in such a way that I rarely had to leave the house. I got a newspaper delivered every day. I used on-line grocery shopping from Tesco, Sainsbury's and Waitrose. All the Christmas presents I bought were gift vouchers from Amazon.

During my four-month stay in hospital Gillian had arranged for carers from Stirling Council to visit Vivien four times a day – at breakfast time, lunchtime, teatime, and last thing at night to tuck her into bed (which in practice was between 7 and 7.30 p.m.). She had also arranged for our Crossroads carer, Caroline, to call twice a week and take Vivien food shopping in the Dunblane M&S. We also now had a cleaner, Gail, who did all the domestic tasks such as laundry and ironing.

We decided to keep everything in place as I was unable to do any housework, partly due to my breathlessness and also because my ribs and breastbone had not yet healed. Even pushing a vacuum cleaner around or attempting to hang up washing caused me agonizing chest pain, so I was quite glad that someone else could do it for me.

I had not experienced much discomfort in my chest after my first cardiac operation in August, but it was a different story the second time round. I can only assume that cracking open my sternum a second time had caused greater tissue damage, resulting in more pain and a longer healing time. The pain was there twenty-four hours a day and was worse at night. I also developed secondary muscle spasms in my back, particularly in bed at night, which also made sleep difficult.

It had been suggested that I take Co-codamol (paracetamol and codeine) to ease the pain, but I had to stop taking this because of the side effects. I had always found that codeine-containing drugs were a problem for me. They always made me feel nauseated and ill and gave me horrendous constipation.

In addition, I soon found that codeine could be a problem if you suffered from epilepsy. One evening I accidentally took two doses of Co-codamol just three hours apart (the minimum suggested interval between doses should be four hours). Soon after this I had a strange feeling in my head similar to what I had experienced prior to one of my fits. I then fell asleep and dreamed I had a fit. I woke with a feeling of anxiety which lasted for some time.

Although clearly I had not actually had a fit, it was almost as though my brain was trying to give me one but wasn't quite managing it because of the Keppra. Out of curiosity I checked out 'codeine and fits' on the Internet and found to my horror that codeine could cause fits even in healthy people, as it lowered the convulsive threshold. Furthermore, it appeared that there was a well-documented drug interaction between codeine and Keppra. To be precise, codeine ingestion caused lower blood levels of Keppra, making fits more likely.

From that point on I avoided taking any drugs containing codeine, as I felt I would rather have a sore chest than a fit. Unfortunately, that left paracetamol as the only drug I could take; non-steroidal anti-inflammatory drugs (such as ibuprofen) were ruled out, as they were contraindicated in heart disease cases. The paracetamol had only a slight effect on the pain, so I got used to disturbed sleep every might.

Before leaving the Scottish Heart Hospital, I had attended a brief lecture on all the dos and don'ts following cardiac surgery. One tip was on how to reduce rib and breastbone pain during coughing: the suggested remedy was to hold a pillow or a rolled-up towel to your chest as tightly as possible to reduce the movement of the bones and hence the pain.

Despite the problems caused by my constant pain, I still enjoyed being home. Besides, I had Christmas to look forward to.

CHAPTER 9

HOME, SWEET HOME

It was wonderful to be home. But I was not the same person who had been rushed to hospital four months earlier. I had lost more than three stone during my stay in hospital, largely because I had little appetite for the poor quality food on offer. My muscles were badly wasted, and I was so thin, I looked like one of the POWs who worked on the Burma railway in WW2.

Prior to my heart attack I had thigh muscles like tree trunks as a result of decades of cycling. Now my legs were like saplings, with weak, flabby muscles. I had a tiny bum like Kylie Minogue, and my arms were like matchsticks. This upper body weakness was a particular problem, as even hanging a coat on a peg was beyond my capabilities. I could just about put a load into the washing machine but had difficulty getting it out and couldn't hang it up to dry.

I couldn't make my bed, as the duvet felt as heavy as a sack of potatoes. Nor could I put on my socks or tie lace-up shoes, as this put too much strain on my tender and weakened breastbone. I could shower myself after fitting an extra grab handle (stuck on with suction cups) and a non-slip mat to the shower cabinet but could not yet use the bath, as I had great difficulty getting in and out.

I still had a great deal of pain in my ribs and breastbone, and my back muscles were in spasm so I had a few sessions with private physiotherapist, Louise Fairlie, whom I had known for more than twenty years. Louise's treatments focused on relieving the painful muscle spasms and improving my flexibility.

I had originally planned to take a short walk every day to build up my muscles, but this proved impossible as the winter of 2015–2016 was especially harsh. Torrential rain, high winds, snow, ice, and sleet seemed to be the norm, and on the few days when the sun did shine, it was bitterly cold, so there were only a handful of days between the start of December and the end of February when I could go for a walk. The single staircase in our house proved a blessing, as going up and down this twenty or thirty times a day strengthened my legs and improved my cardiac function.

It was difficult for me to go shopping, as I couldn't drive, but Caroline (our Crossroads carer) took Vivien to M&S twice a week for a shop, and I backed this up with an online shop at Tesco, Waitrose, or Sainsbury's every week or two.

Now I had to think about what to do about Christmas. Ever since Vivien's stroke we had travelled to Bearsden every 25 December to spend the day with Vivien's mother, May, her sister, Margaret, and her friend, Alice, her daughter Gillian (and boyfriend Richard), and Vivien's son, David. This was now impossible, as I couldn't drive.

A taxi from Dunblane to Glasgow and back on Christmas Day would have been horrendously expensive, and there was also the problem of my frequent need for a pee as a result of taking diuretic tablets. After taking my frusemide, I needed to urinate every fifteen minutes, meaning a one-hour car journey would be impossible. Even if I had got to May's house without incident, I would be sharing her one WC with seven other people. As a result of these problems, Gillian suggested that she would come to us on Christmas day, bringing Richard and David with her, and help me to prepare a Christmas lunch.

I can remember my mother (back in the sixties) putting in a huge number of hours preparing food for Christmas lunch. The turkey (purchased from the Greenock branch of Mac Fisheries) had to be cleaned out, the giblets removed, and stuffed by hand and then roasted for many hours in the oven. Soup and Christmas pudding were prepared from scratch, and everything took ages.

In 2015 it was a different story. Everything could be purchased online and delivered to the house prior to Christmas day. We ate a turkey crown, which required no preparation and cooked in a couple of hours. All the trimmings, like stuffing and pigs in blankets, only required brief heating in the oven. I now rarely drank alcohol but on this occasion enjoyed two bottles of Budweiser. The meal was a great success.

On New Year's Day Gillian drove Vivien to Bearsden so she could spend some time with her family including her brother, Andrew, and his wife, Alex, and children, Simon and Sam, who usually came up to Glasgow for New Year's. Because of my urinary problems, I stayed in the house in Dunblane on my own and enjoyed some M&S party food.

On Thursday, 7 January, I had my first follow-up appointment (since my discharge) at the cardiology outpatient clinic at the Scottish General Hospital. The specialist cardiology rehabilitation nurse who saw me was Linda Tompkins, who had visited me many times when I was in the cardiology ward. Linda was very pleased at how I was doing, took a blood sample, and arranged for me to have a chest X-ray.

The following week she emailed me to tell me that my iron levels were low despite oral iron therapy in the form of ferrous fumarate tablets. I was also still quite anaemic with a haemoglobin level of 11.5 (the norm for a man is 14.5). Her suggested remedy was an intravenous infusion of iron (known as Ferinject), which could be carried out as a day hospital procedure. Afterwards, I could stop taking oral iron.

I agreed to this, and on 26 January, I visited the hospital to have this procedure carried out. It was a wet and windy day, but still I walked all the way from the nearest railway station to the hospital and back, the longest distance (about four miles) I had walked since late July. It exhausted me and left me breathless, but all the same it was a sure sign that I was slowly recovering from my heart attack, and my muscles were strengthening.

Around this time I decided to get my Jaguar X-Type Estate back into running condition. It had been sitting for months in my driveway with a dead battery and four flat tyres. After consulting a local mechanic (Davie McClymont of the Northend Garage), I realized the safest way to charge the battery would be with a trickle charger. The negative lead from the battery to the bodywork had to be disconnected with a spanner and it took two charging sessions of about seven hours each to put enough charge into the battery to start the car. After starting the engine, I had to run it for fifteen minutes to fully charge the battery. All I had to do then was inflate the four tyres to their correct pressures, check the oil level, and input the radio PIN code to put the car back into full running order.

As I had surrendered my driving licence to the DVLA on account of my epilepsy and wasn't going to get it back till at least late November, I couldn't drive the car myself, so I decided to have one of Vivien's carers, Gail, as one of the named drivers. Gail had previously worked as a taxi driver, and the plan was that if she could drive me somewhere about once a week, it would keep the car in good running order. On 22 February Gail drove me to the nearest filling station, so I could top up the fuel tank. It was clear that something was wrong, as there was a loud rubbing noise from the brakes. I surmised that everything had rusted and stuck together during the car's long period of immobility.

Fortunately, the car was already booked in for its annual service with the Stirling branch of Arnold Clark on Monday, 7 March. Arnold Clark operated a pickup and delivery service, so my lack of a driving licence wasn't a problem. In the meantime, I decided the car should not be driven until the rubbing problem had been diagnosed and fixed.

On 24 February Gail drove me in her own car to Killin to collect Kiki, who had been staying with her 'foster mummy' for a few months. I can't say Kiki was pleased to see us, as she was her usual aloof self, but it was great to have her back. The only change in her personality was that she now liked to be stroked, resulting in loud purring, but she still didn't enjoy being cuddled and wouldn't come up on my lap or snuggle up to me in bed as Oscar had done.

By this time I had been attending an NHS rehabilitation class since 9 February. This programme consisted of a one-hour gym workout supervised by the physiotherapists and cardiac rehabilitation nurses, followed by a brief lecture on various topics such as diet and exercise.

Following the first lecture on 9 February, I realized that I had to make a few changes in my daily eating to minimize the risk of a further heart attack. My existing diet wasn't that bad, as I never ate fried food, rarely ate cakes or desserts, and had a low alcohol consumption. Nonetheless, some changes were clearly required, and I took the advice I was given very seriously.

Much to my surprise, eggs and black pudding were now considered OK, as was chocolate. However, I was told I should eat brown rice, brown pasta, and wholemeal bread instead of the white alternatives. Sugar was to be avoided as much as possible, and this meant that daily fruit consumption should be limited. I was to eat as many vegetables as I could and aim for 'five a day'.

Red meat was to be avoided, though chicken and poultry were OK. Oily fish was good but should be limited to one or two portions a week. Polyunsaturated fats such as rapeseed oil should be used for cooking along with a 'one cal' spray, and olive oil was also recommended.

On Wednesday, 16 March, at 2.45 p.m., I had a follow up appointment with my cardiologist, Dr Thomas. He was pleased with my progress and my steadily increasing exercise tolerance and noted that I had no cardiac symptoms. However, he felt a repeat echocardiogram was required, and soon afterwards I received a note by post to inform me that this was to be carried out on Thursday, 7 April, at 11.20 a.m.

I felt a little nervous at the prospect of having another echo. It is the same emotion cancer patients feel when they have some kind of special investigation which will reveal whether their tumour has returned or not, and they are going to live or die. My greatest fear was that a repeat echo would show that the patch inside the heart was starting to peel off, and my heart failure was going to return. However, I knew this was unlikely as I was symptom-free, and my exercise tolerance was steadily increasing.

On the day of the investigation I sat in the waiting area reading my Kindle and wondering how things were going to go. I was taken five minutes early and went into the scanning room, where I had to take off my shirt and recline on a couch while a highly-trained technician put some gel on my chest and pressed a scanning probe (shaped like a shotgun cartridge) against my chest. I could see from her facial expression that something was wrong, and eventually she revealed that the scan had revealed a small leak at the perimeter of the patch, which was causing what is known as a right-to-left shunt (a leakage of blood from the right ventricle to the left ventricle). Clearly it was not causing any symptoms, as I was quick to point out, but she asked me to sit in the waiting area while she showed the scans to Dr Thomas.

A few moments later she returned with some news. Dr Thomas had viewed the pictures and agreed that there was indeed a right-to-left shunt. However, he did not feel that an urgent readmission or further surgery was indicated at present. Instead, he would arrange for two further echoes to be carried out four weeks apart to confirm that the leak was not worsening.

On the bus home from the hospital I worried a little that I might have to go back into hospital or even have a further cardiac operation. But on the other hand, I reassured myself that the problem had most likely occurred within a few weeks of my second operation and had probably been stable since then, as evidenced by my steadily increasing exercise tolerance. All the same, I had an anxious few weeks while I waited for the two further echoes to be carried out. As I had hoped, they confirmed that the leak was small and was not progressing.

I also discovered that the hole was where the patch butted up against the mitral valve. I can understand why this might happen from my experience of fixing punctures in cycling. A small tear in an inner tube can be easily patched, but if the hole is next to the tyre valve, it can be difficult (if not impossible) to patch it, as you will tend to get a leak at the edge of the patch next to the valve. The same problem presumably applies to patching a hole in the ventricular septum of the heart, because if the hole goes right up to the base of a valve, then there is nothing to suture onto.

Despite this problem with my heart, which also had a degree of muscle damage affecting the left ventricle, I was doing well, and by June my diuretic (frusemide) was stopped, which made my life much easier, as I didn't have to keep running to the toilet.

By May I started going out on my bicycle again. To begin with, I could only cycle a short distance and had to push the bike up most hills, but within a few weeks I could cycle to Stirling and back. As the summer solstice approached, I got into the habit of going an early morning ninety-minute cycle run at about 5.30 a.m., usually stopping at the local co-op or Tesco on my way home to buy some essential provisions. On 11 July, as there was a rail strike and problems on the roads caused by the 'T in the Park' rock concert, I cycled all the way to the Scottish General Hospital and back. The staff at the cardiology outpatient clinic were astonished at this feat, as I was supposedly attending a heart failure clinic.

Cycling was building up my leg muscles again and improving my general fitness levels, but I still had to do something about my wasted upper body. Attending the NHS gym session every week helped, as it involved some weight training, but I felt I also needed to do something at home every day to build up my muscles.

Back in April 1981 (when I was only twenty-four) I had purchased an exercise device called a Bullworker X5. I only used it for a few weeks and then put it into storage. Amazingly after thirty-four years it still existed in near-perfect condition in my attic, and after I had given it a quick wipe-down with a damp cloth, I found it to be in full working order.

The Bullworker has an interesting story behind it. For decades, physiologists had known that were two types of muscle contraction, namely isotonic and isometric. An isotonic contraction is one which involves movement of the muscle and adjacent joints. An isometric contraction, on the other hand, involves contraction of a muscle against a fixed (immovable) resistance. In the 1950s two scientists, Dr Hettinger and Dr Muller at the Max Planck Institute in West Germany, discovered that a single seven-second isometric contraction of a muscle produces a maximum stimulation to muscle growth, the same as that achieved with a fairly lengthy workout with weights. This research led to the creation of the first Bullworker by Gert F. Koelbel in 1962. It is essentially a metal tube containing a powerful spring which is compressed by hand grips, or by two pairs of ropes, enabling every muscle group in the body to be exercised isometrically.

It is the easiest way to build muscle, and from May onwards I started using it every morning following my cycle run. Within a few weeks, my muscle strength and size had increased to the point where I was actually more muscular than I was before my heart attack.

Around this time there were other changes in my life. As related in the first part of this book, Vivien's Story, my hypnotherapy and TFT business had been in decline for years, and on 6 April 2016 I formally closed it down. There were a number of reasons behind this decision. First of all, there was little demand for my services. While I was in hospital for four months, I only got four enquiries for hypnotherapy, two from ex-patients. There had also been a huge increase in the number of people offering hypnotherapy services. When I first started my business in 1999 there were only about three hypnotherapists in the whole of the former Central Region (population 310,000); now there were about fifty, including five in Dunblane and fourteen in Stirling. Fewer people could now afford hypnotherapy because of the recession, and it was difficult for me to see people in my house, as carers were coming in all the time, and my consulting room was now used to store online grocery shopping. Lastly, I could no longer see people at the Glasgow Nuffield Hospital, as my contract for room hire had been cancelled because I wasn't seeing enough people. The market for training people in TFT had greatly diminished. For the last couple of years, I hadn't even earned enough to cover the fixed costs of running my business, so for all these reasons I closed down my business in April 2016 and decided to concentrate on writing and looking after Vivien.

My second book, The Craft of Public Speaking, was published on 30 June 2016; my third, Planes on Film: My Ten Favourite Aviation Films, was released on 30 September 2016; and my fourth and most recent book, Dying Harder: Action Movies of the Eighties, was published on 31 May 2017.

On 30 July 2016 we celebrated our fourteenth wedding anniversary with a carry-out Indian meal washed down with some sparkling wine. The following day, 31 July, was another anniversary. It was a year since I had suffered my heart attack. I had undergone two very risky cardiac operations, had nearly died at least three times, had been in a coma for some weeks, and on a ventilator with a tracheotomy. I had developed cardiac failure and epilepsy. Against all the odds, I had survived and regained my fitness. On 28 November 2016 I started driving again.

But I had to face reality. I had a badly damaged heart and would require to take cardiac medications for the rest of my life. There was also the risk that I would have another heart attack, which could be fatal. Exactly how much longer would I live for? Two years, five years, ten years, fifteen years? No one could say with certainty. But there was one positive aspect of all this. I was determined to get myself as fit as possible and stay that way. I would live each day as though it was my last one on Earth. Because one day it would be.

EPILOGUE

We have been on a long and difficult journey together, you and I. We found each other one night in December 1998, two lonely souls thrown together by the fickle finger of fate. Even from the first moment we met, there was a rapport between us, which soon blossomed into true love. From the very beginning we both knew we were right for one another.

As the bond between us grew stronger, our love deepened. We swam together in the warm Mediterranean Sea, held hands under starry skies in Egypt, and walked in the sunshine on all those wonderful foreign holidays, which left us with pleasant memories.

We enjoyed so much together. Walking, cycling, swimming, eating out. Having long conversations. We shared the good times and the bad.

We cried when our beautiful cat Jasper died and consoled each other when my dear mother became demented and went into a nursing home. But we also shed tears of joy, enjoying all the happy moments we had together, like the day we got married in Cyprus and became man and wife.

We had lots in common and enjoyed each other's company immensely. We had so much to look forward to. We planned to see a bit of the world when you retired. We even thought of living abroad in some sun-kissed paradise eventually.

Then one day in May 2011 our dreams were shattered. A tumour deep inside your heart, which doctors had failed to detect, damaged your brain and blinded you in your left eye. It should never have happened. The NHS – which I once worked for and in which we had so much faith – failed you totally in your time of need. I thought I was going to lose you, but a brilliant cardiac surgeon saved your life. Unfortunately, you were left a shadow of your former self.

I rose to the challenge and have done everything possible to make your life as comfortable and fulfilled as possible and to obtain compensation for the terrible mistakes which left you the way you are.

You have no idea of the pain I feel when I look at your blind left eye pointing outwards or see the right side of your beautiful face sagging and your mouth stuck in a downturned expression. It hurts me when I see your once perfectly manicured right hand twisted into a useless claw. And I feel so angry when I realize that it all could have been prevented if the NHS had done its job properly. Then in 2015 I too ended up in hospital with a serious heart condition. You have no idea of the mental pain I endured as I lay as helpless as a baby wondering if you were all right.

The stroke eradicated many of your faculties, but one thing it could not destroy was the deep love and bond between us, which if anything grew stronger. Whatever happens, I will always be there to protect you, love you, and take care of you.

But at the same time there are so many things that I miss. I miss enjoying a meal that you have prepared for me with loving hands. I miss you buying nice clothes for me. I miss seeing your little silver car drawing up outside the house with you at the wheel. I miss the sound of your key turning in the front door lock and you asking me to unload your car for you. I miss seeing you putting on cosmetics in preparation for a night out and wearing all the beautiful clothes that now lie unused in our wardrobes. Above all I miss hearing your beautiful voice and enjoying all the wonderful conversations that we used to have.

For as long as you require care I will be there for you, but I know that one day the time will come when we have both left this physical world, to be reunited in the next one. I know that we will then resume our wonderful conversations. We will certainly have a lot to talk about. I look forward to that day.

APPENDIX 1

SUMMARY OF VIVIEN BARRON'S MEDICAL CONSULTATIONS PRIOR TO STROKE

27/07/2009

Seen by GP. Left hand itchy and red. Thought to be due to touching plant 3 days ago. Erythema of hand noted. Thought to be allergy. Piriton prescribed.

04/08/2009

Seen by GP.
Redness of fourth and fifth fingertips L hand with swelling and tenderness. Vasculitis diagnosed. Oral prednisolone prescribed – 60 mg day for 5 days.

Comment – both above likely to be due to an embolic episode (or two separate episodes).

07/08/2009

Reviewed by GP registrar. Swelling and redness decreasing.

28/08/2009

Seen at A&E Dept at Central General Hospital. R thigh pain. Bursitis of hip joint diagnosed.

Comment – likely to have been an embolic episode.

04/09/2009

Seen by GP registrar. Pain, redness, swelling in left big toe for 3 days. Toe also feels hot. Gout diagnosed. Treated with NSAID.

Comment – likely to have been an embolic episode .

08/03/2010

Seen by GP. Rash on ulnar aspect L hand. 'Purple blanching rash on ulnar aspect fifth finger L hand.' Prescribed betamethasone valerate cream 0.1%.

Comment – another embolic episode.

26/04/2010

Reviewed by GP. Rash on L hand flared up again.

Started on prednisolone 60 mg/day for 5 days.

Bloods ordered – FBC, ESR, U&E, glucose, LFTs, TFTs, complement, RhF, ANCA, Igs.

Comment – another embolic episode.

30/04/2010

Seen by GP. Vasculitis now settled down. Has now been referred to dermatology clinic.

02/05/2010

Seen by out of hours doctor at Central General Hospital. Flare-up of vasculitis. Left lower leg. Patch of mottled skin noted left lower leg. Started on prednisolone again at 30 mg/day.

Comment – another embolic episode.

04/05/2010

Reviewed by GP. Noted that Vivien feels very unwell on steroids. Dose to be gradually tapered off.

05/05/2010

GP emails Dr Brown (dermatology) asking if appointment can be brought forward. Blood tests show moderate leukocytosis.

06//05/2010

Seen by Dr Brown at Dermatology OPD, SRI. Notes recent flare-up of 'vasculitis'. Suggests a gradual reduction in steroid dose. Also notes elevated neutrophil count and raised ESR. Dr Brown unsure about exact type of vasculitis. No follow-up appointment arranged.

Comment – as rash had settled, no biopsy was carried out. However, a biopsy of the area might have revealed myxoma particles.

24/05/2010

Reviewed by GP. Vasculitis now settling, prednisolone to be gradually stopped.

30/05/2010

4.30 p.m. sudden onset attack of dizziness and spinning sensation with vomiting. Seen by Emergency GP. Acute viral labyrinthitis diagnosed. Given IM Stemetil.

01/06/2010

Reviewed by GP. Labyrinthitis now settled.

Comment – likely to have been a TIA due to an embolus from the atrial myxoma rather than 'labyrinthitis'.

03/08/2010

Seen by GP. Flare-up of vasculitis in L hand. Vivien not keen on further steroids due to side effects.

Comment – another embolic episode.

26/08/2010

Seen by GP. Developed rash on right hand. Purpuric rash noted.

Prednisolone restarted at 60 mg/day.

Comment – another embolic episode.

30/08/2010

Seen by GP. Left sided facial swelling. Thought to be steroid side effect.

Comment – likely to have been an embolic episode.

02/09/2010

Vasculitis reviewed by GP.

09/09/2010

Sees Dr Brown (Dermatology) again.

Suggests tapering steroid dose and refers to Rheumatology (Dr Green).

17/09/2010

Seen by GP. Vasculitis flared up again. Dose of prednisolone increased to 30 mg/day.

Comment – another embolic episode.

20/09/2010

Reviewed by GP. Symptoms improved slightly.

24/09/2010

Reviewed by GP. Decides to increase prednisolone to 60 mg/day.

Also in contact with Rheumatology Dept.

Started on alendronic acid, calcium carbonate, and omeprazole (to combat steroid side effects).

29/09/2010

Reviewed by GP.

Steroids to be continued.

06/10/2010

Reviewed by GP. Dr Green saw Vivien that day and has asked her to start azathioprine 50 mg/day in addition to steroids, which will be gradually reduced.

12/10/2010

Seen by GP registrar. Vasculitis worsening again despite medication. Rash L palm.

Comment – another embolic episode.

13/10/2010

Dr Green writes to Dr Brown by fax. Relates to clinic appt on 06/10/2010. Mentions that cause of vasculitis 'unlikely to be found'. Also suggests raised white cell count probably due to steroids.

20/10/2010

Reviewed by GP. Now on azathioprine 50 mg plus prednisolone 30 mg/day.

26/10/2010

Letter from Dr Green to GP. Dr Green mentions that cervical ribs found on chest X-ray, more prominent on right side. He suggests getting opinion from vascular surgeon.

He also says that 'neither Dr Brown nor I have actually seen the lesions and we can't be sure they are vasculitic'.

Comment – Cervical ribs could not be causing the symptoms as the feet had been affected as well and wouldn't explain other symptoms such as facial swelling.

02/11/2010

Reviewed by GP. Rash settling. Now on 50 mg azathioprine and 10mg prednisolone.

19/11/2010

Reviewed by GP. Rash on right finger. Prednisolone now down to 5 mg/day

Comment – another embolic episode.

06/12/2010

GP writes to rheumatologist. Blood results show azathioprine-induced myelosuppression (damage to bone marrow) and suggest azathioprine dose should be reduced.

08/12/2010

Dr Green reviews Vivien at the Rheumatology OPD. Now believes cervical ribs unrelated to symptoms, especially as now told symptoms have also occurred in feet,

Dr Green tells Vivien that she doesn't have vasculitis as 'there is nothing suggesting inflammation' in her blood tests. Vivien asks Dr Green what is wrong with her and he says, 'I don't know.' However, despite his doubts about the diagnosis, she is told to continue with 100 mg azathioprine daily for another six months, when she will be reviewed.

09/12/2010

Rheumatology Dept writes back to say azathioprine dose is fine, as max recommended dose is 200 mg/day.

20/12/2010

Reviewed by GP. Prednisolone now down to 5 mg alternate days. Dr Green recommends staying on 100 mg azathioprine till June 2011. Rash now settled.

Vivien reports pain in thighs, calves, feet for last 5 days. Examination normal.

Possible viral myalgia (muscle pain due to viral infection) diagnosed.

Comment – another embolic episode.

05/01/2011

Reviewed by GP.

Vasculitis now settled and off steroids. Had hot, red swelling medial aspect R foot previous week.

Comment – episode of swelling previous week would be an embolic episode.

24/01/2011

Reviewed by GP. Suffering anxiety, poor sleep, vivid dreams, urinary frequency, hair loss (? side effect of azathioprine). GP writes to Dr Green.

25/01/2011

Letter from Dr Green to GP suggests azathioprine reduced to 50 mg/day for 1–2 months, then stop. Dr Green mentions 8–10 week typing delay between seeing patient and letter going out.

Vivien told (by phone) to reduce azathioprine to 50 mg/day.

17/01/11

Seen by vascular surgeon, Central General Hospital. In letter to GPs she says that she feels cervical ribs are not related to symptoms.

21/02/2011

Reviewed by GP. Azathioprine now down to 50 mg/day. Vivien feeling better. Vasculitis settled.

Also noted pain in left knee. Cause unknown.

Comment – pain in knee likely to have been an embolic episode.

14/03/11

Seen by GP. Rash on face. Possible allergy to azathioprine. Given fexofenadine HCL and topical hydrocortisone 1% cream.

Discussed with other GPs. Agreed that azathioprine can now be stopped.

Comment – rash on face likely to have been an embolic episode.

17/03/11

Reviewed by GP.

Facial rash improving. Also noted R shoulder pain. Slight injury.

Comment – Right shoulder pain likely to have been an embolic episode.

29/03/11

Reviewed by GP. Facial rash improved. Vasculitis also settled.

03/05/11

Seen by GP. 'Funny feeling' in right hand for 2–3 weeks. Unable to perform fine motor skills, e.g. handwriting, putting on make-up. No loss of power or paraesthesia. No headaches/visual disturbance. Neurological examination normal.

Comment – likely to have been a Transient Ischaemic Attack (TIA) or even a small stroke.

18/05/11

Reviewed by GP. Slight improvement in handwriting problem. Examination normal. Examination includes auscultation of carotids and heart. GP suggests problem may be related to cervical ribs but will refer to neurology OPD if no improvement.

20/05/11

Vivien suffers severe right-sided stroke at 8 p.m. (estimated). Rushed to Central General Hospital.

26/05/11

Echocardiogram shows cause of stroke to be left atrial myxoma.

13/06/11

Atrial myxoma removed using open heart surgery at Scottish Heart Hospital.

Summary – between August 2009 and May 2011 Vivien had an estimated **twenty** *embolic episodes.*

APPENDIX 2

The Eleven Errors Which Led to Vivien's Stroke

This appendix summarizes the various errors which led to the tragic outcome. Obviously it has been written with the benefit of hindsight some years after the event, when the correct diagnosis was known and after consulting the scientific literature and a number of medical experts. In writing this rather blunt assessment, I am aware of the difficult clinical situation that many of the doctors were in. For example, faced with an episode of acute muscle pain or facial swelling, most GPs would diagnose the most likely cause rather than thinking of embolic phenomena. Nonetheless, the correct diagnosis was repeatedly missed by various doctors, and it is important that these episodes are recorded for posterity.

Mistake Number 1

Making a diagnosis of vasculitis solely on the clinical appearance.

Vivien was originally diagnosed with 'vasculitis' in August 2009 solely on the clinical appearance of the lesions. No investigations (apart from an ECG) were carried out, probably because the GPs thought it was a localized reaction secondary to a plant allergy and that no investigations were therefore required. In fact, this episode was almost certainly embolic in origin. When Vivien had her next attack of 'vasculitis' in spring 2010, some blood tests were carried out and these were inconclusive. Thus the diagnosis of vasculitis was made solely on the clinical appearance and was never confirmed by laboratory tests such as blood samples and histology.

Mistake Number 2

Prescribing high-dose oral corticosteroids for 'vasculitis' in the absence of a definite diagnosis confirmed by laboratory tests such as raised inflammatory markers and biopsy results.

The only clinical situation in which steroids should be given for suspected vasculitis not confirmed by lab tests would be temporal arteritis (aka giant cell arteritis), in which delay in administering steroids can result in the patient losing vision in one eye. Vivien did not have temporal arteritis. There may be situations in clinical medicine in which steroids may be given empirically, but this is not one of them, as it was treatment for a small, localized lesion that was not life-threatening.

Mistake Number 3

Failure to carry out a biopsy.

In cases of suspected vasculitis, a biopsy can be invaluable, as it can show whether a lesion has a vasculitic or other (such as embolic) cause. In cases of atrial myxoma resulting in emboli, small particles of the myxoma may be seen in biopsy specimens even after a rash has faded. Thus the myxomatous origin of the lesions could have been determined by biopsy. At the very least it would have been possible to determine that they were not vasculitic.

The reason that Dr Brown was unable to biopsy the lesions was because they had cleared up by the time he saw Vivien – and this was partly because she had been put on high-dose steroids by her GP, which may have accelerated the healing of pseudovasculitic lesions.

Dr Brown took the view that since a biopsy was not possible at the time of the clinic appointment, then nothing more should be done about this. But both Dr Brown and Dr Green could have asked Vivien to return to the hospital immediately the lesions returned, allowing clinical examination, photography, and biopsy. A look at Appendix 1 shows that Vivien had many recurrences of the skin lesions prior to her stroke, so if this suggestion had been implemented, there would have been *several* opportunities to biopsy the lesions.

Dr Brown could also have asked the GPs to stop giving her steroids every time the condition flared up, since this acceleration of the recovery of the lesions caused by steroids was probably the reason that he was unable to carry out a biopsy.

Mistake Number 4

Continuing with steroids in the absence of a diagnosis.

There was never any clinical reason for Vivien to be put on steroids, since no definite diagnosis had ever been made. It is puzzling that Dr Brown allowed the GPs to keep treating recurrences with steroids. We know now that this resulted in a masking of the symptoms of her real illness – the atrial myxoma – and her blood tests were also affected. Vivien was off sick from late August 2010 to early December 2010, due entirely to the side-effects of the steroid she had been given, not the 'vasculitis' itself.

Mistake Number 5

Prescribing azathioprine in the absence of a definite diagnosis.

Azathioprine is a dangerous drug. It is similar to anticancer drugs and works by suppressing the immune system. The drug made Vivien ill and caused bone marrow and liver damage.

I would question Dr Green's decision to prescribe it, since no definite diagnosis of vasculitis (i.e. confirmed by lab tests) was ever made. Incidentally, the reason Dr Green decided to switch from steroids to azathioprine was because the steroids gave Vivien insomnia. A better option, though, would surely have been to take her off all medication entirely.

Despite not knowing what was wrong with her, Dr Green kept her on azathioprine and gave her a six-month follow-up appointment. The azathioprine made her very ill, and many of the symptoms she suffered in the next few months were attributed to the azathioprine (when in fact they were probably constitutional symptoms caused by the atrial myxoma). Thus the azathioprine treatment masked the symptoms and signs of the myxoma, just as the steroid had.

Mistake Number 6

Placing too much emphasis on the cervical ribs.

Vivien initially suffered symptoms in her hands but soon developed lesions in her legs (e.g. the attack of 'vasculitis' in her left lower leg on 02/05/2010). It is therefore extraordinary that Dr Green even considered that her cervical ribs could be the cause of her symptoms, since they cannot cause problems in the feet.

His fixation on her cervical ribs seemed to distract him, since he appeared to lose sight of the fact that Vivien was suffering from a systemic illness which required careful investigation. It also affected the decision making of the GPs five months later when Vivien presented with symptoms in her right hand (see Mistake Number 9).

Mistake Number 7

Not considering an embolic cause for the symptoms and failing to order an echocardiogram.

In his excellent review article on the investigation of suspected vasculitis, Dr Ernest Suresh has suggested (see Appendix 3) that it is important to exclude conditions that mimic vasculitis, and he specifically mentions emboli from atrial myxoma. He also mentions subacute bacterial endocarditis (SBE), which is much commoner than myxoma and which would also require an echocardiogram for diagnosis. It should be noted that Vivien had no investigations to exclude the possibility of SBE, particularly blood cultures.

It should also be noted that the rheumatology department at Scottish General Hospital now carries out an echocardiogram in *every case* of vasculitis or suspected vasculitis, as a direct result of this case. A wise move, but as far as Vivien is concerned it is undoubtedly bolting the stable door after the horse has fled!

Mistake Number 8

Misdiagnosis of embolic episodes.

One excuse Dr Green might offer for his failure to order an echocardiogram was that Vivien had not suffered any previous embolic episodes. In fact – with the benefit of hindsight – I believe she suffered *twenty* embolic episodes between August 2009 and May 2011.

As described in the main text, the dizzy turn on 30 May 2010 is likely to have been a TIA caused by an embolic episode, and the 'gout' on 4 September 2009 was almost certainly an embolic episode as well. Details of these twenty embolic episodes are given in Appendix 1.

Mistake Number 9

Failure to order sufficient investigations (apart from the echocardiogram).

The British Society of Rheumatology guidelines on the management of vasculitis stipulate a large number of investigations that should be carried out. Apart from an echocardiogram, they mention pulmonary function tests, the creatinine clearance test, and many other investigations. These aforementioned investigations would not have shown the presence of the myxoma, but a CT scan or MRI scan of the chest (or a total body scan) would have picked it up. These two investigations are sometimes carried out in the investigation of vasculitis cases.

Mistake Number 10

Failure to request a second opinion.

On 8 December 2010 Dr Green told Vivien that he did not know what was wrong with her and gave her a six-month appointment. I believe a second opinion from another rheumatologist and a second dermatologist would have been helpful at that point.

Mistake Number 11

Failure to recognize that a small stroke had occurred.

In late April 2011 Vivien developed a 'funny feeling' in her right hand and some difficulty in doing handwriting and putting on make-up. On 03/05/11 she saw her GP, who found nothing wrong on clinical examination. She was reviewed by another GP on 18/05/2011, who again found no abnormalities on clinical examination but suggested her cervical ribs might be responsible. Two days later Vivien suffered a massive stroke.

With the benefit of hindsight, it is clear that Vivien must have suffered a small stroke (or perhaps a TIA) in late April, and had this been investigated as such, then it is just possible that her later major stroke could have been prevented. The GPs were probably influenced by Dr Green, who had flagged up the cervical ribs. Had he not done so, then they might have considered a stroke in their differential diagnosis and ordered urgent further investigation.

As outlined in the main text, at this point Vivien was running out of time, and even with an urgent referral by the GPs, Vivien might not have had cardiac surgery soon enough to prevent her stroke. But all the same, it is possible that the stroke could have been prevented by an urgent referral to a neurologist or other professionals.

Conclusion

The investigation was a 'tragedy of errors' characterized by multiple mistakes, the worst of which was Dr Green's failure to order an echocardiogram. As one of my friends (a retired consultant) said to me: 'He [Dr Green] did not make a diagnosis, and the reason was because he didn't order enough investigations to enable him to come to a diagnosis.'

APPENDIX 3

LESSONS THAT NEED TO BE LEARNED AND RECOMMENDATIONS

1) The most important single recommendation that has emerged from this case is that anyone who presents with vasculitis or suspected vasculitis must have a *very thorough and detailed investigation*. Further details of all the investigations required in vasculitis cases can be found in the British Society of Rheumatology guidelines on the investigation of vasculitis and also in Dr Ernest Suresh's excellent article on the management of suspected vasculitis ('Diagnostic Approach to Patients with Suspected Vasculitis'). These two documents are freely available on the Internet, and full details are given at the end of this appendix.

2) There is no room for complacency when investigating a case of vasculitis or suspected vasculitis. Vasculitis can be a sign of a very serious (and even fatal) underlying illness.

3) It is also important to remember that a number of conditions can mimic vasculitis. In his aforementioned article Dr Ernest Suresh suggests that the investigation of vasculitis cases should always start by *excluding conditions that mimic vasculitis.*

4) Anyone who presents to their GP with suspected vasculitis should be referred urgently to their local dermatology or rheumatology department. Contact should be made with one of the consultants as soon as possible with a view to receiving advice on management.

5) A full medical history should be taken and a thorough physical examination carried out on anyone who presents with vasculitis or suspected vasculitis.

6) One of the most important investigations that must be carried out in cases of vasculitis and suspected vasculitis is an *urgent biopsy* of the affected area. This can be carried out by the dermatology or rheumatology department, and GPs need to liaise with these departments to ensure that this biopsy is carried out as soon as possible.

7) In cases of giant cell arteritis (aka temporal arteritis) or suspected cases of this condition, where the vision may be threatened, it is acceptable to give high-dose corticosteroids before a definite diagnosis has been established. In general, though, treatment with drugs such as corticosteroids and azathioprine should only be started once a definite diagnosis has been established, based not just on the clinical appearance but on the results of laboratory tests, including raised inflammatory markers and histology samples obtained by biopsy. Vasculitis should never be diagnosed purely on the clinical appearance of the lesions.

8) One potential problem relating to skin biopsies is that the lesions may have cleared up by the time the patient is seen by the dermatologist or rheumatologist. In such cases the patient should be asked to return to the dermatology or rheumatology department the *moment the lesions return* so that an inspection of the lesions and urgent biopsy can be carried out. In addition, it must be stressed that even a biopsy of a fading or just faded lesion can yield useful information, as myxoma particles can remain in the subcutaneous tissues for some time after a visible rash has cleared. Health Authorities and NHS Trusts need to ensure that dermatology and rheumatology clinics have the facility to see an occasional patient at very short notice.

9) An echocardiogram should be carried out in *every* case of vasculitis and suspected vasculitis, not just to exclude atrial myxoma but also to exclude other vascular causes such as subacute bacterial endocarditis as well as to determine whether the vasculitis is affecting the heart.

10) The use of small hand-held ultrasound devices as a partial replacement for the stethoscope should be introduced in the NHS. This would

mean that a missed diagnosis of atrial myxoma would largely become a thing of the past.

11) It does seem odd that in the twenty-first century, skin rashes are merely described in case notes using technical language rather than being photographed. GP practices should have the technology to photograph suspicious skin lesions and then email the resulting photographs to consultant dermatologists to aid in their clinical decisions.

12) Any person who presents with suspected gout should have appropriate laboratory investigations.

13) The government should consider the introduction of a 'no fault' compensation system for medical mistakes, which avoids the necessity for claimants to go to court or to prove negligence.

14) The government should ensure that Health Authorities and NHS Trusts learn lessons from medical mistakes and change procedures if required to avoid a repetition of these mistakes. Details of mistakes made in a particular Health Authority or NHS Trust should be promulgated to all the other Health Authorities and NHS Trusts to enable them to learn from these mistakes. There should be a procedure in place to ensure this happens.

15) Claimants who receive out-of-court settlements should not be required to sign non-disclosure agreements ('gagging orders'), since these prevent frank, open discussion of medical mistakes, which will lead to a lower chance of these errors happening again.

16) A sincere apology from the doctor(s) concerned must be part of the settlement of any medical negligence case.

17) Health Authorities and NHS Trusts should consider introducing written protocols for the investigation of vasculitis (and perhaps other conditions), giving details of all the investigations that must be carried out. This would prevent medical accidents caused by a doctor not thinking of the correct diagnosis, as happened in Vivien's case. Consideration should also

be given to introducing a universally accepted set of national guidelines for the investigation of vasculitis, leading to a national standard for the investigation of vasculitis which doctors should not fall below.

Further Reading

Diagnostic Approach to Patients with Suspected Vasculitis

By Dr Ernest Suresh

Postgraduate Medical Journal. August 2006. 82(1970): 483–488.

British Society of Rheumatology Guidelines on the management of adults with ANCA-associated vasculitis
Available from www.rheumatology.org.uk

APPENDIX 4

Further Reading

Stronger after Stroke: Your Roadmap to Maximising Your Recovery

by Peter G. Levine
Demos Medical Publishing, 2013

My Stroke of Insight

Jill Bolte Taylor
Hodder, 2009

My Year Off: Rediscovering Life after a Stroke

Robert McCrum
Picador, 2010

APPENDIX 5

Useful Addresses

The Stroke Association
www.stroke.org.uk

Chest, Heart and Stroke Scotland
www.chss.org.uk

Action Against Medical Accidents
www.avma.org.uk
This is a charity dedicated to helping people who have been the victims of medical accidents

'Going Forward' Stroke Support Group
'Stroke Club' for people in the Stirling area

www.stirlingstrokesupportgroup.com

The author's website
www.colinbarron.co.uk

American Thought Field Therapy (TFT) Website
www.rogercallahan.com

APPENDIX 6

USING PROGESTERONE CREAM TO HELP RECOVERY FROM STROKES

Anyone who has had a stroke in the last five years many benefit from using topical progesterone cream since it stimulates the development of new neural connections. A few years ago a study was done on soldiers with brain injuries returning from Iraq and Afghanistan, and it was found that female soldiers recovered better and faster. It has been postulated that this is because their ovaries produce progesterone. As a result of this discovery, soldiers of both sexes with brain injuries are now routinely given progesterone by intravenous infusion.

Stroke survivors can benefit from this discovery by using topical natural progesterone cream which can be obtained online from Amazon. I would imagine it could also be purchased from health food shops. One quarter of a teaspoon of the cream should be rubbed on the body every day from the seventh day of each month to the last day of the month in the following sequence:

Day 1 (e.g. February 7th) — *Front of Neck*

Day 2 (e.g. February 8th) — *Upper Chest*

Day 3 (e.g. February 9th) — *Breasts*

Day 4 (e.g. February 10th) — *Inner upper arms*

Day 5 (e.g. February 11th) — *Between shoulder blades on back*

Day 6 (e.g. February 12th) — *Return to front of neck, etc. – continue sequence till last day of month*

These application sites have been chosen because there is less subcutaneous fat in these areas, leading to better absorption. The reason you should vary the application site is because if you stuck to one area the subcutaneous tissues would become blocked with the cream and not absorb so well.

APPENDIX 7

The Perfect Apology

In 2016 the Negotiation and Conflict Management Research Journal published its six-point recipe for the perfect apology, which is as follows:

1) Express regret for what happened

2) Explain what went wrong

3) Acknowledge responsibility for what happened

4) Make declaration of repentance; i.e. say you won't make same mistake again

5) Offer to make amends

6) Ask for forgiveness

REFERENCES

Chapter 11

(1)   Cardiac tumours simulating collagen vascular disease

AP Fitzpatrick, JG Lanham and DV Doyle. British Heart Journal 1986; 55: 592–595

Chapter 13

1)   An Experiment with Time
JW Dunne, 1927. Reprinted 2001.
Hampton Roads Publishing Company.

2)   The Science Delusion
Rupert Sheldrake.
Coronet 2012. Also many other books and articles by same author. See www.sheldrake.org

Chapter 17

1)   The Myth of the Chemical Cure
Dr Joanna Moncrieff

Palgrave MacMillan, 2009

2)   Dr Alastair Dobbin.

www.stepsforstress.org

www.foundationforpositivementalhealth.com

www.positiverewards.com

Chapter 22

(1) 'Erythematous macules on the feet in a case of cardiac myxoma.'
Anne-Claire Bursztejn et al. Acta Dermato venereologiea 2009. Available
on line at www.medicaljournals.se or do Google search on title.

Chapter 23

(1) American Psychological Science Journal.
The (really scary) invisible Gorilla
www.psychologicalscience.org. 29 January 2013

(2) Invisible Gorilla Experiment
See YouTube. www.youtube.com Selective attention test

(3) Miller G.A. (1956). The magical number seven, plus or minus two:
Some limits on our capacity for processing information. Psychological
Review. 63(2): 81-97, PMID 13310704. Also see Wikipedia.

ABOUT THE AUTHOR

Dr Colin M. Barron was born in Greenock in 1956 and educated at Greenock Academy and Glasgow University where he graduated in medicine in 1979. He worked as a junior ophthalmologist for a few years before establishing a private nursing home with his first wife. Between 1999 and 2015 he was a self-employed hypnotherapist and TFT therapist. In 2015 he closed down his hypnotherapy business following a severe heart attack and now writes books and cares for his disabled wife. He has had 150 articles published plus four books – *Running Your Own Private Residential or Nursing Home* (1990), *The Craft of Public Speaking* (2016), *Planes on Film* (2016) and *Dying Harder – Action Movies of the Eighties* (2017). His hobbies include cycling, keeping fit, walking, aircraft, military history, and model-making.